P9-CED-090

ALIEN ABDUCTIONS

Peter Brookesmith

BARNES
&NOBLE
BOOKS
NEW YORK

This edition published by Barnes & Noble, Inc.
by arrangement with Brown Packaging Books Ltd
1998 Barnes & Noble Books

M 10 9 8 7 6 5 4 3 2 1

ISBN: 0 7607 0764 2

Copyright © 1998 Brown Packaging Books Ltd

All rights reserved. No part of this publication may be reproduced, stored
in a retrieval system or transmitted, in any form or by any means, electronic, mechanical, photocopying,
recording or otherwise, without the prior written permission of the copyright holder.

Editorial and design by
Brown Packaging Books Ltd
Bradley's Close
74-77 White Lion Street
London N1 9PF

Editor: Lesley Riley
Design: wda
Project Editor: Brian Burns
Picture Research: Adrian Bentley

Printed in Singapore

CONTENTS

WATCHING THEM WATCHING US

The Background to the Alien Abduction Phenomenon

◆ ◆ ◆

Opposite: At the UFO convention held in Roswell in July 1997, Ray Gonzales waits to compete in an alien costume contest. After 40 years of abduction reports, the bug-eyed Gray has an established place in popular culture.

Small gray aliens are everywhere. At an airport in Dallas, Texas, a blind man is selling trinkets: among them is a keyring with an 'alien' head attached. In a cigar store in a small town in Wales, the black-eyed, domed head of an alien 'Gray' stares out from the lid of a tobacco tin. In New York City, a greetings-card company publishes a series of cards featuring jokey cartoons about aliens. Alien Abductions feature in advertisements for cars, telephone companies and brands of candy.

While I was writing this book I was invited to have dinner with two very old friends. When

Trinkets and jewelry depicting alien faces are now on sale not only where UFO buffs gather – but in markets everywhere in the West.

Alexandra, their teenage daughter, heard what I was working on, she solemnly informed me that she too was an abductee, and gave me a blow-by-blow account of a classic encounter with aliens. By the time she had finished she was clutching her sides with laughter. She knew the script of the UFO abduction scenario by heart, and her tease demonstrated better than anything just how deeply the Grays and their nefarious activities are now embedded in our popular culture.

This book doesn't set out to use incidents like that as 'proof' that alien abductions don't happen.

Drawing by Mona Stafford of the UFO that pursued and then abducted her and her two companions from a car, near Liberty, Kentucky, in January 1976.

It tries to step outside the rituals of the 'believer' versus 'skeptic' debate: for that has long since grown stale, and it often seems that the two sides are shouting so loudly that neither can hear what the other is saying. What the alien-inspired novelties and advertisements and Alexandra's skit tell us is that at some deep level we are fascinated by UFOs and aliens and abductions, and take them seriously enough to make jokes about them. Whether they are real – solid, three-dimensional, physical objects – or not, they are having an effect on us. It seems to me that skeptics should be spending more time asking why this is so, and less denying that abductions happen at all. At the same

time, believers could spend less energy defending the idea that the aliens are from outer space, and recognize that an abduction experience can seem to be absolutely real, and be truthfully reported by an unimpeachably honest witness, without necessarily having happened in any objective sense.

Of course, one can't duck the issues of whether or not the entities people encounter actually are off-world visitors and whether they really are abducting innocent Earthlings and doing unseemly things to them. But the alien abduction phenomenon raises many more questions than these. One can lay out very powerful arguments, backed by the latest scientific findings, against an extra-terrestrial origin for aliens, and still agree with ufologist Budd Hopkins when he affirms that 'despite all the debunkers' theories, all the data [have] not been explained and…an intriguing mystery does remain.'

I've already suggested two aspects of that mystery. If the alien abduction phenomenon is not what it seems to be, why do so many people believe it is, or even entertain its possibility at all? If the phenomenon is not objectively real, what are we to make of the abductees? Are they, as some debunkers have implied, really no more than attention-seeking inadequates who are either hoaxers or sadly deluded individuals? Those that I have met are certainly not, but they insist something very weird and very disturbing has happened to them.

These questions about public fascination and private experience seem to be addressing unrelated aspects of the phenomenon. But in exploring how they can be answered, we shall see how they are indeed connected, and how the public attitude to abductions and the private experience feed off and modify each other. We will also find ourselves exploring the question of what is 'real', and what is not, in human experience and perception. Such answers as are available are not as simple as either believers or skeptics usually allow.

Almost everything about the abduction phenomenon is rather more complex than either side of the traditional argument generally admits. To begin with, there seems to be no such thing as an average abduction. Nor, apparently, is there such a thing as an average abductee. Surprisingly enough, there is also little agreement on the nature or appearance of the aliens who apparently carry out these bizarre kidnappings, and opinions differ considerably as to their precise purposes or intentions – even among their victims.

Every abduction seems to contain specific, and sometimes major, details that are peculiar to the individual involved. How very dissimilar these details can be will emerge from particular cases that we will review in this book. Nonetheless, despite the very real differences between one person's experience and another's, abductions do follow a certain general pattern. Individual accounts of abductions are rather like variations on a theme in music and, like the variations of an exceptionally inventive composer, on first hearing they sometimes seem to bear very little relationship to the foundations on which they are built. It is useful to have this basic scenario in mind when looking at individual cases, and a brief guide to it follows.

The scheme I am following here is based on that noted by folklorist Dr Thomas 'Ed' Bullard in 1987, after an exhaustive analysis of some 270 abduction reports. A very similar pattern was also discerned by Professor Alvin Lawson in 1977 (see Chapter Three). Dr Bullard breaks down abduction narratives into eight segments or scenes: capture, examination, conference, tour, otherworldly journey, theophany, return, and aftermath. Not all of these scenes occur in all abduction reports –

the 'theophany', for instance, is very rare – and according to a small but very visible group of researchers the nature of some of them has altered radically since the late 1980s (see Chapter Two).

A full-blown abduction would go like this:

1. Capture: First, in many cases, comes a UFO sighting, sometimes involving electromagnetic or other physical effects on the witnesses' home or vehicle. It is not always clear exactly how the craft is entered (a phenomenon known as 'doorway amnesia'). Recent abductees often tell of being floated through solid walls or windows and then up a beam of light to the UFO. The interiors of alien craft are reportedly brightly but diffusely lit, often featuring round or curved 'rooms'. They are clinically clean, often with white or metallic fixtures and fittings. The reason for this sterility soon becomes clear, for the next stage in the abduction is a medical examination of some kind – usually a painful one. The abductee is undressed – sometimes forcibly – and may be prepared for the examination by being bathed or immersed in liquid. Witnesses most often report seeing small gray aliens, sometimes together with taller humanoids, on board the UFO.

2. Examination: Mechanical devices vaguely resembling X-ray cameras may be used on the abductee, and appear to scan them physically and, according to some, mentally. Other implements may be thrust into various orifices. Explanations for these invasive operations vary; sometimes the aliens offer no rationale for their behavior. More conventional samples of skin, ear wax or nail scrapings may be taken.

> ◆
> The reason for this sterility soon becomes clear, for the next stage in the abduction is a medical examination of some kind – usually a painful one
> ◆

These examinations may also involve small 'implants' being inserted in or removed from the abductee's body. Victims believe these to be tracking devices of some kind. Others report being forced to have sex with aliens (or being seduced by them), and some women have claimed to have found themselves pregnant as a result. Communication with the aliens is generally telepathic, and many abductees report that the alien in charge of the abduction is different – usually taller, and often more 'human' – from the other entities involved. Some victims also say they feel as if their minds are being scanned telepathically rather than mechanically during the examination phase, often by this 'leader' or 'doctor'.

*3. **Conference:*** Once these ordeals are over, witnesses are allowed to dress and many report having extended conversations with their captors before leaving the ship. At this stage some abductees try to remove an item of the craft's equipment as physical proof of their experience, but the aliens prevent them. Others however are given gifts by the aliens, and sometimes words of wisdom or a 'message for mankind' as well. Frequently, the knowledge they are vouchsafed is to be kept secret and beyond the recall of memory – but, the abductees are told, they will be able to

Truman Bethurum's Aboard A Flying Saucer, *one of several 'contactee' accounts of the 1950s. Their encouters were generally different from today's abductions, although the aliens pass on much the same messages for mankind now as they did 40 years ago.*

remember it when the time is right to reveal it.

*4 **Tour:*** A guided tour around the aliens' spacecraft or part of it. Sometimes this tour includes a visit to alien-human hybrid children, which the abductee may have fathered or borne.

*5. **Otherworldly journey:*** Some abductees also report being taken to visit the aliens' planet, or a base on this or another world; this segment of the abduction scenario may take on a distinctly mystical character, which shades into the relatively rare 'theophany'. In abduction reports that have been gathered since the 1980s, this stage is often replaced by screenings of scenes that are taken to be views of Earth's future, or of the aliens' home planet.

*6. **Theophany:*** The abductee is put in the presence of a figure, being or other manifestation of apparently divine origin or authority. Here again 'messages' or 'wisdom' may be imparted.

*7. **Return:*** The abductee is 'transferred' directly from the craft or 'floated' back to where the aliens first took him or her captive; memories of this stage of the proceedings, like entering the craft, are often very vague. The UFO then leaves at high speed.

*8. **Aftermath:*** After the experience is over and the UFO has departed, the abductee discovers that the events of what seemed like a few minutes' duration turn out to have taken hours, or, in a few cases, even days. Many abductees report no conscious memory of their experience, and some researchers regard this perception of 'missing time' as a primary clue that an abduction has taken place. In the following days or weeks, bizarre UFO-related dreams and memory flashes may occur. Physical symptoms and emotional reactions may afflict the witness.

As I said earlier, some abductees remember little or nothing of their abduction, while others have a clear and complete recollection of events. But how do we know so much about abductions? At what point does someone with little conscious recall of an abduction decide they may be an abductee? How do they make their way to investigators? How do their stories become public knowledge?

Herein lies one of the paradoxes of abduction research, and skeptics have a strong case when they suggest that many 'abductions' are really the joint creations of researchers – in search of evidence for a theory to which they are already committed – and individuals in search of an exotic solution to run-of-the-mill problems. For an abductee to know whom to seek out for advice or investigation, they have to know that abduction researchers exist. So common is knowledge of the phenomenon today that they can be found in the Yellow Pages in large American cities, but before the late 1980s a potential abductee had the choice of living silently with their peculiar experience (assuming they remembered very much of it), actively seeking out a ufologist, or looking for some literature on the subject.

In 1961 Betty Hill, the first American abductee, sent an outline of her and her husband Barney's experience to the National Investigations Committee on Aerial Phenomena (NICAP) after reading a book by its director, Donald Keyhoe. NICAP investigated the case, but the full story of the Hills' abduction came out only when they were hypnotized, initially for medical reasons. Most of the best-known cases of the 1970s emerged because the witnesses saw the NBC-TV movie based on the Hills' 1961 abduction, *The UFO Incident*, and made connections with events (such as 'missing time') in their own lives. Hypnosis had seemed so successful in uncovering what had happened to the Hills that ufologists adopted it as their chief investigative tool in suspected abduction cases. The technique was to prove highly contentious.

As time went on, the books and magazine articles and TV appearances by the investigators generated more enquiries, and more books, and more enquiries. Budd Hopkins's career is a good example of this: the witness at the center of his second book contacted him after reading his first (discussing several alleged abductions), and the central character in his third got in touch with him after reading his second. Since a book about the Hills' case became a bestseller in 1966, the route to an investigator has therefore been littered with opportunities for a potential abductee to become quite familiar with the general outline of what was supposed to happen during an abduction. The more the ufological version of events made sense to potential witnesses, and the more familiar they became with the abduction scenario, the less likely it was that another interpretation would be put upon their experience – especially under hypnosis, for reasons discussed in Chapter Three.

The ufological interpretation of whatever has befallen the witness is further reinforced in investi-

◆

These examinations may also involve small 'implants' being inserted in or removed from the abductee's body

◆

Abductee George Adamski (at left) with journalist Long John Nebel. Adamski's fraudulent stories of meeting angelic spacemen from Venus helped to create a climate of ridicule around any claim to have met aliens.

gators' support groups. These were set up with the laudable aim of providing a forum in which abductees could discuss their experiences without fear of ridicule, but they rarely if ever permit the intrusion of other views. One abductee I spoke to likened one such group he had visited to a religious chapter. The atmosphere in such a gathering, with the fatherly or motherly presence of the investigator, makes it very difficult for a newcomer to escape the pressure to conform and win approval. This too will affect what emerges under hypnosis.

Betty Hill is not impressed with current abduction research, and told me candidly: 'I try to get across to people that they should stay away from hypnosis. You don't want anybody foolin' round with your brain. I mean, you have problems enough to live with, without other people making their contribution. You know these therapy groups?' Betty named a famous abduction researcher and his abductees' support group. 'A

woman called me. She quit. She said she got fed up. That therapy group – it ends up in "I'll show you the kind of sex I had on board the UFO if you show me the kind of sex you had on board the UFO."'

This may be an exaggeration. But in light of the potential drawbacks of the hypnotic technique and all that surrounds it, for this book I interviewed a number of abductees and potential abductees who had not been hypnotized, partly to discover if their experiences were significantly different from those who had (of whom I interviewed several as well). The short answer is that there is no difference worth arguing about. But one of these, David Howard, has an explosive story to tell (see Chapter Four). The circumstances of his abduction and subsequent encounters with alien entities raise an army of fundamental questions that neither the literalist proponents of 'abductions by extra-terrestrials' nor the more obdurate skeptics have even begun to ask.

Why should the aliens who allegedly perform abductions be extra-terrestrial anyway? The answer, such as it is, lies less in the evidence abductees present than in the history of UFOs themselves. Put bluntly, it has always been an *assumption* that UFOs come from outer space. Kenneth Arnold, whose sighting of some odd aerial phenomena in 1947 spurred ufology as we know it into being, finally concluded that what he had seen were some kind of airborne creatures. It was probably not until 1950, when Donald Keyhoe argued the case in an epochal article in *True* magazine, that the general public wholeheartedly adopted the idea that 'flying saucers' were extra-terrestrial. Then, in 1953, former bootlegger and occultist George Adamski published his account of a meeting with a gentle, fair-haired 'Venusian' in the California desert the year before. Adamski, who had previously tried to sell the same story as a work of science fiction, was followed by a rash of imitators.

These 'contactees' had broadly similar fables to tell: they had met beautiful Martians, Venusians and Saturnians who lived in harmonious societies and were deeply concerned about the direction human history was taking. A special worry was the appearance of atomic weapons on Earth. One of these contactees, South African Elizabeth Klarer, claimed to have given birth to the child of her alien lover. Another, British taxi driver George King, averred that he had information from impeccable sources that Jesus of Nazareth was alive and living on Venus; so began the first ufological religious cult, the Aetherius Society. Ufologists have been embarrassed or infuriated by the contactees, and abduction proponents insist that they have no connection with 'their' subjects. The themes of the Earth at risk, interbreeding with aliens and religious mysticism are, however, inseparable from the testimony of abductees.

While the contactees were (largely accurately) denounced as charlatans or seriously deluded, slightly more plausible reports of encounters with UFOs and their occupants flowed in from much more credible witnesses over the next three decades. The first rash came during a huge wave of UFO sightings in France in 1954. Few of these French reports are now deemed reliable, but in 1964 the sighting of two diminutive entities and their landed craft by police officer Lonnie Zamora at Socorro, New Mexico, USA, became embedded in UFO lore as a virtually unassailable case. There were many others, before and after, from all over the world, and not all featured pint-sized aliens, but the entities often seemed to be taking soil samples and otherwise investigating the local flora and fauna. One farmer, Gary Wilcox, from New York State, recalled having a long conversation with two beings about the virtues of different kinds of fertilizer. Then, in the 1970s, there was a wave of reports that seemed to suggest that aliens were mutilating cattle right across the USA. And so within ufology the stage was set for much closer encounters between highly inquisitive but apparently heartless aliens, and human beings. In the late 1970s came the first trickle of reports of abductions in the USA since the isolated cases of Betty and Barney Hill and one or two others in the 1960s.

What it all might mean, and what kind of realities are involved, we shall now explore in earnest.

Author, Budd Hopkins, at The Strange World of Ufomania, NYC, displaying his UFO books collection.

CHAPTER 1

ANATOMY OF A NIGHTMARE

The Variety of Abduction Experiences

◆ ◆ ◆

Opposite: The leader of the aliens who allegedly abducted Betty and Barney Hill in September 1961. The painting, by New Hampshire artist David Baker, was based on the Hills' descriptions and approved by them.

The general public first became aware of the abduction phenomenon in 1966 through John Fuller's best-seller *The Interrupted Journey*, which recounted the experience of Betty and Barney Hill during a trip from Montreal to their home in Portsmouth, New Hampshire, USA, in 1961.

Barney, then aged 39, worked as a mail sorter in Boston, commuting the 190km (120-mile) round trip from Portsmouth each day. Betty, aged 41, was a social worker for the State of New Hampshire. Both were very active in civil rights campaigning and were on their church's United Nations committee. In mid-September 1961 they decided on the spur of the moment to drive to the

Betty and Barney Hill, whose 1961 abduction was the first to be widely reported in the English-speaking world. Later cases tend to be judged by their similarity to this one.

Niagara Falls and home through Canada for a short break. On their return journey, not long after they had left Montreal, weather reports warned of a hurricane moving along the East Coast. The Hills decided on an all-night drive to Portsmouth to avoid the storm. At 9 p.m. on 19 September they crossed the border with the USA. They ate in Colebrook, New Hampshire, and continued south on US Highway 3.

Near Lancaster, Betty noticed a bright light, near the Moon, and getting brighter. Barney suggested it was a satellite gone off course. However, the light didn't go away – indeed it seemed to be pacing them – and several times they stopped the car to see it better. Looking through binoculars,

Barney thought it was an aircraft (he was an 'avid plane-watcher') and suggested various types it might be. They drove on slowly, but now the light seemed to be closer, and circling them. Betty looked through the binoculars and said she could see a huge craft with a double row of windows; she watched it fly across the face of the Moon. At some point, they realized they had driven off the main highway. The light dropped to tree height, and they stopped again. Barney took the binoculars and walked across a field towards the light, and came within 15m (50ft) of it.

He could now tell it was an object 'like a big pancake' with a row of windows. Through the binoculars he could see several occupants, dressed

When Betty and Barney Hill were returning from holiday in 1961, they turned off Route 3 in New Hampshire onto this dead-end road.

in Nazi-style uniforms. Suddenly convinced he was about to be captured, he fled back to the car in terror. As the Hills drove off, they heard a series of beeps, apparently coming from the rear of the car. The couple remembered little after this until they eventually rejoined US3 near Ashland, when they heard another set of beeps. They reached Portsmouth as day was breaking, having taken seven hours to cover the last 300km (190 miles) of their trip. On arrival, Betty noticed some mysterious shiny spots on her car, and found they made a compass needle swing wildly.

Betty reported the sighting to Pease Air Force Base, and began avidly to read all she could about UFOs; within a week she reported their experience to the National Investigations Committee on Aerial Phenomena (NICAP). From 29 September to 3 October she had a series of nightmares in which she saw a group of humanoids blocking US3; she and Barney were then led aboard the UFO they had seen and were medically examined. In late October, in a session with NICAP investigators, Barney realized that their journey from Colebrook had taken two hours longer than it should have done. There seemed to be a period of 'missing time' after the sighting of the UFO.

Barney began to suffer from ulcers, high blood pressure and exhaustion, and developed a ring of warts around his groin. He had psychiatric treatment for a year from summer 1962, and eventually asked his therapist to arrange regressive hypnosis to determine what had really happened on 19 September 1961. He began hypnosis with Dr Benjamin Simon of Boston in December 1963. Betty began separate regression sessions a couple of weeks later.

Both told approximately the same story under hypnosis. At some point south of North Woodstock, Barney turned off US3 onto a minor road. Figures appeared in the headlights, waving them to a halt. They had been roadblocked by gray-skinned, black-haired humanoids with large, wrap-around eyes, small, flattened noses, and blue slit-like mouths. Betty and Barney were taken on board the UFO (Barney was semi-conscious, and had to be dragged to the machine), where they were put in separate rooms and given a medical examination. Betty reported that after a skin sample was taken from her arm, part of a fingernail was cut off, and a hair was pulled from her head, a long needle was inserted into her navel: she was told this was a pregnancy test. The operation caused her considerable pain, which the 'examiner' – who was slightly taller than the other beings – relieved by waving his hand in front of her eyes.

Barney had a circular instrument applied to his groin, apparently for the specific purpose of extracting his semen.

After her examination, Betty had a conversation with the 'examiner', whom she considered the leader of her captors. When she asked where they came from, she was shown a star map with no legend on it, and was given a book as a keepsake of the event. (Later, this was taken from her and she was told she would not remember the experience.) Betty was uncertain as to exactly how she and the aliens conversed. Each understood the other as if they were speaking plain English, but she had the impression that the actual method of communication was telepathic. While the humanoids used colloquial English, they were sometimes confused by very basic concepts – asking, for example: 'What are vegetables? What is yellow?' They seemed to have no notion of time, although they used phrases like 'Just a minute'. They were particularly intrigued by Barney's dentures, and when Betty explained that he had them because of an injury and that many people had them in old age, they failed to understand the idea of aging. The couple were walked back to their car by the aliens, and watched the UFO depart as a glowing orange ball.

Pease AFB confirmed to US Air Force consultant Dr J. Allen Hynek that their radar had shown an 'unknown' in the air at the time and place that the Hills had their encounter. But Dr Simon noted that Betty's account under hypnosis precisely matched the dreams she reported; he concluded that the Hills had had an imaginary experience whose content was based on Betty's dreams, which themselves

> ◆
>
> **Barney realized that their journey from Colebrook had taken two hours longer than it should have done**
>
> ◆

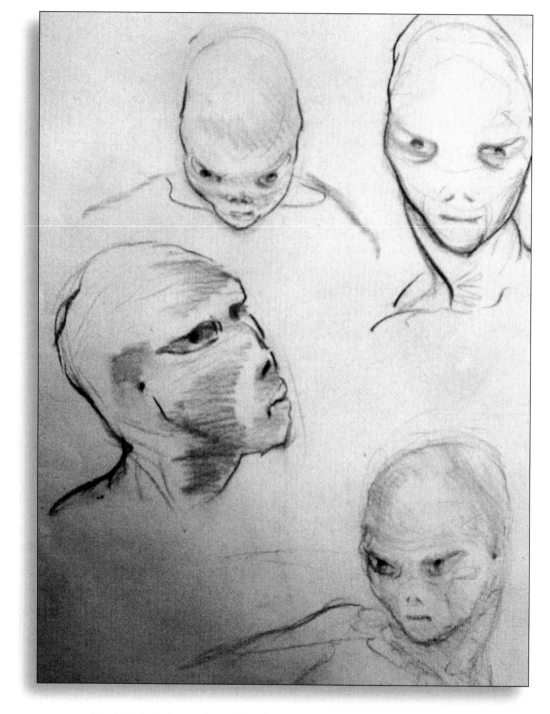

David Baker's impression of the aliens who abducted Betty and Barney Hill.
Described by Barney as gray-skinned, black-haired humanoids with large,
wrap-around eyes, small, flattened noses and blue slit-like mouths, these creatures resemble
the Grays reported by later abductees, but lack their extraordinary all-black eyes
and strange spindly necks.

were caused by fear after a genuine close encounter with a UFO. He also noted: 'Hypnosis is the pathway to the Truth as it is felt and understood by the patient. The Truth is what he believes to be the truth, which may or may not be consonant with the ultimate non-personal truth.'

Betty Hill continued to believe in the reality of her abduction and reported many UFO sightings and encounters after it. (Barney died in 1969 of a cerebral hemorrhage.)

Antonio Villas Boas

This was not the first such case of 'spacenapping' known to ufologists, however. As early as 1959 hints were beginning to reach the USA from Brazil of the case of Antonio Villas Boas (see feature on page 22). Late in 1957 this 23-year-old farmer had first contacted João Martins, a journalist who worked for

Jim and Coral Lorenzen, founders of the Aerial Phenomena Research Organization (APRO), refused, initially, to publish the Villas Boas case in the 1950s.

the Rio de Janeiro magazine *O Cruzeiro*, which occasionally printed UFO-related stories. Martins paid for Villas Boas to come to the city and be interviewed and examined by surgeon and ufologist Olavo T. Fontes. The story was turned down by the magazine, but was eventually summarized in English in a Brazilian ufological bulletin published in the summer of 1962. Coral Lorenzen, who with her husband James had founded the Aerial Phenomena Research Organization in 1952, thought the Villas Boas story so outlandish that she refused to publish it. The first fairly complete version in English began to appear in the British magazine *Flying Saucer Review* in January 1965. In 1967 the Lorenzens printed a slightly more detailed account in their *Flying Saucer Occupants*; a definitive version appeared in Charles Bowen's *The Humanoids* in 1969.

A comparison of the two seminal, 'archetypal' cases of Villas Boas and Betty and Barney Hill illustrates the seeming paradox about abduction accounts that I mentioned in the Introduction. Initially, the two cases seem radically different. Yet despite wide divergences of detail (and of apparent intention on the part of the aliens) they follow the essential pattern of the 'classic' abduction scenario: an initial sighting, an examination and conference with the alien beings (with greater or lesser sexual overtones), the attempt to acquire a 'souvenir', and departure.

Nonetheless, the differences between the two experiences are striking. To begin with, the two sets of abductees could hardly be more diverse in background or occupation. In the Hills' case there was allegedly a period of two hours' 'missing time' from their journey; this has become a key clue to an abduction for later researchers, but Villas Boas suffered no such problem. Nor were his memories of his experience in any way repressed by the

aliens. But most noticeable is the distinction between the reported aliens: a blue-eyed blonde of almost entirely human aspect on the one hand, and gray-skinned, blue-lipped, black-haired creatures on the other. And it would seem that the aliens who landed in Brazil were not adapted to the Earth's atmosphere, as they wore helmets and breathing apparatus outside and inside their craft; but those working in New Hampshire wore none. Both sets of aliens had eyes

Artist Clark Hathaway's depiction of the UFO that descended onto the field Antonio Villas Boas was plowing at night in October 1957.

that seemed unusual to the witnesses. They were elongated and disproportionately large in the Hills' case; whereas Villas Boas's male captors had small, blue eyes, and his seductress's were large, slanted and blue. Notably, neither group of aliens had the bizarre, gigantic, all-black eyes of the 'Grays' so often encountered in later abduction reports. And unlike most Grays, these entities wore clothes – in both cases, apparently some kind of uniform. The aliens who captured Villas Boas 'spoke' in guttural shrieks and made no attempt to communicate directly with their captive; those who abducted the Hills communicated telepathically and easily enough, but were bemused by such everyday matters as colors and time.

Herb Schirmer

For many years, abductees reported equally diverse entities. The seemingly ubiquitous Grays became dominant in abduction reports only in the 1980s - and not everywhere, even then. Consider the following descriptions from the 1960s and 1970s:

Herb Schirmer (abducted 3 December 1967 in Ashland, Nebraska, USA) described his gray-white-skinned captors as standing 1.37–1.52m (4ft 6in–5ft) tall, wearing close-fitting, silver-gray, one-piece uniforms with the emblem of a winged serpent on the right breast; the suit came up over the head to form a helmet, on whose left side was an earpiece with a short antenna. Their heads were thin, with a long flat nose, unblinking oriental – but not especially large – eyes, and thin, unmoving lips. The physiognomy described by Schirmer differs considerably from descriptions of the classic Gray.

José Antônio da Silva

José Antônio da Silva (abducted 4 May 1969 at Bebedouro, Espírito Santo, Brazil) was set upon while asleep in a tent on a fishing trip by several 'men' about 1.2m (4ft) tall. They wore 'shining, light-colored' garments and gray masks 'like dull aluminum' to which breathing apparatus was attached. They had 'human proportions and were robust in relation to their small stature. Their legs

seemed to be thick.' After an 'interminable' journey in a craft shaped like a cylinder set vertically between two saucers, da Silva was confronted by about a dozen unmasked 'homuncules'. A report of the case by investigator Professor Hulvio Brant Aleixo described their apparent leader thus:

> ... *he was extremely hairy. His long tresses, reddish and wavy, fell down past his shoulders to his waist; his beard was long and thick and came down to his stomach. He had wide-set eyebrows, two fingers thick, running right across almost the whole forehead. His skin was light-colored, very pale. His eyes were round, larger than is the norm with us, and of a green shade like the color of green leaves beginning to wither. The orbital cavities of his eyes were deep, the sclerotica were darker in color than his skin, and his pupils were dark. His eyes scarcely ever blinked. José Antônio did not notice any eyelashes....*

◆

The seemingly ubiquitous Grays became dominant in abduction reports only in the 1980s – and not everywhere, even then

◆

The little man's nose, long and pointed, was 'bigger than ours.' His ears were bigger too. The lower part of the ears was the same as ours, but the upper parts were more rounded. His mouth was wide, and, said José Antônio, looked like fishes' mouths. I didn't see a tooth in any of them....'

The beings spoke a 'deep, guttural' language. They communicated with José Antônio through signs, and by making sketches on a light-colored slate. His understanding of what they were trying to say seemed to improve after he had drunk some of a dark green, bitter-tasting liquid that he was offered.

John Hodges

John Hodges (pseudonym; abducted August 1971, in Los Angeles, California, USA) and Peter Rodriguez (also a pseudonym) were leaving a friend's apartment on Dapple Gray Lane in South Los Angeles at 2 a.m. when they saw two brain-like objects on the road in front of Hodges' car. They were as high as a man's waist and apparently alive. The larger of the two 'brains' had a red patch on one side. Hodges drove past the objects, delivered Rodriguez home, and went on to his own apartment.

According to testimony given under hypnosis, the 'brains' then reappeared, before Hodges was able to leave his car. Next, he found himself –with the 'brains' - in a room full of instruments, at which humanoid figures were standing: 'They're tall, skin gray…yellow eyes, very thin eyes, mouths but no lips, funny, flat noses. Their hands have long, thin fingers, six fingers and a thumb. They're webbed, more or less from the palm to the first knuckle….'

The 'brains' were apparently in charge of what was going on, however. Hodges' abduction included prophecies of World War III, which would begin in the early 1980s, followed by nuclear disarmament and 'official contact' with UFOs in 1987. To that extent, the abduction followed a standard pattern.

Charlie Hickson and Calvin Parker

Yet another kind of entity was involved in the experience of Charlie Hickson and Calvin Parker (abducted 11 October 1973, at Pascagoula, Mississippi, USA). The pair were spending the evening fishing off the pier of the abandoned Shaupeter shipyard on the Pascagoula River. At

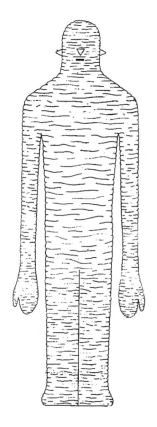

Charlie Hickson's sketch of one of three entities that abducted him and Calvin Parker from the bank of the Pascagoula River in Mississippi in October 1973. Some have suggested the creatures were robots.

about 9 p.m. Hickson turned to get fresh bait, and heard a 'zipping sound'. Hovering close to the ground nearby, Hickson saw, was a fish-shaped blue-gray craft. An opening appeared in the UFO and three 1.5m (5ft) beings floated out of it and toward the anglers. In Hickson's words:

The head seemed to come directly to the shoulders, no neck, and something resembling a nose came out to a point about two inches [5cm] long. On each side of the head, about where ears would be, was something similar to the nose. Directly under the nose was a slit resembling a mouth. The arms were something like human arms, but long in proportion to the body; the hands resembled a mitten, there was a thumb attached. The legs remained together and the feet looked something like elephant's feet. The entire body was wrinkled and had a grayish color. There could have been eyes, but the area above the nose was so wrinkled I couldn't tell.

Hickson later described the hands as crab-like claws, which is borne out in his drawings. The creatures gathered up the two men – at this point Parker fainted – and floated them into the craft. Hickson found himself in a brightly lit room with no visible light source. Parker was taken to an adjoining chamber. Hickson was somehow suspended in the air so that he could move only his eyes, and a free-floating object resembling a gigantic eye moved back and forth around his body, as if examining it. After 20 minutes or so, the pair were floated back to the pier. Hickson landed on his feet. Parker then regained consciousness.

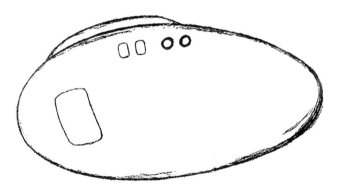

Drawing by Charlie Hickson of the UFO into which he was abducted. Initially, he described the craft as 'fish-shaped'. Other details changed as he retold his story, and he later reported further contact with UFOs.

Patty Roach and her children

In striking contrast to Hodges' abductors, but with one feature in common with the Pascagoula entities, were those who took Patty Roach and her children from their home at Lehi in Utah, USA, five days later, on 16 October 1973. The aliens were very thin, about 1.2m (4ft) tall, with long arms that ended in gloved 'claws' with a very small thumb, and they had large, slanted eyes. They were wearing seemingly fluorescent clothing with Sam Browne belts. In charge of operations on board the UFO to which the Roach family was taken was a 'regular human being' who was 'of medium height, bald on top of his head, with a fringe of gray on the sides, and he wore hornrimmed glasses'. Mrs Roach believed that her 'thoughts were taken' during the abduction.

Carl Higdon

Somewhere between alien, human and the enigmatic 'Men In Black' who are reported to harass UFO witnesses was the being who called himself 'Ausso' and who abducted Carl Higdon – and the five elk that he was hunting – on the north boundary of Medicine Bow National Forest, Wyoming, USA, on 29 October 1974. Ausso stood 1.88m (6ft 2in) tall and weighed about 82kg (180lb), and was dressed in a black suit with black shoes. His belt had a star in the middle of it and a yellow emblem below it. He was 'quite bow-legged', and had 'a slanted head and no chin', and thin hair that 'stood straight up on his head'. Ausso spoke ordinary English and conducted the abduction entirely single-handed. Higdon saw no other alien entities during the event, but he did see five

THE ALIEN LOVER

Antonio Villas Boas

◆ ◆ ◆

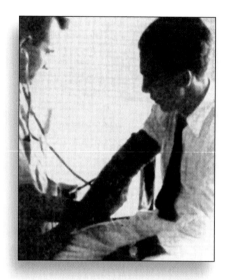

Antonio Villas Boas,
Brazil, 1957.

Twenty-three-year-old Antonio Villas Boas lived with his parents, his brothers and sisters-in-law on a small farm near São Francisco de Salles, in Minas Gerais, Brazil. In the early hours of 16 October 1957 he was out alone, plowing the fields by the light of his tractor's headlamps. He may not have been entirely surprised when, at about 1 a.m., he saw what he described as a 'large red star' descending out of the sky. Ten days before he and his brother had watched a brilliant light approach the farmhouse until it lit up their bedroom, even though Antonio had slammed the shutters closed in fright. And at about 9.30 in the evening of 15 October, when he had been out plowing with his brother, the pair had seen a dim red ball of light hovering about 100m (300ft) above the ground. Antonio had tried to get close to the light to see what was behind it, but it eluded him, darting from one end of the field to the other.

But this time Villas Boas was alone, and petrified, for as the red light came down to about 45m (150ft) above him, he could see that it was an egg-shaped object. As it landed – lowering three shafts as undercarriage – its brilliant glow drowned out the lights of his tractor. The machine had a definite rim, in which were set purple lights. Three spurs were set at the front, lit up with red light. The upper, domed part of the machine was spinning counter clockwise, and as it slowed to land changed color from red to green.

Antonio tried to make off on his tractor, but the engine died. As he started to run across the plowed field, he was grabbed by three entities – none higher than his shoulder, and he is only 1.65m (5ft 5in) tall – and dragged to the waiting craft. He was taken struggling up a flexible ladder into the machine, and found himself in a small, square, brightly lit room with metallic walls.

He realized that there were five small entities present: two kept a firm hold on him. They were wearing tight-fitting suits of thick, soft, unevenly striped gray material, and large, broad helmets reinforced with bands of metal. Pipes led from the helmets to their clothes, two going under each armpit and one down their backs. Thick-soled 'shoes' seemed to be integral to their suits, as did thick, unwieldy gloves. All Villas Boas could see of the creatures' features were their small, pale blue eyes.

Villas Boas later recalled that the sounds they made were 'so totally different from anything I had heard....They were slow barks and yelps, neither very clear nor very hoarse, some longer, some shorter, at times containing several different sounds all at once.... I still shudder when I think of those sounds. I can't reproduce them – my voice just isn't made for that.'

The five diminutive aliens then stripped the protesting farmer of his clothes, and one of them rubbed a wet sponge-like thing over his skin. Then he was led into another chamber, sparsely furnished with a few chairs and a couch. Here the aliens produced 'a sort of chalice', which they used to take a blood sample from their captive. Then Villas Boas was left alone - only to find a weird odor filling the room, which soon had him rushing to a corner to be sick.

Now came the most bizarre part of his experience. Into the room walked a naked woman, whose body was 'more beautiful than any I have ever seen before'. Her hair was smooth and fair, almost white, although her underarm and pubic hair was bright red. She had 'big blue eyes, rather longer than round, for they slanted outward'. Her body, said Villas Boas, was 'slim, and her breasts stood up high and well separated.' What happened next is best told in Antonio Villas Boas's own words:

'The woman came toward me in silence…and suddenly she hugged me and began to rub her head against my face from side to side. At the same time I also felt her body glued to mine….' He became 'uncontrollably sexually excited, something that had never happened to me before.…We ended up on the couch, where we lay together for the first time. It was a normal act and she reacted as any other woman would. Then we had some petting, followed by another act, but by now she had begun to deny herself to me, to end the matter.' At that, Antonio too lost interest - and became angry, as it dawned on him that 'all they wanted [was] a good stallion to improve their own stock….'

Shortly after this the woman was called away. Before she left, she pointed to her stomach, and then at the sky, which he interpreted as meaning that sooner or later she would return to take him away. Brazilian investigators persuaded him, however, that she had simply meant that she would bear their child on her home planet. After this, Antonio Villas Boas was given back his clothes and taken on a tour of the alien craft, during which he tried, and failed, to purloin an instrument as a keepsake. Then he was carried back down the ladder to the ground, from where he saw the UFO disappear into the sky like a bullet. He had been aboard the craft for 4 hours, 15 minutes.

Over the next few weeks Antonio suffered from bouts of sleepiness and nausea. Olavo T. Fontes, a ufologist and also a professor of surgery, interviewed him in February 1958. He gave the young man a complete physical examination and found two 'small hyperchromic spots, one on each side of the chin…resulting from some superficial lesion with associated bleeding under the skin'.

In the years that followed, the case became a classic in ufology, but little was heard about Villas Boas himself. Then in 1978 he surfaced again on a TV program in Brazil - no longer a simple peasant farmer, but Dr Antonio Villas Boas, a sober lawyer with a practice in a small town near the nation's capital, Brasilia, happily married and with four children. Only one item of his testimony changed: the woman had taken a sperm sample from him during their second act of intercourse.

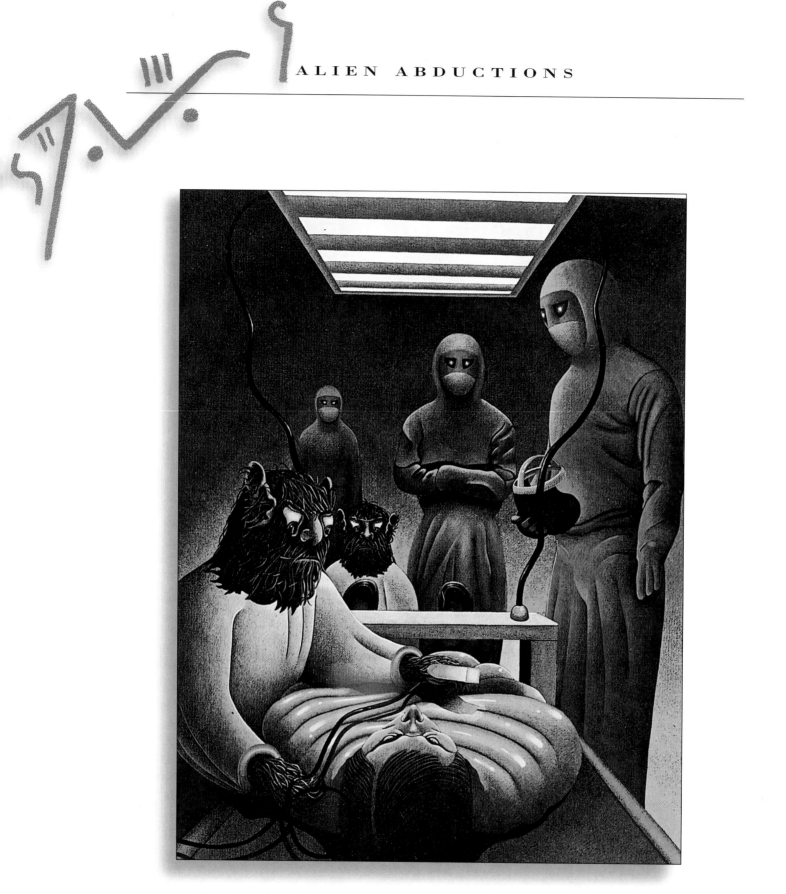

Artist's impression of aliens examining John Avis during his abduction - with his wife Elaine, their two children, and their car - from a country road in Essex, England, in 1974. Distinct types - some say races - of aliens have been reported aboard UFOs by abductees since, but no others have recalled these particular entities. The Avises' experience also included the appearance of a prophetic, Christ-like figure, which does not feature in other reports.

other humans on the planet – or place – that he was taken for a brief, non-intrusive examination, during which he remained clothed and standing. The craft Ausso piloted resembled a transparent cubicle, which Higdon estimated to be about 2m (7ft) square. In Sweden eight months previously, a witness known as 'Anders' was abducted while walking to his home in Lindholmen at night; this time the aliens were 'semi-transparent'. They were about 1.88m (6ft 2in) tall and looked 'like Indians' – that is, people from the Indian sub-continent. He had the impression they were wearing hoods, as he did not notice their ears or hair. There was a 'hazing glow' around them, and they communicated with each other 'by a series of musical tones'.

The Avises

On 27 October 1974 (just two days before Carl Higdon was abducted in Wyoming), still another, entirely different, set of entities lifted John and Elaine Avis, their children and their car from a country road in Essex, England and into a craft. Under hypnosis John Avis recalled three tall (over 1.8m/6ft) 'controllers' or 'watchers' who appeared to direct the activities of smaller – and considerably uglier – alien creatures. The humanoid 'controllers' wore one-piece silvery suits that also tightly covered their heads and masked their lower faces. Avis could make out only slanted pink eyes that seemed to have no pupils, high cheekbones, and the shape of a long nose beneath the masks. He was actually examined, however, by two grotesque creatures wearing white surgical gowns and wielding small, pen-like instruments. They were hairy, bearded dwarves with triangular eyes, beaked noses and slit-like mouths – in the original investigator's words, 'not dissimilar to humanoid bats' – and had

hairy, claw-like hands. Elaine Avis's descriptions of the aliens matched those of her husband.

Not all the people mentioned above experienced a complete playing-out of the basic abduction scenario. Carl Higdon, for instance, was told that he was 'not what they needed', and the encounter was cut short. Even when many or even all of the standard scenes do occur, they can differ enormously from case to case, just as the appearance of the aliens may. In the accounts above the entities are variously tall, short, bald, hairy, clothed, unclothed, and nearer or further from being typically human in general conformation. They communicate – or don't – in distinctive ways. What is conspicuous is the peculiarity of their eyes. They are not all the same, but (with the exception of the possibly eyeless creature seen at Pascagoula) they are all striking. They tend to be larger than what the witness considers usual, almost always slanting, and often overpowering in their effect.

Barney Hill, for example, was almost overwhelmed by the aliens' eyes that he saw through binoculars on the side of US Highway 3: 'Oh, those eyes! They're in my brain!' he exclaimed under hypnosis. He felt they kept following him as he returned (or fled) back to the car. Later, when the aliens were standing in the road, blocking the way, he recalled:

> They won't talk to me. Only the eyes are talking to me. I – I – I – I don't understand that. Oh yes – the eyes don't have a body. They're just eyes.... I know what it is. It's the

◆

What is conspicuous is the peculiarity of their eyes. They are not all the same but … they are all striking

◆

Cheshire cat in Alice in Wonderland. *Ah, I don't have to be afraid of that. It disappeared too...only the eyes remained....I'm not afraid.... The eyes are telling me, 'Don't be afraid'.... All I see are these eyes.... I'm not even afraid that they're not connected to a body. They're just up close, pressing against my eyes.*

Artist Clark Hathaway's painting of Barney Hill's view of the aliens through binoculars emphasizes the creatures' bizarre eyes – which, Barney said, were 'in his brain' at the time and, later, 'talked' to him.

In Lewis Carroll's classic, incidentally, the Cheshire Cat vanishes all but for its *smile*, and not its eyes – but Barney Hill was not the last alien abductee to liken alien eyes to those of a cat.

Sandy Larson (abducted 26 August 1975 on Interstate 94, about 70km/45 miles west of Fargo, North Dakota, USA; see Chapter Two) echoed Barney's sense that the alien's eyes were hypnotically powerful. Asked by ufologist Dr J. Allen Hynek what was the particularly strange thing about the face of her alien examiner, she answered: 'The glaring of the eyes. It seemed like their eyes could control my brain.' Beneath the variations of specific details, then, we can see a common theme. What we do not see in these early cases is the solid-black eyes of the Grays, although their pallid skin color crops up not only in the Hills' experience but in the quite dissimilar creatures that the Pascagoula pair encountered.

The Grays seem to have emerged as the dominant form taken by aliens in the USA with the publication in 1981 of Budd Hopkins' book *Missing Time*. Six years later, when Whitley Strieber published *Communion*, their prevalence started to become international, in parallel with the massive publicity effort the publishers put behind the book. At the Abductions Study Conference held in Cambridge, Massachusetts, USA, in 1992, British ufologist Jenny Randles drew attention to a curious difference that by then had become clear among American, British and European abduction reports. Randles had observed that the three types of entity most commonly encountered in abductions seemed to favor certain parts of the world.

Three main groups of entities appear in the British sample [Randles reported]. These are the 'Grays' (the small large headed type most common in American abduction literature), the 'Nordics' (tall, often blond-haired, blue-eyed entities with cat-like eyes...), and 'humans' (figures that are fairly normal in height and appearance and in several cases were described as wearing beards or looking 'just like you or I'.

These are the percentages that Randles found

	Human	Nordic	Grays	Others
Britain	44	35	12	09
USA	12	06	73	09
Europe	15	25	48	12

when she compared the British experience with those in the USA and Europe:

Six times as many Grays seemed to be visiting the USA, and four times as many were reported in Europe, as were arriving in Britain, whereas six times as many Nordics were visiting Britain and more than four times as many were seen in Europe as were encountered in the USA. Between three and four times as many 'humans' were reported in Britain as in Europe and the USA.

Randles drily commented, 'The differences are very marked. It should also be noted that many of the relatively few British encounters with the "Grays" have been reported post 1987, when major publicity for Whitley Strieber's experiences with these figures began to invade British culture.' She also observed that among the 'other' British cases were 'several robot-like creatures and one described as pieces of jelly (Jell-o) lumped together.'

If one heavily promoted book influenced British experiences, it may be expected to have had a similar effect in the USA and Europe. We will explore the implications of this possibility in later chapters, for it raises real and difficult questions about the extent to which abduction reports – if not necessarily abduction experiences – are influenced by popular culture and society at large.

In the context of ufology, the significant presence of 'Nordics' in British and European cases should have been slightly embarrassing to American abduction researchers. The Nordic alien entered UFO lore in the 1950s, when a number of now generally discredited characters made a living by maintaining that they had met such off-world

> ◆
>
> **the significant presence of 'Nordics' in British and European cases should have been slightly embarrassing to American abduction researchers**
>
> ◆

GUARDIANS OF THE EARTH

Betty Andreasson

◆ ◆ ◆

Betty Andreasson and her husband Robert Luca say they have been abducted, separately and together.

In the foggy evening of 25 January 1967, Betty Andreasson, then 30, was at home in Ashburnham, Massachusetts, USA, with her seven children and her parents, who were there to help out while her husband was in hospital recovering from a car accident. At about 7 p.m. the lights failed. Betty saw a pink light glowing through the kitchen window. Her father saw small creatures, 'just like Hallowe'en freaks', in the yard. When the lights came back on, most of Betty's family were frozen in a kind of catatonic trance, but she and her 11-year-old daughter Becky saw four 1.2m (4ft) tall entities enter the house – materializing through the closed door. Betty, a devout fundamentalist Christian, thought they must be angels. The beings were typical 'grays', with oversized pear-shaped heads, large eyes, and hands with only three digits. They were wearing skintight, dark blue uniforms with a bird-like emblem on the left sleeve, and gloves and high boots.

Betty remembered nothing more about this event until she underwent hypnotic regression. In 1975 she wrote to the Chicago-based Center for UFO Studies, describing her experience, and her letter was passed on for investigation to the Mutual UFO Network based in Massachusetts.

Under hypnosis in early 1977, Betty recalled that the leader of the grays informed her telepathically that his name was Quazgaa and that the aliens needed 'food…tried by fire, knowledge tried by fire'. After a slightly farcical misunderstanding that saw Betty carefully burning some meat on her stove, she gave him a copy of the Christian Bible; in return he gave her a 'thin blue book' with 'luminous white' pages. The aliens asked her to follow them so that she could help them 'help the world'. Betty agreed reluctantly, and was led outside to an oval craft. Aboard it, she was given a painful physical examination: a long needle was thrust into her navel, and a probe into her nose, from which a 'prickly' object about the size of buckshot pellet was extracted.

Next she was put on a chair, hoses were attached to her nose and mouth, and a transparent, airtight cover was placed over her. Gray fluid filled this 'container', and Betty felt a pleasant pulsating sensation. The fluid was then drained away, and two aliens led Betty out of the craft down a dark, rocky tunnel, through a mirror to a lifeless landscape, where everything, even the air, was colored red. Walking between square buildings, she was alarmed to see lemur-like creatures without heads but with eyes on stalks climbing over them.

The party passed through a circular membrane into a new setting imbued with green. In the distance Betty saw a beautiful city; nearer was a pyramid-like structure with a sculpted head at its apex. At the end of their path was a display of airborne crystals, giving out a brilliant light. But blocking the way was a 4.5m (15ft) tall bird, radiating intense heat. This vanished, but in its place was a fire. Out of its ashes crawled a fat worm. Betty then heard a powerful voice (which she believed came from God) telling her she had been chosen 'to show the world'. What that meant would be forthcoming later: 'The time is not yet. It shall come.' The party then returned to the craft, Betty was sealed up again, and she eventually found herself being led out of the UFO into her back yard once more. Quazgaa told her that 'secrets' had been 'locked' in her mind. Inside the house the family was still in suspended animation. The aliens led them to their beds, and left. The encounter had lasted an estimated 3 hours 40 minutes. Unfortunately, the book given to her disappeared 10 days after her experience (but not before she had shown it to Becky), and she had no recall of 'formulas' implanted in her mind by Quazgaa. Voice-stress and psychiatric tests showed Betty Andreasson to be sane, sincere and reliable. Many aspects of Betty Andreasson's account reflect religious and other symbolic images, and Quazgaa's final message to her echoes common Christian themes:

> *...unless man will accept, he will not be saved, he will not live... All things have been planned. Love is the greatest of all. They do not want to hurt anybody – but...because of great love, they cannot let man continue in the footsteps that he is going.... They have technology that man could use.... If man will just study nature itself, he will find many of the answers that he seeks.... Those that are pure of heart, that seek with earnestness will be given.*

The case investigator, Raymond Fowler, suggested at first that these were deliberately used by the aliens to win Betty's confidence. Betty herself was convinced the entities were 'messengers of the Lord' and involved with the Second Coming of Christ, and that the experience was 'an initiation' of some kind.

Further hypnotic sessions in the years after 1977 revealed that Betty had first been contacted by the aliens at the age of seven, when they gave her a hint of things to come. At the age of 12 she received a similar message, and was first abducted a year later. On this occasion her left eye was removed while a 'glass pea-sized object' and 'one or more tiny glass-like slivers' were implanted in her head. She was also shown glass or ice-like 'sculptures' of animals and plants that came to life briefly when she touched them. She would understand, she was told, when she got 'home', and 'Home is where the One is.' The One existed behind a 'Great Door', which Betty entered in an out-of-the-body state. Betty had another contact in 1961, with messages of reassurance, and approval of her Christian faith.

After further minor encounters, Betty and her second husband (fellow abductee Bob Luca) were abducted together in 1978. They had an out-of-the-body experience (OBE) and were, along with many other humans, temporarily transformed into beings of light beyond the Great Door. In 1986, an alien induced another OBE in Betty. She floated over a vast crystalline landscape as a huge bird passed above her. As Raymond Fowler describes it: 'Her abductors again told her that they were caretakers of the forms that life had taken on our planet [and] their abductions were...done to monitor environmental effects on the body and to achieve the restoration of the human form. Again they stressed...that the balance of nature on earth was in jeopardy.'

◆

Her abductors again told her that they were caretakers of the forms that life had taken on our planet

◆

types, most of whom said that they were greatly concerned about the future of humanity and issued messages of love, peace and harmony. These aliens supposedly came either from Venus, Saturn or Mars, or from totally unheard-of planets such as Clarion or Meton, which were usually within our local solar system. American abduction researchers have been careful to distinguish these 'contactees' and their beautiful blond 'Space Brothers' from the 'real' abductees and 'real' aliens that feature in their accounts. And yet here were the Nordics in Britain and Europe, no longer issuing moralistic messages to self-advertising 'contactees', but busily abducting ordinary folk against their will and to their general embarrassment. So here are yet more questions: where, precisely, can one draw the line between the old-style contactee stories and the later reports of abductees? And to what extent, if any, is the abduction phenomenon a continuation of both close encounter cases and contactee stories?

The difficulty was already emerging in the 1960s and 1970s. This is apparent in the dramatic content of the abduction accounts of that era. By 'dramatic content' I mean the whole of what happens to an abductee while encountering aliens, and whatever meaning one can glean from that, regardless of whether or not the experience is objectively real.

One theme that has continually, if not consistently, appeared in abduction accounts from the beginning is sex – or, more accurately, reproduction. This displays itself in modern accounts as the notion that aliens are either manipulating human genetics or are using humans to breed alien–human hybrids

> ◆
>
> **Carl Higdon speculated that he was 'not wanted' by the aliens because he had had a vasectomy**
>
> ◆

(see Chapter Two). It was either a truth revealed or an idea established by the Villas Boas case, and echoed in the Hills' experience, when the aliens – or 'UFO people', as Betty Hill calls them – told her they were giving her a pregnancy test, and apparently extracted semen from her husband Barney. Herb Schirmer recounted under hypnosis in 1968 that aliens told him they 'had a program known as "breeding analysis" and some humans had been used in these experiments'. Carl Higdon speculated that he was 'not wanted' by the aliens because he had had a vasectomy. Many early cases, however, elaborate though they are in other respects, have no sexual overtones at all.

If the human future – and perhaps that of the aliens – is represented by reproduction in abduction accounts, it is presented in other ways too. John and Elaine Avis recalled being shown a holographic image of the Earth ruined by pollution, after which a robed figure appeared, holding a sphere, which they were asked to touch. Elaine was told: 'This is the seed of life, our past and your future, our whole existence. Accept this from us for yourselves, your children and your fellow kind.' A robed figure appeared to José Antônio da Silva, too, after the dwarf-like creatures who had taken him captive broke his rosary, but da Silva refused to reveal the message or messages this personage gave him, and was distinctly coy as to its identity.

An almost entirely symbolic vision of the future was given to Betty Andreasson (see feature on page 28) in 1967, in the consumption by fire and rebirth of a huge bird – an exact replay of the Egyptian version of the myth of the phoenix. During hypnosis in 1977 she made it clear that this intimation of fundamental renewal was linked to the Second Coming of Christ, which the aliens suggested was very close. She has also reported further experiences in which concern for the future has been expressed in both sexual and environmental terms. Witnessing the removal of a human–alien hybrid fetus from another abductee, she was told that 'as time goes by, mankind will become sterile. They will not be able to [re]produce because of the pollutions of the land and the waters and the air....'

Whether sexual or otherwise, the notion of alien intervention in human affairs – not just the affairs of the abductee – is present throughout these accounts. But abductees are by no means uniform in ascribing motives of kindly concern to the aliens. A whole folklore has grown up among ufologists since the late 1980s about the evil intentions and activities of aliens and the reasons for abductions. Known collectively as the Darkside Hypothesis, these stories draw on beliefs that UFOs and aliens essentially bode ill for humanity,

Artist Clark Hathaway's painting The God Worm *combines several images from Betty Andreasson's account of her unique abduction in 1967. In this experience, Mrs Andreasson viewed airborne crystals, witnessed the consumption of the Phoenix by fire and its rebirth as a worm, and heard the voice of God.*

and on conspiracy theories and political paranoia from both inside and outside ufology. This outgrowth is beyond the scope of this book, but it is worth looking at the abduction account that seeded it; for it illustrates the distinctly indifferent perspective – to the point of cruelty – that even some early abductees perceived in alien activity.

Myrna Hansen

Driving home on a road near Cimarron, New Mexico, USA, one night in the spring of 1980, 28-year-old Myrna Hansen and her six-year-old son saw five UFOs descending into a cow pasture. Until hypnotically regressed, she had confused memories of a close encounter, and noted a time loss of some four hours. She was regressed on 11 and 12 May 1980 by Dr Leo Sprinkle.

According to Ms Hansen's accounts under hypnosis, two white-suited figures emerged from one of the UFOs and proceeded to mutilate one of the cows in the field with a knife 45cm (18in) long. When she got out of the car and objected, she and her son were captured and taken to separate ships. She continued to resist but was forcefully undressed and given a physical examination, including a vaginal probe that reportedly later produced a severe infection. The procedure was interrupted by what appeared to be a tall, jaundiced human, who apologized and ordered the aliens punished. He then took Ms Hansen on a tour of this and possibly other UFOs. The last one seems to have taken flight, as she was next led out into a landscape that she believed she recognized as being west of Las Cruces, about 500km (300 miles)

◆

The procedure was interrupted by what appeared to be a tall, jaundiced human, who apologized and ordered the aliens punished

◆

south of Cimarron. Here she was taken into what seemed to be an underground base, where she managed to escape her captors briefly; she was soon horrified to find herself in a room full of vats in which were floating human, animal, and possibly alien body parts.

She and her son were reunited, and both were put through a further painful process involving loud noises and blinding lights. Ms Hansen recalled the aliens saying they had to make '"necessary alterations" in order to take me back'. After this mother and son were returned to the UFO and flown (with their car, which was also aboard) back to the site of the abduction.

The imagery thrown up by the regression is certainly gruesome, and the aliens' treatment of Myrna Hansen is both perplexing and callous; despite their belated apology they insisted that what they did to her, and to the cattle, was 'necessary' if 'regrettable'. She had the very strong feeling, nonetheless, that they had made some kind of error both in abducting her in the first place and in their procedure – which she called 'torture', saying, 'I feel like I've been in Auschwitz.' The overriding impression one gets from the full transcript of the hypnosis sessions is that the aliens were absolutely indifferent to Ms Hansen, although agitated about the consequences to themselves of their 'mistake'.

This detachment has been remarked on by many abductees since, but the most elaborate account of it I have heard comes from 'Kathy' who, besides being abducted, made friends with 'Sphere', a piece of alien technology, when she was 12 years old. Her story has not been published before, so it is worth considering at some length. It is far from being a standard abduction history, and has not been acquired through hypnosis. It draws

*Abductee Kathy's drawing of the UFO that
descended on Lake Becker, British Columbia,
to suck up a huge column of water while she and her
companions watched in terror. The UFO sent out a
robotic scout – an intelligent machine in the shape of
an airborne sphere – that at first seemed hostile but
soon befriended Kathy. She believes her companions
may have been adversely affected by the encounter:
all but one are now dead.*

together a number of motifs that we've already seen in the accounts above, as well as opening up some new ones that we will consider in later chapters.

Kathy's initial abduction took place when she was two or three years old (see feature on page 34), from which time she suffered frequent nightmares and showed a fear of the dark and a terror of being left physically alone. She refuses to discuss details of her unhappy early years, but does reveal that even in company she felt separate from other people: 'I had friends for school work, or to work with, but personally – no.' This sense of isolation lasted into adult life. 'When I first went to

work in a factory,' Kathy says, 'I never said a word to anybody, not a word. They thought that I was a deaf mute.'

Kathy was abducted numerous times as a child. 'There was a very specific routine to my experience with the little people. I would spend some time in the round room, which I later learned was the inside of a craft. I would be taken along with a group of other children of various ages to another "place" far away from where I was. It was at this other "place" that extensive examinations and "true" learning would take place.'

By her own account, Kathy, though very bright when young, still found her alien education daunting.

It's difficult to describe the fully interactive and continuous communication that goes on during these abduction experiences. Ideas and concepts flow as fast as the brain can manage. The flow of communication is so fast that words are simply not used as a medium. I can only compare it to the buzzing of bees where you are forced to listen to each and every vibration of every single bee's wing that makes up the symphony of the hive. This isn't to compare these little people as bees, only to show that their complexities are far beyond normal human experiences.

I had no control over the timing of these experiences, nor of the duration and other factors of the experiences. [Afterwards] I would be returned to approximately the same place as I had been. To all outward appearances, I was the same as I had been before the experience.

A SCHOOL IN SPACE

Kathy

◆ ◆ ◆

Kathy (pseudonym), now a factory safety supervisor living in Toronto, Ontario, Canada, was first abducted in 1951 or 1952, when she was no more than two or three years old. She and her family were living in a remote gold-mining camp at Bralorne, British Columbia. On a picnic with her mother, Kathy wandered off into the forest. As she recalls it:

> *I walked along this wide trail for a short distance. I stopped to think about where I was....*
> *At that moment, three little men in shiny dark blue suits came along and one of them took*
> *my hand. I wasn't carried far at all, perhaps only a few hundred feet to a clearing in the*
> *forest. There, the group paused momentarily before a bright yellow light glowed in the air*
> *around us from above. In a short few seconds, there was a whirl of sparkles in the air around*
> *us. One at a time, we were raised up into the air. The next thing I remembered, I was standing*
> *in the yellow light in a little gray room with other little people who had differently colored*
> *suits. A few of the little men talked while others sitting at the end of the room were busy with*
> *controls of different types.*
>
> *[After some time] I was taken into a room that had cloth walls, a table and a large*
> *bathtub. I was lifted onto the table and many things were done to me. My clothes were*
> *removed and I was told to sit quietly. Other people came in and gathered around the table I*
> *was sitting on. There were several people who seemed to know what to do and others obeyed*
> *their commands implicitly. When they had finished what they wanted to do to me, they left.*
>
> *One of the people stayed behind. That person said it was time for my bath. I was picked up*
> *and carried over to the large bathtub. I was given a bath in a large tub of cold liquid. I was held*
> *by my heels and lowered head first into the salty cold water. I began crying because of the pain*
> *from my heels caused by how I was being held. Still gagging on the awfully tasting water, I was*
> *raised up and the hands holding my heels were repositioned further up my ankles. Again I was*
> *lowered into the terrible water for a few long moments. Then, I was held up and dried quickly.*
>
> *Then I was taken into another room. I saw other children of various ages, all of them*
> *older and larger than me, playing there. We quietly introduced ourselves to each other. After the*
> *introductions, we talked quietly about where we were from. They all named cities and towns*
> *where they lived while I had difficulty describing the mining camp I was from. The children*
> *were from different places, but they all spoke the same language. All of them had been*
> *unhappy or unwanted where they had lived. When offered the chance to live with the strange*
> *people, the children agreed, hoping for a better life. None of the children could have imagined*
> *how different everything would be. Whatever they thought about the strange people after*

moving to their new home, couldn't make any difference. The children were well aware that they couldn't ever return to their old homes. I was told many things and I learned many things more. When all was said and done, I was allowed to say goodbye to all of the children. We hugged or shook hands, said a few brief words. Then, we left that place and went into the round room again. I was told more things to remember and it was made sure that I could repeat most of what I had remembered. I was put into the little round room of the yellow light. A few moments later, I was standing on the ground in the same clearing in the forest.

This experience left me with many fears and other terrors that lasted for years after the event. I was afraid of the dark, of being left alone and a host of other things that left me crying a lot. I didn't have a very nice childhood.

The next experience I can remember happened while I was at school in 1954. Early one misty autumn morning, I

Composite drawing by Kathy of scenes from her childhood in a remote gold-mining camp in British Columbia in the 1950s and 1960s.

became enchanted with the sight of dew forming on the underside of the leaves of grass. I was so intensely lost in this little realm of experience that I failed to hear the school bells, the students moving to their classes and all. From somewhere, a voice questioned me about what I was doing and why. I answered as best I knew how. The next thing I looked up to see little people in one of the round rooms. These people seemed to know me well and I began a two-hour-long experience instead of going to school.

During this experience, implants were placed in her body. Kathy was again abducted in 1956 and 1958, and after 1964 she continued to be abducted at two- to three-year intervals. There were two basic kinds of experience: a 'routine' abduction in which the aliens would monitor the state of her mind, body and implants, and others in which the aliens imparted enormous amounts of information. During one such experience, Kathy says, she had her left eye replaced to modify her perceptions. 'I see high into the infra-red as a direct result. I can see, like, if there's a row of trees, and there's a car parked in there, if it's well hidden, I can see the heat. If the lights turn out, I won't be blind at all.'

Her last abduction was in 1975. Then, in 1976, an electric shock at work destroyed her implants. This meant that the aliens were incapable of finding her, and her abductions came to an end.

'For two short years, I was unimaginably capable of anything I chose. There was nothing I couldn't explore or play with'

Kathy regards her early abductions as preparation for her later experiences. She once told me, abductees 'have to be conditioned from a very early age to accept the massive and interactive experiences that they will have during their lives – to be "specially prepared" to deal with some of the things that take place during a normal encounter.'

On 17 August 1961, bike-riding in the mountains near her home at Bralorne, British Columbia, Kathy and her companions watched astonished from the shore of Lake Becker as a gigantic flying saucer descended to 15m (50ft) above them and began to suck a huge column of water from the lake. Kathy was close enough to the craft to be noticed by the crew, and a small white sphere shot from the UFO, approached and interrogated her, communicating directly to her optical and aural nerve centers. She insisted she was harmless, answering its questions in such a way, she says, that it perceived her as a tree trunk. The UFO departed, but the sphere followed Kathy and her friends home and then hovered outside her room overnight. 'It was 28in [40cm] in diameter. I was able to see that it was a kind of metal and that it was real to my touch and all of my senses. It was an artificially sentient life form.'

Kathy says that all of the ships the aliens use are sentient. 'Although they are created, they have intelligence and understanding far beyond human capabilities. Still, the aliens themselves consider their ships and other things as no more than smart things.' For Kathy, 'Sphere' was much more than a 'thing'. 'As far as I was concerned, my friend was an individual with a personality whom I could relate to. And I know that at times, other people saw my friend also. Some people would see a bright light source, or a metallic globe, or simply a blur in the air when it chose to remain invisible. It would be about a billion and half years in advance of us. I came to an agreement with it – if there was no interference with my friends and family, I would be its pet.'

Kathy makes it plain that the relationship was not exactly equal: she was treated as a kind of plaything by Sphere. Nonetheless, under the terms of her deal she could explore Sphere's capabilities and enormous data banks, and was given a priority clearance that allowed her to join the humanoid crews of the saucers on their missions. To prevent her being missed while on these trips, Sphere edited out her friends' and family's memories of her extended absences. 'For two short years, I was unimaginably capable of anything I chose. There was nothing that I couldn't explore, or play with. There wasn't anything I couldn't do. There wasn't anything that could hurt me in any way. I owe all that I am to a lot of help. I figure [that I absorbed] 100 years of experience and 1000 years of culture compressed in two years with my friend. There's so much information stored in my genetics that it's incredible.'

Sphere was part of an alien expedition to the Sun. 'That involves a city ship, like 500 miles [800km] long, a multitude of motherships upwards of a mile to 10 miles [1.6km to 16km] long, and a host of little ships.' Kathy wasn't told where these visitors to our star came from, but she did learn that there are several distinct kinds of aliens taking part in the 'Sol Expedition'.

Kathy spent hours and sometimes days at a time in the company of Sphere. 'I had daily encounters with it. I had to go to school. At the end of the day I'd come home, have milk and cookies or something like that, then walk up the hill to my favorite pine tree and interface through a direct laser link, like a blue thread of pure light.'

The learning process was made easier in part by manipulating the implants Kathy says were placed in her body in 1954. Her description of these confounds the usual reports of metallic objects offered by many abduction researchers.

With Sphere's help in 1961, I was able to reconfigure the access to five implants in my body to my own frequencies and for my own uses. The implants are primarily a tagging device used to track and monitor any particular human. All a craft has to do then, is to fly close to the subject to see the implant reactivate and send its stored information to the craft. They are entirely dependent upon the human's own blood supply for electrolytes and potassium to keep it going. It is a kind of little lifeform that has been tailored to become a perfect communications device.

I could...read minds with them. I was given the opportunity to become a technician. I'm super-good at analysing patterns, so I became a logic technician for the Sol Expedition. Our minds are like recorders, like a tape cassette. You can go back to your first memories. In a few seconds to two minutes, I would go through someone's entire mind, analyse every memory that they have, change their mental conflict values, edit memories, take care of things you wouldn't believe.

These operations were apparently conducted even when Kathy was in class at school. They were made possible by the laser link between Kathy's implants and the Sphere, which relayed information and instructions between the schoolgirl and the person who was the object of her attention.

Thanks to Sphere's patronage, Kathy was able to join the alien crews on their ships. On one occasion she assisted in the repair of a 'Starseed' space station based 'somewhere near the inner levels of the coronosphere of the Sun'. The station, Kathy reports, was in need of a routine visit by the aliens 'to gather rare elements and to perform necessary checks of the fully automated base'. She was away on this trip for three days.

In September 1961, Kathy stowed away on a craft that she had been invited to watch as it gathered up abductees. For hours she managed to escape the notice of the crew, although her unexpected presence apparently interfered with the proper functioning of the ship.

In such activities, interspersed with journeys on the aliens' craft and with continual access to Sphere's data banks, two years flew by. Kathy says that by the spring of 1964, she was 'a very spoiled and solitary kind of person. I had a momentary attention span and definitely unusual interests. Only Sphere could make me happy with the ongoing infinite access and capabilities that far exceeded normal human standards.'

Then, while searching through the 'memory-strings' of certain 'unusual and powerful people', Sphere came across a rumor about a child with a sentient ball. 'Sphere investigated further and found a string of memories to another person. The trail led through a host of organizations and many people devoted to investigating unusual sightings, stories and so on. Sphere discerned the possibility of my involvement in the investigations and that I could be in danger.' There was a strong hint, as Kathy understood it, of government involvement.

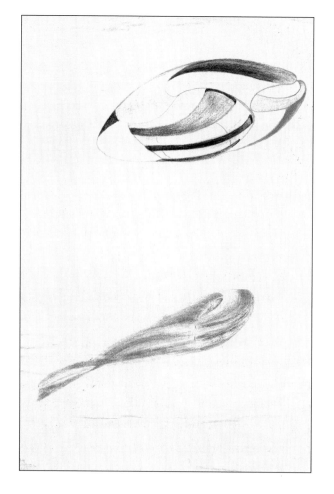

Drawings by Kathy of what she calls 'prettyships' – single-seat craft used mainly for pleasure and recreation by members of the aliens' 'Sol expedition'. On one occasion she saw a number of these machines destroyed as their pilots flew too close to the Sun, apparently deliberately risking their lives in acts of derring-do.

'It was simply a no-win situation for me if the investigations were to continue until I would be found. In that case, I would probably have to deal with special agents of all kinds. And, there were politicians and other powerful people who would have had dire intentions for both Sphere and me.'

Eventually, the net closed in. One Saturday afternoon, Kathy was sitting with Sphere under her favorite tree at the top of a steep gravel and sand slope. The ravine she was overlooking was about 30m (100ft) deep and about 800m (half a mile) wide. At the bottom of the ravine ran a gravel road. Kathy saw a black car stop on the road. Two men jumped out of the car, and began climbing the slope up to where she was sitting. The Sphere moved away from Kathy. When the men approached her, Sphere warned them that to proceed further was dangerous. The men kept on coming, despite a further warning.

Then one of them tried to reach out to touch Sphere, possibly to grab it. Sphere reacted by exploding. The two men were blown back, straight out into the air above the steep slope. They fell about half way down the ravine. Kathy saw that one had broken an arm; both were badly bruised and scratched but, otherwise, 'reasonably functional'. The two men ran as fast as they could back to their car and sped away. Sphere lay in two halves, smoking, on the ground.

'I cried steadily for a week afterwards,' recalls Kathy. 'Three kids of about eight to ten years old came and took Sphere's pieces to be buried in deep sand. They promised to bury Sphere deeply and to keep the secret with their lives. I haven't seen them since, nor do I know where they took Sphere's pieces to be buried.' Kathy's association with Sphere had already set her apart from her peers and her family. After this loss she became still less sociable:

I became very solitary and morbid, avoiding all possible contact with people as much as I could. I made friends with wolves that ranged in the nearby mountains. I would run with them for days at a time. I much preferred their company to that of humans. There were times that my family went to the beach. I would go along, spending most of the time by myself. I would swim as fast as I could in the water, and dive deep often. Only complete exhaustion and hypothermia would get me out of the water.

I still think of myself as a solitary sort. There are many occasions that I have to interact with people. I have resolved myself to be as polite and as presentable as possible in the presence of anyone. Seldom have I enjoyed the luxury of being overly emotional about anything. And, I keep on the move as much as possible. I haven't stayed more than five years in any one place nor with the same employer for long. I continue as I must, I do what I do. I really need warranty work done on my defective implants.... I would rather be there than here anyways. And I hate being a human being, especially since I know there is better.

Kathy does not believe the aliens are concerned about humanity. 'We are incidental, entirely. We take salmon, they take us. What's the difference? They don't even consider us a sentient life form, we're too stupid. This planet was once a garbage dump for some old race or something, and we're the mold growing on it. Nothing more than that.'

The way she expresses the thought suggests she agrees with this alien view. At the same time, she has 'no idea' why the aliens do what they do. In this, she is at odds with today's best-known researchers into abductions, although her knowledge of alien ways would seem to be far more intimate than theirs. What they think, we shall examine next.

Aliens taking part in the 'SOL' expedition:

◆ ◆ ◆

◇ **Grays:** most often these are the technicians and crew members of ships. The most advanced of these are preened for specific duties in the sciences and medical fields. They are the result of genetic engineering.

◇ **Clones:** these are the worker class of crews and other technicians. Usually they have genetic defects which prevent them from assuming duties associated with superior Gray classes.

◇ **Cyborgs:** these are altered humans, lobotomized and altered for specific purposes to make the best use of their short life-spans of six months to possibly a few years.

◇ **Preying Mantis:** an insect-like being that oversees many specialized areas of research projects and is the only being to use a 'psychotronic probe' to directly access anyone's mind or personality. Most often this being is disguised by altering the perceptions of anyone viewing it.

◇ **Firebeing:** a guardian of the ships that inhabits sealed up areas. They are terrifically hot and have very long lifespans of thousands of years.

◇ **Reptoids:** reptilian species of aliens about which I know very little.

◇ **Unknown1:** a very tall and capable being. Noted for high intellect and long lifespan.

◇ **Nordics:** very humanoid looking beings. They are noted for their tall and well-formed body structure, as well as high intellect. Most often, they have commanding positions.

◇ **Berserkers:** a class of aliens that are only guardians or protectors of the entire expedition. They are very advanced military troops kept in reserve in case of war conditions.

CHAPTER 2

THE ALIENS' AMBASSADORS

The World According to Abduction Researchers

◆ ◆ ◆

Opposite: Travis Walton is 'zapped' by an intense beam of light from a UFO
visiting the Apache-Sitgreaves National Forest in Arizona, in 1975 – as depicted
in the movie Fire In The Sky, *based on Walton's story.*

According to some leading American researchers, abductions have been going on since at least the late 19th century. Dr David Jacobs, for example, a professor of history at Temple University in Pennsylvania, has said that he believes they began in around 1897, at the same time that newspapers in the USA were filled with stories of sightings of mysterious, gigantic airships. Their source, owners, inventors and operators were never discovered, and no man-made airship had flown at that time.

Several researchers, including Dr Jacobs, believe that abductions run in families, so that if one could

Dr David Jacobs, one of the best-known proponents of the view that abduction claims are literally true.

hypnotize or by some other means investigate the forebears of a child abducted by aliens today, one should find evidence of abductions stretching back over as many as four or five previous generations.

Looked at from this point of view it, appears, initially, that the abduction phenomenon has a long and consistent history. But if one instead regards the phenomenon from the point of view of how our knowledge of it has developed, then a rather different picture altogether emerges. Before 1957, there was only a very small number of reports even hinting that abductions had taken place. Memories of abductions that allegedly occurred before that date have surfaced – more often than not under hypnosis – only since the mid-1970s.

So, the first point to note is that the modern UFO era, which opened in 1947, was well under way before even the earliest abduction claims were made. The second is that the mid-to-late 1970s were a watershed in terms of media exposure and public knowledge of abductions and, indeed, of UFOs. Those years were also a watershed in the way aliens were perceived, and a time in which abduction accounts began to undergo subtle changes that did not stabilize for about a decade.

This process can be seen at work if we take a survey of the landmark publications on abductions and close encounters of the third kind. As we noted in Chapter One, the two outstanding reports of the 1960s – the Betty and Barney Hill case, and the Villas Boas case – portrayed very different kinds of alien. We've also seen how accounts from both sides of the Atlantic, above and below the Equator, threw up a startling variety of reported alien forms. Despite the differences in the details of abductees' reports, however, the underlying pattern of the abductions was essentially the same.

Scattered among the first reports to be published, however, were strong hints of things to come. On 11 December 1957, before either the Villas Boas case had been investigated or the Hills had even been abducted, *The Citizen* - a newspaper printed in Prince George, British Columbia, Canada - published an article about an unnamed man who had walked into the paper's office and given a reporter the following story.

> ◆
>
> **So, the first point to note is that the modern UFO era, which opened in 1947, was well under way before even the earliest abduction claims were made**
>
> ◆

The man had served with the US Army in Austria in the early 1950s; walking home one evening in 1951 or 1952 he was accosted by a helmeted figure who paralyzed him with a pencil-like object. The entity placed a square black plate on his chest and pulled him to a 45m- (150ft-) wide UFO. 'I wasn't actually in the air, but my full weight wasn't on the ground. It seemed as if I was light,' recounted the man. Somehow, although the man 'couldn't move or walk', they entered the craft through an opening in the top. The UFO took off, flew past the Moon, and landed on a planet that the man thought might be Mars. At the landing field he saw other UFOs parked, two of which also contained human beings. They did not respond to the man's attempts to draw their attention. After a brief absence, the entity returned and flew the ship back to where he had taken the man captive. The paralysis was lifted and the black plate removed, and the UFO flew off. The man described his captor in terms that have, in many respects, since become commonplace in abduction accounts:

He had no hair at all.... His head was [a] sort of cylinder form. A very high forehead, with big eyes. You could see lots of little eyes in the two big eyes. It seemed to me [they] looked like the eyes of a fly. No nose at all, just two holes. He had a very small slit for a mouth. It looked like he had skin; it was sort of white. There were two holes for the ears. His skull was very large. The torso was formed kind of like a tin can. The legs were of proportionate length. His arms were a little bit shorter than our arms.... His hand seemed to be three long fingers. I couldn't see any neck, but he was wearing material that was like silver but wasn't shiny.

The eyes of this creature seem distinct from those of the 'Grays' that dominate modern accounts, until one recalls how often Grays have been likened to insects (latter-day abductees are frequently reminded of the praying mantis). But in some respects, the story – including an 'otherworldly journey' in which other humans are unresponsive – is strikingly modern, even if the purpose of the abduction remains obscure by today's standards. As Charles Bowen, editor of *Flying Saucer Review*, wrote in 1967, even if this story is 'just fantasy', then 'it must be agreed that the author possessed not only a fertile mind, but also a touch of the prophet.'

Travis Walton

This tale languished in obscurity for decades; but while full-scale treatments of abductions were rare in the 1970s, a few major cases hit the headlines and filled the pages of ufological magazines. One was the Pascagoula event of 1973, detailed in Chapter One. The most celebrated, and probably still the most controversial, abduction of the decade befell Travis Walton in the Apache–Sitgreaves National Forest in eastern Arizona, USA, at around 6 p.m. on 5 November 1975.

Walton was one of a crew of woodcutters returning home in darkness from a work site in the forest between the towns of Heber and Snowflake. Before their pick-up truck had cleared the trees, the men saw a disk glowing 'milky-yellow' about 6m (20ft) wide and 2.5m (8ft) high hovering in a clearing. There seemed to be panel-like geometric forms on its smooth surface. The crew responded with mixed emotions – most of them fearful. But Walton was excited, and intrigued, by the spectacle. He said later that he was afraid he would 'miss a once-in-a-lifetime

opportunity ' to see a genuine UFO at close range.

Even before the driver, Mike Rogers, had brought the truck to a grinding halt, Walton had leapt from the vehicle and was running toward the object. He stopped at the edge of the circle of light the disk was casting onto the ground. The object was giving off strange beeping and soft rumbling sounds. When it began to wobble (and get noisier), Walton finally became afraid, and he turned to run back to the truck. His buddies then saw him struck by a blue-green bolt of light that lifted him,

Travis Walton in 1985. He claimed to have been a captive of aliens for five days after apparently being snatched by a UFO almost under the noses of fellow workers; polygraph tests supported his story.

spreadeagled, into the air, and threw him backward some 3m (10ft). Walton hit the ground right shoulder first, and lay still. All that Walton himself recalled of this moment was hearing a 'crackling' or 'popping' sound, then feeling 'a numbing shock...like a high voltage electrocution' that particularly affected his head and chest. Overcome with terror like the rest of the crew, Mike Rogers gunned the truck's engine and drove off in panic. After a few minutes' reckless driving, Rogers swerved to avoid a pine tree; the truck skidded sideways, and was jolted to a stop by a pile of dirt.

After gathering their wits, the men decided they had to go back for Walton. As they prepared to leave, Rogers thought he saw a streak of light through the trees, which he took to be the UFO leaving. The loggers had some difficulty locating the clearing where the UFO had hovered, and when at last they came upon it there was no sign of Walton, and nothing else about the place seemed unusual. They

Clarke Hathaway's painting Going Up *shows his conception of the view from the alien spacecraft as Travis Walton lies unconscious in the forest, prior to being brought aboard.*

drove south to Heber and, with emotions still running high, told the police there what had happened. A somewhat patchy and disorganized search for Walton ensued.

The police began to suspect that Travis Walton may have been murdered, and became increasingly unhappy with the UFO story. But after five days, Travis phoned his brother-in-law. In a faint, confused voice, he said: 'This is Travis. I'm at the Heber gas station, and I need help. Come and get me.' Then, sensing disbelief in the silence on the line, he screamed: 'I'm hurt, and I need help badly. You come and get me.'

Walton said later that after being struck senseless by the blue-green bolt of light from the UFO, he had recovered consciousness in a diffusely lit hospital-like room. He had a metallic taste in his mouth, he was thirsty, his vision was blurred, his body ached and he had difficulty in breathing the heavy, humid air. As his eyesight came into focus, he saw a softly glowing, seamless white metal rectangle above him. A plastic rocker-like device held him from armpits to ribcage. He was still fully clothed. Three non-human figures, clad in loose,

The gas station and telephone booth outside Heber, Arizona, where Travis Walton alleged he was 'dropped' by the aliens after his abduction.

one-piece orange suits stood nearby. As he described them:

They were short, shorter than five feet [1.5m], and they had very large, bald heads, no hair. Their heads were domed, very large. They looked like fetuses. They had no eyebrows, no eyelashes. They had very large eyes – enormous eyes – almost all brown, without much white in them. The creepiest thing about them were those eyes. Oh, man, those eyes, they just stared through me. Their mouths and ears and noses seemed real small, maybe just because their eyes were so huge.

Walton struggled to his feet and shouted and lunged at the figures, who backed off and left the room.

Walton himself then ran out of the room and down a curving corridor. He went into another domed room, which had a high-backed, pedestal chair made of metal in its center, with a panel of control buttons on its right armrest. Whenever Walton approached the chair, the light in the room faded and the walls seemed to become transparent, revealing an encompassing star-spangled blackness. When he sat in the chair, he later wrote, 'the effect was like sitting in a chair in the middle of space'. He spent some time experimenting with the controls on the chair, making the display of stars rotate and freeze. He was interrupted by what appeared to be a tall, tanned, sandy-haired and muscular man, who had 'strange, bright golden-hazel' eyes, and was wearing a bubble helmet.

He silently led Walton through a tiny 'metal cubicle' and into a hangar-like space. Light glowed from some of the panels forming the walls. The craft he had left looked like the disk seen in the woods, but larger. Other craft were parked nearby. Walton – asking questions that were not answered – was taken into a room where there were three more good-looking humanoids, also wearing helmets; one was a woman. Smiling, but without speaking a word, they lifted Travis onto a table. He began to struggle but they forced him down and put something like an oxygen mask on his face. He awoke to find himself lying face up on a highway near Heber, 15km (10 miles) from the scene of the original encounter. He briefly glimpsed a round white light hovering over the highway before picking himself up and telephoning his brother-in-law.

The arguments over the investigations that followed (by ufologists – including supporters who turned into skeptics – die-hard debunkers, journalists of various shades, and even the police) have tended to distract attention from the experience Travis Walton claimed to have had. Walton failed one lie-detector test, but passed another. All but one of the logging crew also passed polygraph tests – and there were special reasons why that one failed. Some aspects of Walton's story have never been explained. Why did he show no bruising from his impact with the ground when he was zapped by the light beam? Why were his fingerprints not on any of the telephones in the Heber gas station?

Veteran American ufologist Jerome Clark, in an admirable, comprehensive treatment of the Walton case, points out how some of the inconsistencies can be explained, and notes that there is 'a mountain of supporting circumstantial evidence which so far even the most committed debunkers have been unable to topple'. If the Walton case was a hoax, says Clark, then it was 'among the most skillfully and intricately executed in UFO history. If it is not, then its implications – for all of us – are

extraordinary indeed.' The consensus among ufologists was that the Travis Walton case was at the very least unexplained, and for many – and many more for whom ufology was merely a spectator hobby – that was almost as good as saying that it had happened exactly as Walton described. The case, coming close on the heels of a cluster of others in the mid-1970s, did much to raise both the profile and the status of abductions among ufologists.

One of the group of smaller aliens that Travis Walton reported seeing while aboard a UFO – as drawn by Mike Rogers, leader of the logging crew that witnessed the initial stage of Walton's alleged abduction.

The furor surrounding the Walton affair gave the abduction phenomenon unprecedented publicity and established the image of what are now called Gray aliens in the public mind. Walton's experience also introduced the notion that the aliens work with other races of beings, some of whom may actually be human. The Patty Roach case of 1973, mentioned in Chapter One, featured a human male wearing horn-rimmed glasses and was investigated by Dr James Harder, who shortly afterward became closely involved in the Walton case on behalf of APRO. But Patty Roach's experience was not publicized until 1977, when an account of it appeared in the first book since John Fuller's *The Interrupted Journey* to devote itself entirely to abductions. This was Jim and Coral Lorenzen's *Abducted!* and it brought the stories of Patty Roach, Carl Higdon, Sandy Larson and others to the non-specialist audience.

The case of Sandy Larson (see feature on page 48) is particularly interesting for the way it too introduces themes and motifs that were to become part of the standard lore of abductions as reported by leading researchers of the 1980s and 1990s. In this account, for the first time, an abductee reports the following items: being floated through a solid wall on the way from bedroom to alien spacecraft; nausea and dizziness at critical points in the experience; floating to a secluded area where the real business of the abduction gets under way; and the immobilization

Jerome Clark offered a paranormal explanation for abductions in the 1970s, but now regards himself an agnostic on the subject.

or 'switching off' of the abductees' companions during the aliens' intervention.

While Sandy Larson's story contains unusual features, such as the apparent removal of her brain from her head 'to connect something back different' and the mummy-like appearance of the aliens, it would seem in retrospect to provide confirmatory evidence of the reality of earlier as well as later cases. There was, for instance, her insistence on the terrifying power of the aliens' eyes, the episode of 'missing time', and the 'otherworldly journey' through a desert landscape, and the almost universally noted impersonality and indifference of the abductors toward their captive.

By 1980, half a dozen books – including one by Walton himself – had appeared dealing with abductions, either as collections of several cases or full-length studies of individual experiences. That was a measure of the phenomenon's increasing respectability. But the abduction phenomenon remained both a puzzle and something of an embarrassment to many leading ufologists. While America's foremost ufologist, J. Allen Hynek – who was well known for his reservations about UFO experiences involving entities – could cautiously endorse the reality of the Pascagoula incident, there seemed then to be little apparent pattern to abductions or reason for

◆

Sandy Larson's story contains unusual features, such as the apparent removal of her brain from her head 'to connect something back different'

◆

THE SINGER AND THE MUMMIES

Sandy Larson

◆ ◆ ◆

Sandy Larson, a country singer, her 15-year-old daughter Jackie and 20-year-old Terry O'Leary (Jackie's boyfriend) set out from Fargo, North Dakota, USA, at 3.15 a.m. on 26 August 1975 to drive 300km (190 miles) west to Bismarck, where Mrs Larson was to take a test for a realtor's license later that morning. All three were sitting in the front seat of the Larsons' 1970 Plymouth Barracuda, and O'Leary was behind the wheel.

About 70km (45 miles) from Fargo on Interstate 94, the travelers saw a brilliant flash light up the sky and heard what seemed to be unusually loud thunder. Looking south, they saw eight or so 'orange, round, glowing objects' flying north and east, and losing altitude. The UFOs were as bright as the Sun, with 'puffs of smoke around each one'. When the UFOs were about 50m (150ft) away from the car, several of them shot away at high speed. No one noticed where the others went. O'Leary said that, at this point, 'It seemed like I was standing still.... It seemed like I was hardly movin' in the car and I was doin' at least fifty [80km/h]. Just seemed like I was frozen for a second.' Recovering from their surprise at the sighting, the trio realized that Jackie was now in the back seat of the car. It seems she was unaware of having made the move. At a Tower City truckstop, a few kilometers down the road, O'Leary reported the sighting to the Highway Patrol, who laughed it off. Sandy Larson now noticed the time was 5.23 a.m. The journey so far had taken at least an hour longer than it should have done.

On 20 October 1975, Mrs Larson watched The *UFO Incident*, an NBC TV movie based on the experiences of Betty and Barney Hill, and was struck by their episode of 'missing time'. Through a local UFO investigator she made contact with Jerome Clark, who in turn recruited Dr Leo Sprinkle of the University of Wyoming in Laramie to the investigation. Over several days in December 1975 and again in January 1976, Sprinkle and Clark spent time in Fargo questioning Sandy and Jackie Larson under hypnosis. (Terry O'Leary, who was by then estranged from Jackie, refused to undergo hypnosis.) They pieced together the following account of the event on Interstate 94 the previous August.

◆

When the UFOs landed, the Larsons' Plymouth was 'stopped automatically' and then somehow 'pulled up' to one of the craft

◆

When the UFOs landed, the Larsons' Plymouth was 'stopped automatically' and then somehow 'pulled up' to one of the craft. Sandy Larson began to feel dizzy, and had the sensation of floating, and then numbness. She was floated into the UFO, and next remembers 'lying on a long, narrow table and seeing [O'Leary] strapped against a vertical "table" that seemed to be attached to a wall.' Jackie was not present: she was apparently being held paralyzed by a force field outside the UFO.

Sandy's clothing had been removed, and an 'alcohol-like substance' had been applied to her body by an instrument of some kind. She saw only one alien, who was 1.8m (6ft) tall, had 'metallic' arms and 'a glow about his head and shoulders, and may have been wearing some kind of rubber suit. At one point 'he' turned around to adjust some controls, and the back of his head lit up. Communication was by telepathy. The creature's most striking feature was its face: 'It's not like a face,' said Mrs Larson. 'It's like a...like Band-aids over a head or wrapping.' She then consistently called the alien 'the mummy'. Its eyes, however, were visible:

the 'particularly strange thing' about the face was the 'glaring of the eyes. It seemed like their eyes could control my brain.'

The alien took an X-ray through her stomach, and used something 'like a little knife or like a cotton swab' to scrape the inside of her nose. And, she said, 'It felt like they were separating me.... Felt like they reached their hand on the top of my head and took the brain out and set it beside me.... It was like they could draw it right out. Like there was plugs that they could unplug, and then pull it right out.'

'Did it feel as if it was thoughts that were being pulled out or feelings that were being pulled out?' asked Dr Sprinkle.

Estelle Parsons plays Betty Hill in the 1975 NBC-TV movie The UFO Incident. *Seeing the film caused Sandy Larson to wonder if she, too, had been abducted.*

'It was like they wanted to connect something back different, when they put it back,' answered Sandy, obliquely confirming that her physical brain and not just its contents had been removed 'for a minute'.

After about half an hour inside the UFO, Mrs Larson and O'Leary were floated back to the car which, with Jackie inside, was in a ditch. They somehow got the vehicle back on the road. At that point their normal memories, and their journey, resumed.

When Clark and Sprinkle arrived to investigate the August experience, Mrs Larson told them of a UFO sighting followed by strange but only vaguely recollected 'dreams' that she had had on 2 December 1975. Under hypnosis in January 1976 she recalled waking between 3 and 4 a.m. to see two small beings, otherwise identical to the one she had seen in August, beside her bed. They 'magnetized' her and then floated her through the solid wall of her room and through the streets of Fargo to a field some blocks away. Here an orange UFO was hovering. Next, she remembered her nude body being encased 'like maybe inside a cube of ice' as she was floated through a bare, desert-like landscape. In the solitary building there she was released from the cube and conversed telepathically with the occupant, who wanted to know about life on Earth and 'about people's minds'. Mrs Larson was to 'give him a report on everybody I meet'.

After this she was floated back to the UFO, where she passed through a tunnel of brilliant white light; on emerging, she could see the Earth. The UFO returned to its previous landing ground, and Sandy Larson was floated back through the streets to her house, through the wall, and into her bedroom. She then thought about taking a shower to wash off 'alien germs'. Apparently reading her mind, the entities asked her what soap was. She took them to her basement laundry room, showed them some soap powder, and gave them a green cupful of it, which they took away when they left shortly afterward, having seen Mrs Larson back to her bedroom.

them. Hence the embarrassment. The very weird-ness of the phenomenon demanded a rationale.

Coral Lorenzen's contribution on the subject to Ronald D. Story's *UFO Encyclopedia* published that year concentrated on a process that several abductees had reported undergo-ing – 'thought stealing', as she termed it. She also noted a 'startling likeness' in the humanoids being reported by various abductees. The implication was that striking differences would have been less surprising.

Then, in 1981, Budd Hopkins published *Missing Time* – an anthology of cases he had investigated over the previ-ous few years. Hopkins was a well-regarded New York artist who had become increasingly absorbed – some would say obsessed – by the abduction phenomenon. As the title of his book suggested, Hopkins considered a period of 'missing time' in someone's life to be a primary clue to an abduction, especially if it was associated with a UFO sighting. Taking his cue from the rôle of Dr Benjamin Simon in the revelation of Betty and Barney Hill's experience, Hopkins regarded regressive hypnosis as the key to unlocking whatever had occurred during that unaccounted-for interval. In his research he had enlisted the aid of several professional psychologists, who were also versed in hypnotic techniques. The book related the stories of seven people whose abduction memories had emerged under hypnosis, and referred to many more, some previously unpublished. All seven reported being taken by the entities that today we call Grays. The similarity of the aliens that only a year previously had startled Coral Lorenzen was now standard fare.

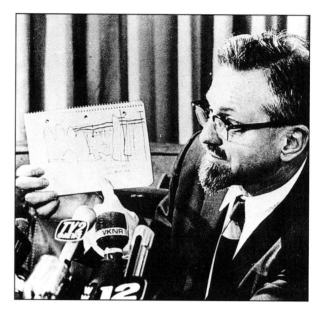

Dr J. Allen Hynek, longtime consultant to the USAF on UFOs, only cautiously endorsed the abduction scenario, accepting no more than that certain individuals had had frightening and inexplicable experiences.

Unlike previous studies, *Missing Time* pulled together common strands in these experiences and subjected them to what Hopkins called 'specu-lations both grim and hopeful'. The book not only catalogued symptoms that could indicate an abduction might be hiding in someone's past; it suggested – albeit tentatively – the motives and purposes behind the phenomenon. And some features of the abduction experience that have now become standard in the findings of other researchers were revealed for the first time.

Virginia Horton

Among these new aspects of the phenomenon was the hint that it represented a long-term monitoring program on the part of the aliens. Hopkins was struck by the number of abductees

> ◆
>
> **Among these new aspects of the phenomenon was the hint that it represented a long-term monitoring program on the part of the aliens**
>
> ◆

who reported being taken in childhood – and then again, in later life. On each occasion, they said, they met the same individual entities when being examined or interrogated on board the UFO. In this regard, the major case Hopkins cited was that of Virginia Horton, who in 1950, at the age of six, had acquired a deep gash on the back of her leg while collecting hens' eggs on her grandfather's farm in Manitoba, Canada. Curiously, she recalled, the wound caused her no pain – but she had no idea, at the time or later, what had caused it. Hopkins regarded this strange gap in her memory as the equivalent of a period of missing time, and hypnosis uncovered a story of being taken by gray-skinned aliens who treated her gently, explained their presence on Earth in terms of an exciting adventure, and asked permission to make the incision in her leg so that they could 'take a little, teeny piece of you home'. The aliens described the operation as 'a combination of a souvenir and a way of getting to know [Virginia] better'. The encounter included plenty of banter and laughter. Hopkins began to regard unexplained scars as another sign of abduction.

Virginia Horton introduced another fresh concept into abduction lore with her account of her second abduction. This occurred in 1960, when she was 16 years old, on vacation in Alsace, France, with her family. (She may also have been abducted when she was 13, but her only recollection of this was a dream.) The family had gone on a picnic in the woods, and at some point Virginia and her brother walked off among the trees by themselves. Somehow the pair became separated, and Virginia next recalled being in the company of a gray-brown deer with unusually large, bright eyes. She had a telepathic conversation with it. It was saying goodbye.

Budd Hopkins, whose successful career as an artist in New York was overtaken in the 1980s by his interest in alien abductions. His books helped to change the way ufologists regarded and assessed the phenomenon.

That pretty deer that I was so fond of. It was like my best, long-lost friend. I didn't want him to go away. He said he had to.... I think he said he'd see me again.... I'm describing it as if it was a mystical experience, but it didn't feel that way.... How I found him and how the communication happened I can't remember.... I do remember my parents had been calling me. And, in fact, that is what the deer said – 'Your parents are calling you...you've got to go back and have your picnic,' and I said, 'There's no rush!'...then it just sort of dematerialized, disappeared. And...when I got back, I had this blood on my blouse. Just a little. Just where you would if you had a nosebleed.

The deer, it transpired under hypnosis, was in fact an alien, bidding Virginia farewell after she had been abducted into a 'top-shaped' ship parked among the trees; when she returned to her family they had become concerned at her long absence.

This seems to be the first account in the literature of a 'screen memory'. Although the scene Virginia recalled is distinctly odd, the theory is that a false memory of some mundane event prevents the conscious recollection of details of the abduction. Hopkins wondered if the screen memory was perhaps induced by the aliens themselves, or perhaps by the abductee's mind, to obliterate the shock of the abduction experience.

Hopkins suspected he had discovered another example of this process at work in a fellow artist whom he calls 'Mary'. She had been present when Hopkins told some of Virginia Horton's story to a gathering of friends at his house on Cape Cod, in 1979. A week later, she told him of 'one of the strongest memories of her childhood' – an event that also took place in 1950, when she too was six years old, in Chapel Hill, North Carolina.

Mary was playing in a neighbor's garden when she saw a hummingbird – 'the most beautiful thing I had ever seen. It was absolutely gorgeous' – and decided to capture it in a glass jar. She fetched the jar, caught the bird, and then went back into the house to show off her prize. But the jar was empty. And her leg was bleeding, although without any pain. Mary thought the wound had left no mark, but Hopkins asked if he could check, and found a hairline scar on her left calf, in virtually the same place as Virginia Horton's scar. When Hopkins completed *Missing Time*, investigations with Mary under hypnosis had failed to break through what she perceived as a 'wall' in her memories 'that she could neither see through nor outflank'. Hopkins was undaunted by this, however. After six hypnotic sessions, he felt, any prosaic cause for the scar 'would most likely have emerged by now'. He was further encouraged in his suspicion when Mary told him of strange dreams she had had of being on a spaceship and (like Betty Hill) being shown a star map.

Hopkins was also among the first to identify the reason for the peculiar and unnerving procedure that the aliens had carried out on many abductees, of poking a thin, sharp instrument up their noses and well into their sinuses. Comparing reports from his own and others' subjects, and noting that tiny objects seemed to be either inserted or extracted during this operation, Hopkins concluded that these might be monitoring devices. Virginia Horton recalled just such an operation taking place during her abduction in France. The blood on her blouse was the result.

Also brought to the fore in *Missing Time* was Hopkins's speculation that the aliens' long-term program was directly connected to human genetics. This was not an entirely new proposal, for (as we saw in Chapter One) there were powerful hints of something of the kind even in the very earliest abduction reports. The first specific

> ◆
>
> **The deer, it transpired under hypnosis, was in fact an alien, bidding Virginia farewell after she had been abducted**
>
> ◆

mention of the idea was made in 1968, when Herb Schirmer recalled under hypnosis that the aliens had told him that they had 'a program known as "breeding analysis" and some humans had been used in these experiments'. But Hopkins was the first to put this theme at the center of the alien agenda. He even toyed with the thought that some kind of cloning was going on.

Virginia Horton was again the source of this suggestion, for during her second abduction the aliens had talked to her about 'how important biological diversity is', and she had met 'a sort of female friend' who was 'more like my age' and

Artist Michael Buhler's concept of an alien implant being inserted through the nose. The devices are said to help the aliens track their victims.

seemed 'like she was a relative that got to come along and meet me'.

To ufologists one of the most surprising revelations to emerge from Hopkins's research was the number of his subjects who had no conscious recollection of a UFO sighting before or after their abduction. One had no more to bolster his suspicions than a dread of a particular stretch of highway in Maryland and a memory of missing time. Another remembered only seeing a flare of blue light inside his house, which was followed by a sudden eerie hush, and going outside for a few minutes to investigate, with a loaded pistol in his hand. When he returned, the

TV program he had been watching had changed, which suggested that he had been gone much longer than he thought.

Not surprisingly, *Missing Time* generated considerable controversy. We will see what skeptics and debunkers made of it in the next chapter. For those who were inclined to view UFOs and their occupants as genuine alien visitors, the book was a godsend, because it, at last, made *sense* of the abduction phenomenon. Furthermore, the sanity – even ordinariness – of the witnesses was endorsed by psychologist Dr Aphrodite Clamar – who had hypnotized several of the subjects – in an afterword to the book.

Throughout the 1980s and 1990s the question of whether abduction experiences have a psychological basis was batted back and forth between believers, skeptics and those somewhere in between, and it is to Hopkins's credit that this necessary debate began – and that it came to engage trained and professional psychologists. In the end it had established to almost everyone's satisfaction that the abduction experience is not the product of psychosis or mental or emotional damage or dysfunction. Which is to say that while psychotics may have abduction experiences, reporting an abduction is not in itself an indication of madness, delusion or other less disabling mental illness.

More vexed and contentious is the question of whether it has its origins in the psychology of normal everyday life. Hopkins himself used his contacts among mental health professionals to explore the question, and wrote in 1985:

> *I think it is fair to say that I have spent more time exploring the possibility of a psychological explanation for abduction accounts, have consulted more psychiatrists and psychologists on the subject, and involved a wider array of these professionals in actual investigations than most researchers. And no psychological explanation, even tentatively, has resulted.*

Not everyone, today, would concur with that all-encompassing claim, and we will look at some of the ideas that have been put forward to account for abductions in terms of the psychology of the sane and normal in Chapter Four.

Hopkins had thrown into relief some of the consistent and persistent elements of the abduction experience, and discovered – or introduced – some new ones as well. But a similar exercise across the whole UFO phenomenon had been conducted a dozen years previously by ufologist and computer expert Dr Jacques Vallée. His *Passport to Magonia*, published in 1969, drew attention to the similarities between traditional fairy lore and all aspects of UFO encounters. It was never clear whether Vallée believed that UFO reports, from strange lights in the night to full-blown abduction accounts, were really a form of folklore in modern technological guise, or that fairy stories were an ancient repository of UFO reports phrased in terms of the limited technical understanding of days gone by; or were simply two aspects of some other, shadowy, third phenomenon. In any case, others saw the possibilities in all three interpretations, for Vallée made the parallels between the two bodies of accounts plain enough. Given the internal consistency of so many abduction reports and their correspondences with traditional tales, the matter of whether abduction accounts were a

---

♦

while psychotics may have abduction experiences, reporting an abduction is not in itself a sign of madness, delusion or other less disabling mental illness

♦

Dr Thomas 'Ed' Bullard, who first formally analysed the sequence of events in abduction accounts. To him, their consistency suggested the reports were of real events.

concluded, as those that were consciously recalled.

Bullard maintained that elements in a genuine folk story will tend to vary when they can, but this symptom of folklore was absent from abduction accounts. He wrote:

> *If the beings look alike from case to case, if they do similar things in approximately the same order, if different witnesses report the same mental and physical effects over and over again, then abductions take on the appearance of a coherent phenomenon. The more unanimous the descriptions, the stronger our reason to believe that diverse witnesses experienced the same kind of event.*

He has also said that

> *Abductions...combine a bedeviling mixture of implausible, surrealistic elements with seemingly physical events. As a folklorist, I am impressed by the many parallels between abductions and fairylore, shamanic initiations, near-death experiences and the like. I could easily conclude that these parallels 'prove' a common and probably psychological origin. But as a folklorist, I am also impressed by the consistency of the accounts, when variation is the hallmark of folklore. If parts of a story can vary, they probably will. The parts in an abduction story do not, so I have little confidence that these narratives belong to oral tradition.*

species of modern folklore gained fresh urgency in light of Hopkins's findings.

Aided by a grant from the Fund for UFO Research (FUFOR), Dr Thomas 'Eddie' Bullard, who had earned his doctorate in folklore at the University of Indiana, made a monumental study of that question. He trawled the literature for every abduction case he could find – nearly 300 in all – up to 1985. In the course of his analysis, which was published in 1987 as *UFO Abductions: The Measure of a Mystery*, he recognized the underlying structure of abduction accounts described in the Introduction. He discovered that beings resembling the Grays feature in the overwhelming majority of them. Accounts retrieved through hypnosis are in all major respects the same, he

In his FUFOR study Bullard favored neither a literal nor a psychological interpretation of abductions – in either case, he felt, they justified 'continued and serious research' – but he has elsewhere confirmed that he leans toward an extra-terrestrial explanation for the phenomenon, saying that 'the consistencies, physical evidence, multiple-witness cases... leave me with no choice but an objective event for the answer. The explanation of extra-terrestrial activity serves the evidence well enough in most cases, so I have to give this explanation serious consideration.'

Bullard's qualified endorsement of 'the aliens' as objectively real, his painstaking research, and his academic standing, gave an authority to the belief that abductees are reporting the literal truth, an endorsement that has stood many ufologists in good stead ever since.

Debbie Tomey

The same year, 1987, that saw Bullard's research published also saw a new book by Hopkins on the market. *Intruders: The Incredible Visitations at Copley Woods* largely chronicled the extraordinary story of 'Kathy Davis', real name Debbie Tomey, who has since published a book of her own with her sister. Tomey contacted Hopkins late in 1983 because she had read his earlier book, *Missing Time*, and hoped he could help explain some strange events and a period of missing time that had happened on the evening of 30 June that year.

The central encounter of the book, which prompted Tomey to write to Hopkins, started when she saw a ball of light in the yard of her parents' house in a suburb of Indianapolis, Indiana. Later, on her way to visit a neighbor, she checked that all was well outside. There was no lightball to be seen and everything seemed in order, although the pool house door, previously open, was now closed. She then drove to the neighbor's house.

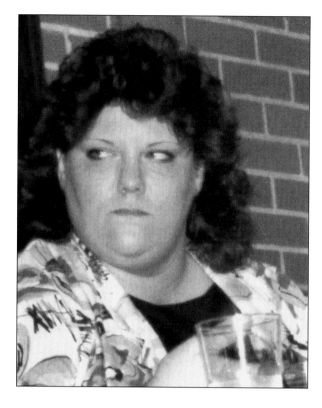

Debbie Tomey – also known as 'Kathy Davis' – whose experiences suggested to ufologist Budd Hopkins that an alien-human breeding program lay behind abductions.

While Debbie was out, her mother, inside the house, saw a strange translucent light, the size of a basketball, alongside the pool house. She could see the bird feeder through it, and there was no beam coming from it or falling toward it (as there would have been with a flashlight). Then it 'sort of faded out, all at once'. She called the neighbor's house where Debbie was visiting, and Debbie returned to investigate, prowling around the grounds for 10 minutes or so with her father's shotgun in her hands. The time was then about 9.30 p.m. Once again she found nothing amiss, apart from her dog hiding fearfully under one of the family's cars. It was a hot, humid night, so Debbie set off for a friend's house for a moonlit swim.

Budd Hopkins holds up a collection of photographs of scars and other physical marks that appear to have been inflicted by aliens during abduction episodes.

She should have arrived at her destination no later than 10 p.m. if she had spent only 10 minutes patrolling her parents' garden, yet it was 11 p.m. by the time she got to her friend's house. Undeterred by the hour, Debbie, her friend and another companion returned to the Tomeys' home and slid into the swimming pool. Then, they all began to experience odd sensations, such as inexplicable coldness, and a fogging of vision or a highly localized haze; there was an unusual halo around the electric lights. All three felt nauseous at about the same time.

Hopkins learned that the Tomeys' closest neighbors had also noticed some unusual events

that evening. They had seen a brief flash of light in the direction of the Tomeys' house and had felt a low vibrating sound. Their own house shook and a chandelier moved slightly. There was interference on the TV, the house lights dimmed, and the digital clocks in the house had to be reset. The neighbors thought there had been a small earth tremor. The next morning, on the Tomeys' lawn, was a burned circle with a long line of burned grass leading away from it and ending in a sharp curve. The scorched patch was about 2.5m (8ft) in diameter, and the line was about 15m (50ft) long.

Under hypnosis, Debbie recalled that when she had gone to investigate the strange light her mother had seen, she was hit by a blast of radiation and abducted aboard a UFO. Like others before her, she had had a probe inserted into her abdomen and an object was implanted in her head through her ear. Some kind of suction device was also applied to her.

According to Tomey's further memories retrieved under hypnosis, aliens first visited her when she was a child, and when she was six implanted a device in her head so that they could keep track of her. (She and other members of her family had similar, mysterious scars on their legs, which Hopkins attributed to cell-sampling by the aliens.) This event was hidden behind a screen memory of visiting a strange house, in which an alien appeared in the shape of a small boy.

As a teenager, Debbie allegedly became pregnant, but the pregnancy ended suddenly and mysteriously. Under hypnosis she recalled that before her pregnancy, aliens had visited her,

> ◆
> **she had had a probe inserted into her abdomen and an object was implanted in her head through her ear**
> ◆

performed an 'uncomfortable' and intimate proce-dure, and left. Some months later they returned and removed her fetus. This was the first recorded instance of an alleged 'missing fetus' – a temporary, alien-induced pregnancy. This was a theme that was to reappear many times in abduction literature.

Years afterward, by which time she had married and had two children – and had been abducted on several other occasions, too – the aliens returned again and briefly presented her with a little girl who 'looked like an elf or an angel'. This was, apparently, her extra-terrestrially induced daughter. Debbie Tomey was not the only woman who, Hopkins soon believed, had been impregnated by ufonauts, but her pregnancy was the first to be reported.

There were other odd features to Debbie's later abductions – aliens float-ing through walls, for instance – but perhaps the most significant after the revelation of the aliens using her as a surrogate mother were the indications Hopkins picked up that her two (terrestrial) sons had also been abducted, and the signs that her mother and sister were also involved in the 'program'.

Hair-raising and gruesome as the 'Copley Woods' case was, it provided Hopkins with a ratio-nale for alien intervention in human affairs. The aliens' hitherto mysterious interest in their victims' reproductive systems – the gynecological examina-tions and the probes into women's navels, and the seductions or mechanical extraction of semen from men – now made sense. The aliens were using people to breed hybrids of their species and ours. Why they should need to do so, no one knew,

> ◆
>
> **the aliens returned again and briefly presented her with a little girl who 'looked like an elf or an angel'**
>
> ◆

although on the outer fringes of ufology there was no lack of speculation about 'dying races', govern-ment entanglement in a dark conspiracy with the aliens, connections with mysteriously mutilated cattle, and worse.

Whitley Strieber

An altogether more optimistic interpretation came from Whitley Strieber, a highly successful American author of science-fiction and horror novels. But *Communion*, which on publication in 1987 promptly shot to the top of the *New York Times* bestsellers' list, and for which Strieber report-edly received a one million dollar advance, was a different enterprise altogether. For one thing, it was categorized as non-fiction. More significantly, its subject matter centered on a painful abduction experience he had undergone over Christmas in 1985, along with other encounters with what he referred to as 'the Visitors'. These were classical alien abductors on the one hand, but with significant divergences from conventional UFO entities on the other. *Communion* catapulted what (with a few exceptions) had been a relatively obscure occur-rence and the province of specialists into front-page prominence. For better or worse, the book brought abductions out of their ufological closet, and there would be no stuffing them back.

As Christmas 1985 approached, Strieber had every reason to be savoring his success. Two books that he had written with fellow Texan James Kunetka, *Warday* and *Nature's End*, had been bestsellers. Films of two of his solo novels, *The Wolfen* and *The Hunger* (the latter starring Catherine Deneuve, Susan Sarandon and David Bowie), had either been released or were in development. With money coming in, an apartment in Greenwich Village and a delightful rustic cabin in upstate New York, the transplanted Texan, his wife Anne and son Andrew should have been enjoying the good life.

Instead, Strieber was displaying distinct symptoms of paranoia. Despite having installed a state-of-the-art alarm system at the cabin, he kept a loaded shotgun by the bed. Before turning in for the night he would check the closets and look under the bed, although for whom or what he wasn't exactly sure. On the night of 26 December, however, he was given an unexpected and unwanted clue, when his 'Visitors' arrived (see feature on page 60).

The experience, only fitfully recalled in conscious memory, eventually brought Strieber in contact with Budd Hopkins. Under subsequent hypnosis, a relatively 'typical' alien abduction emerged. But as Strieber explored his own memories, some reaching back to childhood, he came to doubt that such visitations were as literal and physical as Hopkins obviously believed them to be. Indeed Strieber's experiences have been so strange and varied that any attempt to summarize or categorize them, especially in a short space, is doomed to failure. Strieber would ultimately conclude that what he dubbed the 'Visitor experience' was instructive and, he said, the Visitors 'must be counted the allies of our growth'. Such ideas would prove anathema to established abduction researchers such as Budd Hopkins and David Jacobs. Strieber's conciliatory, almost worshipful, view of the Visitors

The archetypal 'Gray', as it appeared on Whitley Strieber's Communion.

smacked of apostasy and heresy, a throwback to the days of the contactees and their heralding of the 'Space Brothers', entities who supposedly had humanity's best interests in mind. Like the contactees of the 1950s, Strieber would eventually warn of impending ecological and planetary catastrophes on Earth, unless mankind changed its collective ways.

But another aspect of the abduction experience reported by Strieber would rapidly gain currency with conservative researchers. This was the claim that, far from being random, one-off events, abductions actually began in early childhood and continued into adulthood. Strieber was instrumental in introducing the notion that individual abductions were a constantly recurring affair. Once visited, you were almost sure to be revisited – repeatedly.

Strieber has had other inexplicable experiences, and anomalous phenomena were also reported by guests to his New York cabin. One of the earliest strange tales to circulate in association with Strieber was told by Bruce Lee, a senior editor at William Morrow, shortly after the company had published *Communion*. While browsing in a prominent New York bookstore, Lee saw 'a man and a woman, bundled in mufflers, hats and long overcoats' pick up a copy of Strieber's book and thumb through it. 'He's got it all wrong – look at that,' one of them said, speaking 'in what sounded like educated Upper East Side Jewish

TRANSFORMED BY VISITORS

Whitley Strieber

◆ ◆ ◆

Whitley Strieber, author
of Communion, *who claims*
contact with the aliens
since childhood.

Author Whitley Strieber's first conscious memories of being abducted began over the 1985 Christmas holidays, which he and his wife Anne and son Andrew were spending at their isolated cabin in upstate New York, USA. On the night of 26 December, Strieber was awakened by what he described as 'a peculiar whooshing, swirling noise' from downstairs, as if a subway had suddenly disgorged its passengers in his living room. Instead of investigating, he went back to sleep, only to reawaken when something entered the bedroom – 'a compact figure' less than 1.2m (4ft) high with 'two dark holes for eyes and a black down-turning mouth' – and rushed to his bedside.

Although Strieber would soon encounter the 'classical' Gray described by other abductees, this bedroom intruder was different. For one thing, it was *dressed*, whereas Grays typically appear either nude or in form-fitting body suits. According to Strieber, it had 'a smooth, rounded hat on, with an odd, sharp rim' that jutted out on the side he could see. From shoulder to midriff was a square breastplate with concentric circles on it, and below that another rectangular plate, which covered the entity from its waist to its knees.

The creature was accompanied by a horde of dwarves in dark-blue coveralls with 'wide faces [and] glittering, deep-set eyes, pug noses, and broad, somewhat human mouths'. Strieber was raised out of bed by these creatures, then carried downstairs and outside, into a clearing in the woods.

From here he was lifted into the sky and transported into a 'messy round room' where he found himself surrounded by more entities, one of which smelled vaguely of cardboard and cinnamon. Clothes were strewn about the moldy interior – a sharp contrast to the experience of most abductees, who report being examined in an almost surgical, antiseptic environment. An entity crouched in front of Strieber and opened a small box containing 'an extremely shiny, hair-thin needle mounted on a black surface'.

'If I had been afraid before,' Strieber wrote later, 'I now became quite simply crazed with terror.' Aware that the entity intended inserting the needle into his brain, he complained that 'This place is filthy,' and followed that with the protestation: 'You'll ruin a beautiful mind.' The entities ignored his objections. The next thing he knew there was 'a bang and a flash'.

Worse was to come. Strieber was soon transported into another room, where he was shown 'an enormous and extremely ugly object, gray and scaly, with a sort of network of wires on the end. It was at

The entrance to the 'Secret School' in the San Olmost Basin, San Antonio, where Strieber maintains he and other children regularly met alien entities in the 1950s.

least a foot [30cm] long, narrow, and triangular in structure.' This grotesque object was inserted into Strieber's rectum, where it seemed 'to swarm into me as if it had a life of its own. Apparently its purpose was to take samples, possibly of fecal matter, but at the time I had the impression that I was being raped, and for the first time I felt anger.' For all his fear and anger, however, Strieber came to see his 'Visitor experience' as ultimately beneficial.

Strieber has written four books about his encounters with the Visitors (he prefers not to use the word aliens, and resists the idea that they are extra-terrestrial): *Communion* (1987) *Transformation* (1988), *Breakthrough* (1995), and *The Secret School* (1997). The last concentrates on Strieber's childhood experiences in the city of San Antonio, Texas, USA. The 'school' was in a wooded area, the Olmos Basin, near his family's stately home, where Strieber and other children would gather at night to be taught by a tall figure in a hooded cowl. At times a sort of helmet – what we would now think of as a virtual reality visor – was placed over Strieber's head and he was shown scenes of the ancient past and far future, vistas of unearthly landscapes, including the surface of Mars. At one point, he said, he traveled into the future, into a semi-abandoned yet semi-inhabited and devastated San Antonio.

At the end of the book, Strieber produces a series of predictions based largely on his understanding of the Secret School's teachings. Some examples:

Our present system of government, made unstable by debt, public disaffection, and the vast chasm between its secret and public sectors, will change radically in the context of economic disruptions brought on by serious environmental difficulties of various kinds....

As science becomes increasingly honest, open, and powerful, it will begin to detect the presence of a deity in an incontrovertibly factual manner. At that point, a Niagara of joy will flood the world as the species consciously joins the companionship for which it was created....

Fusion is perfected as an energy source and we will want to mine the Moon for fuel, but there will be an obstacle to this that will be overcome only through profound personal and social evolution....

We will meet people from other worlds, the barrier between the living and the dead will collapse, and it will become possible for the individual to store and process huge amounts of knowledge.

> ◆
> **This grotesque object was inserted into Strieber's rectum, where it seemed 'to swarm into me as if it had a life of its own'**
> ◆

Artist and designer John Velez's depiction of the 'examination' phase of an abduction. Velez himself has a long history of UFO sightings and strange encounters with alien entities, and bases this artwork on his own experiences. Besides performing physical tests at this stage, the aliens may indulge in a 'scanning' procedure in which, abductees believe, their minds are being read.

accents'. The rest of their wardrobe included tinted glasses through which large 'dark, almost almond-shaped eyes' could be glimpsed.

Lee told New York reporter Tracy Cochran that he approached the couple and asked what was wrong. While the man ignored him, the woman seemed to emanate 'complete loathing, hatred'. Shaken, Lee quickly left the store. Had he merely encountered two pranksters - of which, like most large cities, New York suffers no shortage - staging an impromptu scene for his benefit, unknowing of who he was? Or had Lee bumped into the legendary Men in Black, those shadowy, seemingly only half-real figures not infrequently reported by other UFO witnesses?

Equally puzzling - and even more ambiguous - are the childhood experiences reported by Strieber in his 1997 book, *The Secret School*. Paranormal events are not unusual in the lives of abductees, but researchers such as Budd Hopkins and his associate David Jacobs do not address them in their case studies. Debbie Tomey and her sister Kathie revealed in their jointly written book that their family has 'always' been plagued by poltergeists and other bizarre manifestations, but there is no mention of this in *Intruders*. Strieber's acknowledgment of such elements in his own life, and his tendency to contactee-style prophecy, have probably estranged him from 'conventional' ufologists as much as the kind of personal differences that caused a famous rift with Hopkins. Strieber's accomplishment was initially to bring abductions before the public; but his admission that the phenomenon has a wider context than ufology may turn out to be the greater achievement.

Following on from Hopkins's *Intruders*, historian Dr David Jacobs produced the next conventional elaboration of the aliens' activities during

Sketch by Albert Bender of the first Man In Black (MIB) in ufological history. Possibly real, perhaps apparitions, MIB mysteriously harass those connected with UFOs.

abductions. Jacobs had written a well-received history of UFOs and ufology that had been published in 1975, had met Hopkins in 1982, and become increasingly intrigued by the abduction phenomenon. He spent many hours observing Hopkins at work. In 1986, having learned hypnotic techniques, he began direct investigation himself. In 1992 he published *Secret Life* (which in the UK appeared a year later under the title *Alien Encounters*), which did not so much extend the general understanding of abductions - the reasons they were happening – as it shaded in details of the aliens' techniques during abduction, and revealed some fresh ones.

Screen memories figured heavily in Jacobs's cases, as did the 'sophisticated' equipment that his subjects reported the aliens using in their medical-cum-gynecological examinations. The reproductive process, Jacobs found, was what he called the 'primary' feature of his abductees' experiences, and other episodes in the scenario to which Ed Bullard had given more or less equal weight, such as the conference with the aliens, the tour of their craft, and the 'other-worldly journey', were relegated to secondary or, even lower, to 'ancillary' status, and were now often revealed to be a facet of the breeding program. In many cases the 'tour' was reduced to a visit to an on-board nursery, where the aliens expected the abductee, pretty much on command, to 'bond' with her hybrid offspring. The imparting of secret or esoteric knowledge, and even genial banter, that had characterized the conference stage of the encounter for earlier abductees, gave way to video-like displays of apocalyptic scenes of destruction and environmental collapse.

> ◆
>
> **the 'tour' was reduced to a visit to an on-board nursery, where the aliens expected the abductee, pretty much on command, to 'bond' with her hybrid offspring**
>
> ◆

While Jacobs considered the 'child presentation' scene, in which humans were shown their alien progeny, to be a secondary feature of his subjects' accounts, its details and its frequency among his sample of abductees still amounted to a new development in ufologists' apprehension of what occurred during abductions. At virtually every stage of their experiences, Jacobs's subjects were producing highly specific and detailed accounts where once vagueness had often reigned. As a result, they also produced new insights into primary aspects of the abduction experience, although these often raised fresh questions about the aliens' intentions.

The process of mind-scanning, for instance, which previous abductees had reported in various guises from time to time, became more prominent and more consistent in form; and the form itself was new. Among Jacobs's subjects it involved a slightly chilling scene that occurred after tissue samples had been taken and implants inserted or removed, and before the reproductive phase began. The apparent leader of the aliens leaned over the abductee and gazed deeply into his or her eyes for some time; the abductees all felt that their minds and emotions were being read. Jacobs revealed another new and curious facet of these episodes: a number of his subjects reported that their feelings of outrage, loathing and helplessness toward the aliens changed in the course of the procedure to ones of acceptance and love. This mental and emotional exchange (and alteration) would be followed by the equivalent of the 'conference', after which ova or sperm were collected, embryos implanted or fetuses extracted, and related affairs attended to.

This revised abduction scenario as Jacobs unfolded it was a far darker thing than even Hopkins had suspected (and light years away from Whitley Strieber's optimistic vision). Matters became still bleaker as the two researchers discovered that abductions tended to run in families: an abductee's children, parents and even grandparents were found, on closer inspection, to have been abducted or at least to show many of the overt signs and symptoms of being abductees. And in 1992, Hopkins and Jacobs, with sociology professor Ron Westrum, published the results of a huge survey in the USA

Professor of psychiatry Dr John Mack, whose account of his research into abductions brought a mixed response from ufologists and scorn from his medical colleagues for its rejection of conventional scientific method.

that, they believed, indicated that as many as 3.7 million Americans had been abducted. Not only was the phenomenon horrible; it was apparently occurring on a massive scale.

While Jacobs and Hopkins were refining the elements of the abduction scenario, a new and academically distinguished investigator had appeared on the scene. John Mack, a Pulitzer-prizewinning Harvard professor of psychiatry, had long been interested in 'alternate realities' and, through a friend of a friend, was introduced to Hopkins in January 1990. Like David Jacobs, he sat with Hopkins for months listening to sessions of hypnotic regressions, learning the appropriate techniques, and familiarizing himself with the abduction scenario at first hand. By 1993 he had interviewed and regressed some 80 abductees himself, and completed a lengthy book that went into exhaustive detail about 13 of his subjects. Given the earlier ructions between believers and skeptics over

the purely psychological content or origin of the abduction experience, most of ufology was agog to hear what he had to say. And given his academic prestige, and with abductions now firmly part of popular consciousness thanks to Whitley Strieber, his book - soberly titled *Abduction: Human Encounters With Aliens* - was comprehensively reviewed by publications from local weeklies to *Time* magazine when it appeared in 1994.

Mack succeeded in impressing nobody. Conventional reviewers were appalled at his casual rejection of Western science, which he considered inadequate to the task of understanding the phenomenon and should therefore be abandoned, and his apparently unqualified acceptance of anything his subjects told him: that they had been reincarnated many times, that they were part alien (see feature on page 66), that the aliens were grooming them to be leaders and guides for the remnants of humanity after some unnamed but almost imminent global catastrophe. The list of oddities went on and on, and it disturbed many leading ufologists too. Mack's professional status, experience and knowledge should have been brought to bear to make the subject respectable - and the cause had been betrayed into the arms of New Age vaporousness. No one would believe *genuine* abductees were being taken by *real* aliens, and bring abductions within the ambit of established scientists, when someone of Mack's standing was endorsing this kind of nonsense.

In light of ufology's bemusement with Whitley Strieber, however, one wonders whether this was only what distressed ufologists. For Mack had

> ◆
> No one would believe genuine abductees were being taken by real aliens...when someone of Mack's standing was endorsing this kind of nonsense
> ◆

AN ALIEN ON EARTH

'Paul'

◆ ◆ ◆

When he was about 25, Paul (pseudonym) underwent relaxation/hypnosis sessions with a mental health professional to explore the possibility of sexual abuse in his childhood. The therapist believed this might explain certain highly disturbing, apparently paranormal experiences in Paul's life. No memory of sex abuse emerged, but he did recollect 'encounters with unusual beings' going back to the age of two or three. In this earliest memory he was taken from his bedroom by Grays, and examined aboard a spaceship; as one of the creatures ran its fingers over his leg, he felt a sudden pain, then numbness, as if his leg had had 'something injected into it'.

Paul found the therapy unproductive, and he believed his retrieved memories were disturbing his therapist, as was alleged poltergeist activity at her home, for which he felt somehow responsible. In 1994 he made contact with Dr John Mack at Harvard University, who began his investigation by exploring under hypnosis an encounter Paul had already partly recalled, which occurred when he was six years old, in 1972.

Paul remembered the arrival of a UFO and then being greeted with hugs from two groups of diminutive aliens. Next, he was on a ship, with stars visible from it, and aliens in attendance. They had huge dark eyes with no visible irises, a hairless head, a nose 'flat like an ape' and a mouth with 'scales round it, like plates on [their] lips'. Paul estimated he had already been on the 'spacecraft' about 70 times, although on this occasion he was given a standard tour of the UFO, as if he had never been aboard before.

It was then explained to him that he was in fact an alien spirit in a human body. 'I am a cross between...what I've known as me and the brothers who were with me, what the human beings would call an alien.' Paul – who from then on veered between speaking as an alien and as a human being – said that the aliens – the 'TA' people – 'have evolved over a long time but differently from humans'. There are many dual-identity aliens on Earth. 'I'm more than a TA person. I'm more than a human being. More people are finding out how in between they are themselves.'

His 'home' planet is very peaceful, and the aliens are 'here to integrate' with humans. But, he said: 'I'm trying...to help you, but I'm under attack....We came and we were killed by many of you....You people are too violent...too hostile. There's so much life, yet human beings want death.'

The aliens do not understand human destructiveness. When Dr Mack asked if the intrusive procedures aliens use during abductions are an attempt to learn about this, Paul said that was a part of the reason, and that 'the "poking" and looking are for the purpose of understanding, helping, and "adjusting".' In Dr Mack's words, 'It appears to the aliens [Paul says] as if we have deliberately chosen death over life, and their experiments are in part an effort to understand our perverse, stubborn ways as well as a kind of intervention to move us along the difficult path from destruction toward creation.'

The aliens – the 'TA people' – said they came here thousands of years ago, and communicated with the dinosaurs, who had great intelligence – 'smarter than humans' – and even powers of precognition. 'They were

Dual Identity *by John Velez:*
The artist's impression of the belief
expressed by numerous abductees that
they are, in fact, part alien.

able to have an understanding, a compassion towards the future of your existence.'

In a later regression Paul was 'shown the world' by a hooded figure with a pointer and 'all these people are dying. He's telling me I'm going to fix it.' He recalled a battle in a cellar, at the age of 12, with what 'some people call Satan'. At the age of nine he was abducted and a piece of bone was removed from his leg, in an operation that was painless and bloodless. The aliens told him they 'want me to form a group that can meet with them' to enter into 'an "exchange" of love'. The aliens 'may have shown me where the creational force is'. Paul also claimed to have 'notebooks full' of information on the 'unbelievable' healing technology of the aliens. They are, for example, able to bring their dead fellows back to life in certain circumstances.

Paul reported that in his alien identity (but also aged nine as a human) he was taken in an alien ship to a UFO crash in a desert; there were dead aliens that 'men in uniforms' had shot. Paul and his companions were there to retrieve, and revive, the dead, but the human military arrived to take away the crashed ship and the alien bodies, so the rescue party had to make good its escape.

Dr Mack immediately identified this scene with the so-called Roswell Incident of 1947, when according to UFO legend an alien craft crashed in New Mexico. However, Paul was not born until 1966. Dr Mack speculated aloud about 'consciousness as a kind of "continuous fabric" that allows you to go "anywhere under certain conditions".' Paul agreed, and added:

The memories are there, but it's kind of like you push back out again, and you take form again ... like ... you feel that independence because you're so focused into one direction, into one purpose, like coming back molecularly and drawing from everything, drawing from all because of what you're connected to.... The lines that you have to where you're really from are ominous power. It's enormous! But, like, since you're pushing forward you forget what's behind you.

Paul was convinced that he was on the rescue ship at Roswell in 1947. Dr Mack was inclined to agree, and explained how this could occur in terms of consciousness being 'the primal source of creation' and 'a kind of hologram of universal sourcefulness which can create matter and form itself'. Confirmation of a kind of Paul's abduction experiences came from 'Julie', who met and recognized him in Dr Mack's abductee support group. She said she had met Paul many times previously on the alien spacecraft. Here, he appears as a 'rock solid', 'very centered' individual, with an overpowering personality that 'exudes love'.

◆

15 months later,
in February
1991, Hopkins
received a letter
from two men
claiming to be
police officers.
They said that
they had seen
Mrs Cortile's
abduction

◆

committed a heresy similar to Strieber's: he had exposed the weirdness that lay all around the abduction phenomenon, by quite properly presenting his case histories in all their strange particulars. His gullibility did no favors to those – seemingly absent from his sample – who had had strange and deeply disturbing abduction experiences, and who remembered them without benefit of hypnosis, and wanted some answers. But for those interested in steering a course between Hopkins's and Jacobs's commitment to an outright nuts-and-bolts interpretation and the presumption that abductees as a class were more than slightly batty, Mack's efforts were not entirely wasted. They provided a somber warning of the pitfalls awaiting those who abandoned scientific objectivity, and an indication of how the phenomenon could be hijacked to suit almost anyone's private emotional and psychological agenda.

Linda Cortile

Over the years in which abductions had been reported, there had been a number of cases in which several people claimed to have been gathered up together by the aliens. But one item of evidence was painfully lacking in the battle to prove the physical reality of intrusive alien activity: an independently witnessed abduction. In 1996, Budd Hopkins published *Witnessed*, his long-awaited report on the experiences of Linda Cortile, some of which he had been discussing for years at meetings and conventions. The case, he felt, provided that much-needed extra dimension - not one, but several, objective and unrelated witnesses to a truly startling abduction.

Linda Cortile (pseudonym), a 45-year-old New Yorker, began regressive hypnosis with Hopkins in April 1989. She suspected that she had been abducted by aliens when in her twenties. Then, at the end of November 1989, she was apparently abducted again.

Linda Cortile had gone to bed at about 3 a.m.; her husband was already asleep. She began to feel a paralyzing numbness creeping from her feet up her body, which from previous experience she knew was a prelude to an abduction. She tried unsuccessfully to wake her husband. When a gray entity appeared in the room, she threw a pillow at it. Then she became totally paralyzed, and her mind went blank, although she vaguely recalled someone palpating her spine. The next thing she knew she was falling down onto her bed from a great height.

Under hypnosis, Mrs Cortile recollected that three or four aliens had come into the room. Then she had been 'floated' through the closed window of her 12th-storey apartment by the aliens, had entered a blue beam of light, and was taken aboard a craft that was hovering above the building. She was given a medical examination, then taken back and dropped onto her bed from mid-air. Her violent return failed to wake her husband. Fearing he and her two sons had been killed by the aliens, she checked their breathing with a mirror held under their noses. They were unharmed.

About 15 months later, in February 1991, Hopkins received a letter from two men claiming to be police officers. They said that they had seen Mrs Cortile's abduction, from a car parked under the South Street Viaduct, near her apartment house. She had floated 'like an angel' through the air into the UFO, which was 'about three quarters the size of the building across'. Then the UFO had gained altitude, flown over the South Street Viaduct, and plunged into the East River a short distance from the Brooklyn Bridge. They had considered visiting the block to find the woman. They were particularly concerned to know if the victim was alive and well, for they had waited 45 minutes but not seen the UFO emerge from the river. The officers signed themselves Richard and Dan.

Hopkins warned Mrs Cortile that she might be visited by the pair, and why. The news upset Linda, for it seemed to confirm the objective truth of an experience that she had hoped was imaginary. Some weeks later she reported that Richard and Dan had called on her, and that they were relieved to find her safe. They refused to speak to Hopkins in person, for fear of public exposure, but agreed to contact him.

Soon afterwards Hopkins received additional letters, drawings of the event and a taped account from one of the officers. He explained that they could not meet Hopkins because he and his partner were in fact Secret Service agents. On the night of the abduction they had been escorting Javier Perez de Cuellar, then Secretary-General of the United Nations, when their limousine broke down. They had pushed it to within a couple of blocks of Mrs Cortile's apartment house. De Cuellar had also witnessed the entire episode. Hopkins concluded that the aliens had been deliberately demonstrating their powers and the reality

New York housewife Linda Cortile, whose abduction in 1989 turned out to be anything but routine.

of their presence on Earth, to a person of international standing and influence. In short, the limousine's breakdown had been the aliens' doing, too.

Linda Cortile experienced two more abductions in 1991, but not by aliens. One afternoon in April, Richard and Dan forced her into a car while she was out walking and asked her a series of bizarre questions. They demanded that she remove her shoes to prove she had toes because, they said, aliens had no toes. Mrs Cortile somehow noted that the car was being followed by another vehicle. Hopkins later traced its license plates to diplomatic missions to the United Nations.

On 15 October 1991, Linda was kidnapped by Dan, who shoved her into a red Jaguar and drove her to a beach house on Long Island. There, he made crude advances to her and made her put on a white nightgown like the one she had been wearing when abducted. Mrs Cortile managed to tape-record some of this encounter, which was cut short when Richard arrived and managed to sedate Dan. She later received a letter from Dan. Apparently written from a mental institution, it was clearly not the work of a sound mind.

Between these two events, in mid-September 1991, Hopkins received a letter from Dan that entirely changed the emphasis of the case. According to this, Dan, Richard and de Cuellar had gradually recalled further details of the early morning of 30 November 1989, and now realized

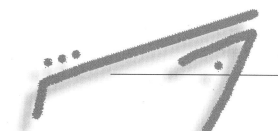
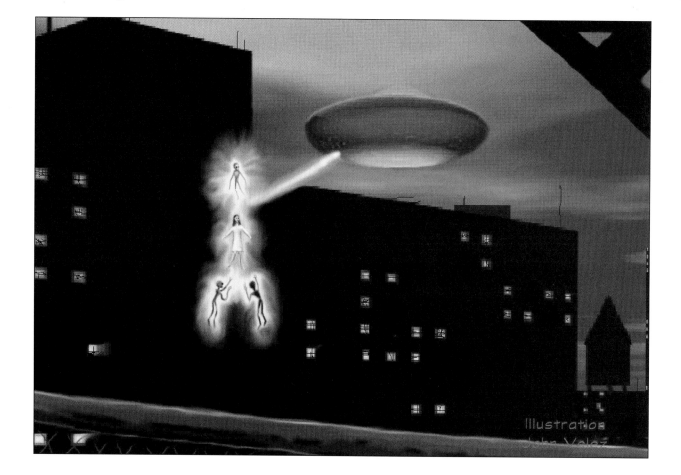

John Velez's impression of Linda Cortile being 'beamed up' from her apartment house on the Lower East Side of New York City to a waiting UFO. One of the alleged witnesses to the event described Mrs Cortile as looking like 'an angel' as she floated through the air.

that they too had been abducted. They were taken to a seashore, where they watched Mrs Cortile and several aliens, carrying scoops and illuminated pails, digging in the sand. Linda appeared to be speaking the aliens' own language. Then she and the aliens walked up to the three spectators, and Linda held up a dead fish and said 'in a bold voice – "LOOK AND SEE WHAT YOU HAVE DONE."' When Dan asked her who she was, one of the aliens answered: 'Lady of the Sands.' Hopkins later hypnotically retrieved virtually identical details of this scene from Mrs Cortile, along with much more

about the aliens' concern over pollution, which was destroying life in the oceans.

In November 1991 Hopkins received a letter and drawings from a retired telephone operator in her sixties whom he calls 'Janet Kimball'. Her car had mysteriously, temporarily, failed as she crossed Brooklyn Bridge into Manhattan, within sight of the Cortile apartment, on the night Mrs Cortile was abducted. The bridge lights had blacked out, and the other cars on the bridge also broke down. Mrs Kimball claimed to have seen the UFO, the party of aliens and Mrs Cortile being floated into the craft, even though the UFO was shining so brightly that she had to shield her eyes from it. Hopkins also found two other witnesses who had seen a red UFO in the vicinity of Linda's apartment, and a fellow resident of the block who on the night of Linda's abduction had been awoken by a brilliant light flooding the inner courtyard.

Also in November 1991 Mrs Cortile met Richard again, and he expressed some romantic interest in her. From letters Richard wrote to Hopkins and from conversations and hypnotic regressions with Linda, it then transpired that Linda and Richard had been abducted together since childhood. There was even a suspicion that Linda's son Johnny had been the product of this 'bonding'.

In May 1992, Richard sent Hopkins two samples of sand that he had kept from his 1989 encounter. One he had managed to purloin, after it had been 'processed', while on the alien craft. The other was taken from his shoes. Electron micrographs of the samples show the particles of 'processed' sand are much smaller than those from Richard's socks.

In October 1992, Linda's son Johnny had a conversation with a benign elderly gentleman who subsequently had a gift of an old-fashioned deep-sea diver's helmet delivered to the Cortile apartment. Hopkins showed Johnny some 20 photographs of prominent men of about the same age, and the boy identified Javier Perez de Cuellar as his benefactor.

In November 1992, Hopkins discovered a member of his abductee support group, Marilyn Kilmer (pseudonym), and Mrs Cortile had had strikingly similar dreams in which Johnny had been abducted; apart from the two women, Perez de Cuellar was also present, wearing blue striped pajamas. Linda kept thinking of de Cuellar as her father.

Hopkins concludes that the events of 30 November 1989 were 'an attempt to convey to a major political leader a benign alien concern with earth's ecology.' Perez de Cuellar has publicly denied being abducted.

In many ways the 'Linda case' sums up the state of abduction research. To those convinced of the material reality of alien interventions in human affairs, it presents an almost watertight case. To skeptics, it reeks of hoax and delusion. Why they take that position, and reject most other items on the alien agenda as well, we shall ponder next.

The Brooklyn Bridge:
a witness said the bridge's lights
failed during the course of Mrs
Cortile's abduction.

CHAPTER 3

SITTING IN JUDGEMENT

The Skeptics' Response to Abduction Claims

◆ ◆ ◆

Opposite: Examination stage of an abduction, as shown in 'Beyond The Veil', a 1996 episode from the TV series The Outer Limits. Skeptics have long maintained that abductees' imagery is often drawn from the media.

The debate between believers and skeptics over alien abductions has been frequently acrimonious. Neither side is entirely free of responsibility in this. Budd Hopkins has accurately summarized the hardline skeptics' argument as follows: 'Since UFOs don't exist, abductions can't occur...', a position he regards as a 'rigid belief system'. The longest-serving UFO skeptic, Philip J. Klass, can certainly appear immovably prejudiced when he asserts that abduction claimants are 'little nobodies trying to get on TV'.

At the same time Hopkins himself displays a certain intransigence when he calls those who persistently question the reality of abductions 'fana-

Philip J. Klass, the scourge of abduction claims, makes his peace with an alien at a conference in London in 1997.

tical', 'bigoted', and 'blatantly dishonest'. His colleagues Dr David Jacobs and Dr John Mack have made more sweeping statements in support of their chosen subject. Dr Jacobs proclaims: 'No significant body of thought exists that presents strong evidence that anything is happening other than what the abductees have stated.' And Dr Mack declares: 'No plausible alternative explanation for the reports of abductees, which are sometimes corroborated by physical evidence, has ever been discovered.'

By looking at what the skeptics say, we can judge whether Hopkins's ire is justified, and whether the literalist interpretation of abductees' experiences is as solidly founded as Jacobs and Mack grandly

73

UFO photographed in January 1971 by Woody Akins at Charlotte, South Carolina. A hypnotized witness can easily be led to 'explain' such a strange sight by means of an abduction fantasy.

insist. We can also see whether the skeptics themselves fall short in logic, evidence, and justice.

One of the major objections skeptics have raised against the evidence for abductions by aliens is to the way much of it is acquired: through hypnosis. Jacobs calls hypnosis 'an indispensable tool in unlocking memories of an abduction', and the cases he, Mack and Hopkins present in their various books have all been extensively investigated by putting their subjects in trance and 'regressing' them to the occasions of their alleged encounters.

Aviation journalist and UFO skeptic Philip J. Klass was one of the first to argue that abduction

researchers were woefully naïve about the pitfalls of hypnosis, in *UFO Abductions: A Dangerous Game* (1989). Like others who have doubted the efficacy of the technique, he first reviewed the famous, but sadly never repeated, experiments of Dr Alvin Lawson, John Herrera and Dr Bill C. McCall in 1977. The trio recruited 'creative, verbal types' from the student population of the Los Angeles area, ensured they had little or no prior knowledge of ufology, and gave them the bare bones of an abduction narrative. Dr McCall, a very experienced clinical hypnotist, then put them into trance, and asked them for details of their abduction.

As ufologists, Lawson and Herrera had expected 'real' abduction accounts and their subjects' inventions to differ greatly, and that the 'imaginary' stories would be rather stunted at that. But the imagined abduction reports matched the allegedly real thing in detail after detail – which the students needed no prompting to provide. For instance, one recounted being taken aboard a UFO marked with insignia and being examined by two aliens, one of them reptilian. Another described encountering a UFO in the mountains, and being drawn up to it through a beam of light. The 1.8m-(6ft-) tall aliens took a skin sample and immediately healed the wound. A third student found himself in a clear bubble inside a Saturn-shaped UFO, where the light was a green glow and there was a constant, 'hypnotic' hum. Aliens were described as communicating by telepathy, being faceless, and kindly but businesslike. High-technology probes were used in the examination phase; some subjects said they were strapped onto tables, while others were simply 'paralyzed'. There was the familiar statement (or order) that the victims would forget their ordeal. When asked about their responses to the imaginary abduction the subjects even reported such changes as a more open mind, improved personality and generally good feelings.

Lawson considered there were 'no substantive differences' between 'real' and imagined abduction reports. The experimenters did, however, note several differences between their subjects and 'real' abductees. The imaginary abductees did not emerge from the experiment believing the experience was genuine. They showed little emotional response to the events they described; they had no physical effects; and they suffered no long-term emotional effects (including dreams and nightmares).

Whether they were inspired by the imagination, by the subconscious or by imagery generated by natural neurological functions, these false abduction memories demonstrated how difficult it was to tell just what kind of 'truth', if any, emerged from hypnosis. The case of Christy Dennis (see feature on page 76) was to make the point inescapable.

In 1981 she had described her 13-day sojourn on another planet with beautiful, tall aliens, which she had recalled under hypnosis. In 1983, she confessed publicly that she had invented the entire story. Her motives had been pure enough: deeply concerned at the possibility of nuclear catastrophe, she reasoned that more people would attend to her message on behalf of world peace if it came from wise and benevolent extra-terrestrials. Unfortunately, most who took her seriously were 'more interested in sensation than in sensibility' – they wanted to hear about the aliens' way of life, not 'their message to Earthlings'. Unable to bear the pressure of her position, and realizing 'just what kind of a messed-up life you can get if you continue with these things', she decided to come clean and apologize to those she had deceived.

No less revealing than Christy Dennis's motives was the reaction of Dr Leo Sprinkle to her confession. When Sprinkle had originally hypnotized her, he called her account 'one of the most remarkable abduction cases I've come across'. In a memo accompanying her admission in 1983, he wrote:

I confess I am as puzzled by Christy's recent statement as I am puzzled by her original statements...but I do know that

> ◆
> Lawson considered there were 'no substantive differences' between 'real' and imagined abduction reports
> ◆

KIND OF METAPHYSICAL

Christy Dennis

◆ ◆ ◆

For many years, professor of psychology Dr Leo R. Sprinkle has hosted an annual meeting for contactees and abductees in Laramie, Wyoming, USA. On 23 May 1981 a young housewife named Christy Dennis, from Phoenix, Arizona, described to those attending that year's conference her extraordinary, extended experiences at the hands of aliens. Although she did not mention it during her address, Ms Dennis had originally produced much of her testimony under hypnosis administered by Dr Sprinkle.

Christy had suffered a broken hip in a car accident and was confined to bed. Bored by television, she had been reading books on 'metaphysics'. After reading about techniques for inducing out-of-the-body experiences (OBEs), she decided to try one of the procedures herself. As the exercise progressed, she found she was 'dematerializing'. 'It scared me,' she told her audience. 'I pulled out of it, and there was a huge sonic boom and the windows rattled – I didn't know what happened!' Despite her fright, Ms Dennis tried the exercise again the following night. Once again she began to feel as if she was dematerializing:

I thought to myself, 'What in the world is going on?' I got the impression that I wasn't alone; I said, 'Who are you and what's happening?' And this voice said, 'Well, it takes a few minutes to transfer you. If we take you too swiftly from the point where you are to where you are being transferred to, there could be a explosion which could create a destruction of the dwelling in which you now exist.' And I thought, 'Wow! This is too much!'

Christy sat up in bed, and there was another 'huge sonic boom'. It woke the rest of the family. Next day, Christy phoned a physicist friend to find out if what she had been told during her OBE 'had any validity'. She received advice that few physicists might recognize: 'Sure, some scientists have already proven this,' he said. 'They send atoms backwards in time, they move them from one point to another, and there are implosions....' Christy wondered what she was 'playing with here', but the 'physicist' suggested she could go through with it and find out: 'Maybe you can tell me what is going on.'

As she began the exercise the next night, she realized she was putting out a message: 'If somebody can help me, to get myself straightened out, I sure would appreciate it.' The feeling of dematerialization began again, and then: 'Suddenly, I found myself face first in some sort of cushion. This was really a shock, because I was lying on my back; because I had busted a hip, and I couldn't turn over.' But she managed now to turn herself over onto her back, to see a glowing cone above her, getting dimmer and dimmer. 'It had a coil wrapped around it and a dish behind it. I was inside a cylinder, with this cushion on the bottom, with a little opening on the side where I could crawl out. I tried to crawl out and fell, because my hip hurt.'

At this point a 'being, in some kind of space suit with a bluish glow around it' came into the cylinder and asked Ms Dennis if she was damaged. She snapped back that she was already damaged before she got there. The being was about 2.6m (8ft 6in) tall, with golden hair, olive-bronze skin, 'perfect features' and, Christy learned later, was female. She then plied the entity with questions: 'How did I get here? What am I doing here? Where am I? Who are you?' The alien silently helped her up.

'It really frightened me when she touched me because somehow this bluish glow created some kind of a field around her. She reached out...and she never really connected...I mean, there was never really any contact made.' Christy was carried down a long corridor to what would be her 'quarters' for the time she was with the aliens, for she was already on another planet. She was told she was in quarantine because of the microbes she carried, and because of her 'primitive and disruptive emotional vibrations'.

In her room Ms Dennis found she had tape, movie and TV equipment that would play

Christy Dennis, having read about techniques for inducing an out-of-body experience, or OBE, decided to try one for herself. To the accompaniment of a sonic boom, she suddenly found herself 'dematerializing'.

material from any time period, indeed anywhere, she wanted, if she pushed the right buttons. The bed in the room was equipped with a sleep inducer, which she was told 'not to mess with' lest it cause brain damage. Christy Dennis's abduction was particularly unusual because she stayed with the aliens for 13 days:

I went to another planet...called Encore Receiving Station.....I was told they did 'spectral scanning': they would scan different parts of space for certain energy levels [that] had to be of biological life forms...then they would 'lock in'. They would scan this individual's life, and see what kind of life the person had, and what kind of life pattern the person was going to follow, and if [they were] going to have some sort of disaster or an accident or something....

They could bend time, so if they found somebody was going to die in a few years, they would run their scanner up to that point, lock in on it, and beam the person up from that point...they would ask these persons if they wanted to perform in an experiment to help man to evolve by learning new ways of communicating...or if they wanted to continue their karmic experience and go on to another life and go back to the point from which they picked them up, which they called, interestingly, their 'native position'.

Despite learning something of the aliens' technical knowledge, Ms Dennis did not have 'the mental capability to understand' much of the data. The aliens would often remark that their equipment worked on 'a principle that your culture has not yet evolved'. The aliens often expressed concern about the future of humanity.

she demonstrates in her behavior some of the characteristics of us UFO contactees [Sprinkle believes he himself has been abducted], including a concern about our planetary plight, and a certainty that, at various levels of 'reality', intelligent beings are developing a wider interface with society....[but] I do not know of a simple psychological explanation for the complex information she has provided.

It would appear that Dr Sprinkle could not quite believe that Christy Dennis was altogether a hoaxer. The 'simple psychological explanation' on her side is that she made her story up – disproving hypnotists' oft-repeated claims that subjects cannot deliberately lie when in trance. As for Dr Sprinkle, Klass was to remark dryly, '...because no Earthling has ever visited an extra-terrestrial civilization and returned to describe the experience, the most experienced abductionist has no criteria for discriminating between fact and fantasy.'

Back in 1977, ufologists were dismayed at Lawson, Herrera and McCall's conclusions – in Klass's words, they were 'as welcome as a skunk at a garden party'. In response, critics have fastened ever since on the differences the experimenters noted between the 'genuine' and the 'imaginary' abductees' reactions to their experiences. But all these effects on 'real' witnesses ultimately derive from the initial belief that the experience is real. And the possibility that their experiences are real must be a consideration in the minds of those who consult researchers who specialize in abductions. Thereafter, everything depends on the way the hypnosis itself is carried out.

Klass weighed in with sizable quotations from a world authority on the subject, professor of

Psychologist Dr Leo Sprinkle, in 1981 listening to an abductee at a conference in Laramie, Wyoming.

psychiatry Dr Martin T. Orne, to demonstrate that abduction researchers were very poor hypnotists.

Orne emphasized the key, commonsense point that nothing derived from hypnosis should be regarded as true without independent verification. It is, of course, in the nature of most abductions that little about them can be verified. The risk, Orne pointed out, is that under pressure to provide information, an hypnotic subject will confabulate – fill in gaps in relevant memory with fantasies and fragments of related memories. Close questioning in pursuit of details would produce details aplenty, but with 'a marked decrease in accuracy'.

Yet we find that abduction researchers do just this all the time. For example, in *Secret Life* (1992), David Jacobs describes a man who under hypnosis at first recalled a raven-haired, 'beautiful young woman...coming over to him for...a sexual liaison'. Jacobs's response is revealing:

Through meticulous questioning about the minute details of her actions and her appearance ('If her head is on your upper

*Close-up portrait of 'Jordeye', David Howard's main contact, and friend,
among the alien races he has met during narcoleptic dreams of abductions and close
encounters. Howard's abductions occurred only in his dreams, and they precisely
mirrored descriptions given by 'real' abductees.*

chest, can you see the top of her head?'), *the false memories fell away and the* *abductee independently [sic] realized that* *it was her black eyes that he had been* *describing and not her hair. In fact, she* *had no hair at all.*

This is presumably an example, and the result, of asking 'proper' questions, which earlier abduction investigators, Jacobs says, did not know how to do:

Even when competent hypnotists were *called in on cases, they were not well* *versed enough in abduction research to* *ask the proper questions. They could not* *tell if the subject was 'filling in' with false* *information.... And because investigators* *did not know exactly what happened* *during an abduction, they could not* *identify false memories purposely placed* *in the victims' minds.*

Where proper questions end and leading ones begin, Dr Jacobs does not say, any more than he justifies the profoundly unscientific principle he seems to be enunciating here: that no one should undertake any investigation unless its results are known beforehand. Nor does he explain how he and his colleagues can distinguish between real and false abduction accounts, given that both are just that – accounts. What is happening, skeptics suspect, is that researchers ignore or discard accounts (or parts of them) that do not fit their preconceived ideas of what an abduction *should* be like. Certainly I myself have seen Dr Jacobs dismiss as 'confabulations' witnesses' drawings of aliens they had encountered, purely on the grounds that they did not conform to the standard

description of Grays or Nordics.

More disturbingly, Dr Orne goes on to say, false material can be confabulated from discussions before the trance session, leading questions, unconscious suggestions, voice inflections and other clues provided by the hypnotist to what he or she was hoping to hear. The confabulations would then form a seemingly genuine part of the subject's normal waking memory.

Speaking of therapists who use hypnosis to search out evidence of sexual abuse in childhood, Dr George Ganaway, professor of psychiatry at Emory University, Atlanta, Georgia, USA, has also warned that

memories can be distorted, even created, *in susceptible minds by the tone of voice,* *phrasing of a question, subtle non-verbal* *signals, and expressions of boredom,* *impatience, or fascination. In short...in* *some cases...therapists [are] creating the* *very problems they hoped to cure.*

In *Witnessed* (1996), Budd Hopkins describes many occasions on which he talks through episodes that he wishes to explore with the principal witness, Linda Cortile (see Chapter Two), before then hypnotizing her. A particularly egregious example occurs when he is hoping to confirm that Linda, her son Johnny, and Marilyn Kilmer, a member of his abductees' support group, were all abducted at the same time. After a lengthy discussion, Hopkins hypnotizes Linda and insists over and over that she look at the person on the aliens' examination table. Eventually Linda admits that this figure is Johnny.

Orne had proved experimentally that he could instill false memories many times. It was particu-

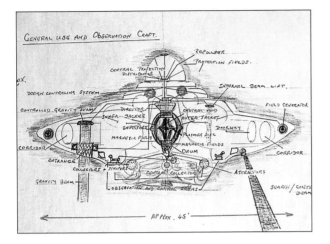

Plan of a 'General Use & Observation Craft' from the planet Dut, as drawn by David Howard – who in highly detailed, vivid dreams has visited the planet. He claims little prior knowledge of UFOs or abductions.

larly easy to instill even very trivial pseudo-memories (let alone something as disturbing as an abduction) into periods of time when little or nothing was happening in the subject's life, because there were no competing memories to screen out or rearrange. Orne gives being asleep as an example, but performing routine or semi-automatic tasks in a tedious environment (such as driving at night) offers little competition either.

Orne also insists that no one other than the subject and the hypnotist should be present during the trance session 'because it is all too easy for observers to inadvertently communicate to the subject what they expect, what they are startled by, or what they are disappointed by'. Klass notes that Hopkins was always present in the days before he conducted his own hypnotic sessions. In some regressions of Sandy Larson (see Chapter Two), no less than three people were firing questions at her, and all were committed ufologists. As for corroborating evidence, Mrs Larson showed no scars or other

side-effects from having her brain temporarily removed and 'rewired'.

While Hopkins and Jacobs insist they do not lead their subjects, John Mack seems to regard confabulation as a positive bonus. In *Abduction* he calls it 'a co-creative intuitive process' which, he disarmingly remarks,

> *may yield information that is in some sense the product of the inter-mingling...of the consciousnesses of the two (or more) people in the room. Something may be brought forth that was not there before in exactly the same form. Stated differently, the information gained in the sessions is not simply a remembered 'item,' lifted out of the experiencer's consciousness like a stone from a kidney. It may represent instead a developed or evolved perception....*
>
> *From a Western perspective this might be called 'distortion'; from a transpersonal point of view the experiencer and I may be participating in an evolution of consciousness.*

Unimpressed by this grandiose and somewhat conceited rhetoric, Dr David Gotlib commented tartly in the *Bulletin of Anomalous Experience*:

> *[Mack] admits that much of his case material makes little sense 'in the framework of the Western ontological paradigm' [i.e. in scientific terms]. His solution is to discard that paradigm in favour of one in which anything is possible, where 'familiar words like "happening," "occurred" or "real" will themselves have to be thought of differently,*

less literally perhaps.' Nowhere in this book is it explained how we are to change our definitions of these words or concepts. This argument is an oft-repeated 'stopper' which effectively excludes any attempt at logical or rational analysis of his argument.

Julie Presson, partner of Clarke Hathaway (see Chapter Five), is a qualified clinical hypnotherapist, a specialist in past-life regression, and a witness to some very odd paranormal phenomena. She is scathing about the way today's most prominent researchers lead their subjects. In discussions with me she pointed out that hypnotic subjects should be given only minimal direction or encouragement. Questions should be as vague as possible ('And what is happening now?'). Even a seemingly innocuous question such as 'What color are their eyes?' is suggestive to the respondent and can provoke confabulation. To the respondent, the eyes and their color become important; and so does pleasing the hypnotist with an acceptable, specific answer. No one who has the slightest acquaintance with the work of Hopkins, Jacobs or Mack can be unaware of the kind of eyes aliens are supposed to have.

One of the investigators of the Patty Roach case (see Chapters One and Two) was Kevin Randle, since renowned for his research into the 1947 Roswell Incident. He is now convinced that leading questions and 'priming' of the witness by his colleague Dr James Harder were responsible for the story Mrs Roach told under hypnosis. In the first session she apparently showed no emotion as she explored her experience, which caused Harder some concern. During a break over

◆

Julie Presson...is scathing about the way today's most prominent researchers lead their subjects

◆

ice-cream, he proceeded to regale her with the details of Betty Hill's abduction (see Chapter One). In the next hypnotic session, Patty showed all the appropriate emotional reactions as she told of a classic 'gynecological examination' during her 'abduction'. Kevin Randle believes today that the trigger for Mrs Roach's experience was sleep paralysis, a common but distressing occurrence, which I discuss in a later chapter.

Betty Hill, whose story set off the American abduction saga, is herself highly critical of the *kind* of hypnosis offered by today's leading abduction researchers. The hypnotic state they achieve is not, she says, the deep trance induced by clinical hypnotists such as Dr Benjamin Simon, nor are subjects given post-hypnotic suggestions to forget their accounts until the next session, as she was. The result is a highly suggestible subject. Further,

Betty and Barney Hill (seated) under clinical hypnosis induced by Dr Benjamin Simon (standing).

Betty Hill told me, she is convinced that while alien-induced amnesia is accessible only through deep trance, it will – like any post-hypnotic suggestion – wear off in due course. 'All a real abductee needs is patience,' she says.

Those abductions Betty Hill regards as genuine have not required hypnosis, and the abductees can always immediately recall what happens until boarding the craft and what happens on leaving it. She rejects the increasing numbers of 'UFO-less' abduction reports, and deploys a formidable wit at the notion that aliens can float up and down blue light beams or drift unscathed through walls and windows – 'They're people! like us! the laws of science apply to them too!' Their biology precludes cross-breeding and hybrid children. Not only out-and-out skeptics have doubts about the latest elaborations on the basic abduction scenario.

One of the aliens' many claimed talents is the power to cover their tracks by altering the memories of their victims. Allegedly, the aliens insert 'screen' memories of innocuous events into abductees' minds, to prevent victims remembering the truth and revealing the aliens' activities. In Chapter Two we saw how, as a teenager, Virginia Horton consciously recalled meeting a deer in a wood; but hypnotic probing by Budd Hopkins 'revealed' the deer image as a screen memory of an alien, which in turn led to the unraveling of an abduction story.

The notion of screen memories was first conceived by the founder of psychoanalysis, Sigmund Freud. In his opinion, they were usually very vivid memories but of something strangely trivial, which covered up genuine but repressed memories of either distasteful or unbearable events. And, he noted, the screen memory was a transformation of the origi-

Anonymous abductee's painting of a Gray. This one is familiar with time, but many aliens reportedly do not understand this and other very basic concepts.

nal event and always left symbolic clues to the 'repressed material' it camouflaged.

In borrowing the concept, the abductionists have subtly altered it. While transferring the power of repression and substitution to the aliens, they leave aside the awkward symbolic connection between the two kinds of memory that Freud was able to use in order to winnow real from concocted events. Hopkins, Jacobs and Mack also ignore – if they ever knew about – an important point Freud makes in his original (1899) paper:

...these falsified memories...must have originated at a period of life when it has become possible for conflicts...and impulsions toward repression to have made a place for themselves in mental life - far later, therefore, than the period to which their content belongs.

Nowhere in the abduction literature is this reported to be the case. According to ufologists, a screen memory is generated at the same time as the event it conceals. However, the skeptics remark that, if screen memories exist at all, there is no need to call in the aliens as their agents. The human mind is all you need since, everyone agrees, abduction is a traumatic experience, the memory of which you may well want to repress, if you can.

Why should aliens be held responsible, then? Because, say skeptics, it makes the aliens seem more powerful, more otherworldly, and more frightening. And it is the abduction researcher's rôle to rescue the abductee from this dark, fear-filled forest. In a provocative essay in *The Gods Have Landed* (1995), sociologist John Whitmore identifies the strategy: 'In standard captivity narratives victims are often rescued by a morally perfect hero who destroys the victim's tormentors; in abduction tales the hero is the researcher-hypnotist, who alone knows the chilling agenda behind the victim's capture.' The dark side of this knightly derring-do is a persistent casting of women, in particular, in humiliating rôles that they are encouraged to believe are part of genuine and continuing events. In commandeering 'screen memories', the literal-

◆

it is the abduction researcher's rôle to rescue the abductee from this dark, fear-filled forest

◆

Sigmund Freud, the founder of psychoanalysis. Skeptics say ufologists misunderstand and distort Freud's notion of 'screen memories' when they attempt to defend retrieving memories of abductions through hypnosis.

ists not only traduce Freud but contradict a key facet of his concept. As J. La Planche and J.-B. Pontalis define it in *The Language of Psychoanalysis* (1985), a screen memory 'leads back to indelible childhood experiences and to *unconscious phantasies*.' (Emphasis added.) This compares interestingly to what Dr Bob Hinshelwood, clinical director of the Riverside Mental Health Service in Richmond, southern England, told me:

In principle...a Freudian would tend to regard the [abduction] phenomenon as a visitation from the patient's inner world, his unknown inner world, his unconscious in Freud's terms.... His reporting a visitation from outer space would seem likely to be a disguised (dream-like) externalization of the 'return of the repressed'.

In other words, if Freud was right, an abduction memory may itself be a species of screening event!

This is borne out too by Professor George Ganaway's account of screen memory. 'Therapists,' he is reported as saying, '...must always try to avoid implanting memories...either through suggestion or expectation, because once a suggestion is seeded it can sprout into an elaborate "screen memory" that serves to block out the patient's ambiguously painful but relatively unremarkable childhood experiences.'

Ganaway cited the example of 'Sarah' who 'remembered' seeing 12 children bound, raped and brutally murdered in a satanic ritual. It turned out eventually that this was a mask for her childhood terror when her grandmother insisted on reading grisly details from detective magazines to her. 'Sarah invented the "screen memory" of...mass murder in an attempt to preserve her grandmother's image as a loving, protective figure,' Ganaway concluded.

When they have not ignored them, ufologists have responded to such doubts and criticisms by pointing to the large number of abductions that have been fully recalled without hypnosis. This argument, skeptics reply, would be a trifle stronger if the published pro-abduction literature contained any evidence that *hadn't* been gathered under hypnosis (and some may point unkindly to the

case of Christy Dennis). At best it shows only that the human imagination is all that is needed to generate an abduction account.

Then, counter the believers and their supporters, consider the times hypnosis has been used to break through amnesia or retrieve obscure details that have helped to solve crimes. In his unpublished essay 'The Abduction Conundrum' (1996), music critic and ufologist Greg Sandow – one of the few balanced commentators with a sympathy for abduction reality – cites three instances reported in the academic literature:

◆
consider the times hypnosis has been used to break through amnesia or retrieve obscure details that have helped to solve crimes
◆

◆ *William S. Kroger and Richard Douce of UCLA studied how police departments used hypnosis, and declared: 'Hypnosis was of value in providing investigative direction, and, in the [23] cases described, has led to the solutions of major crimes.' ('Hypnosis in criminal investigation,'* International Journal of Clinical and Experimental Hypnosis.*)*

◆ *A team from the University of Arizona reported that hypnosis had successfully been used to restore the memory of a man suffering amnesia after he'd been raped. ('Amnesia as a consequence of male rape: A case report,'* Journal of Abnormal Psychology.*)*

◆ *David Chamberlain – though this does seem hard to believe – hypnotized children and their mothers to retrieve memories of the children's birth. The children had no conscious birth memories, but their accounts were similar*

THE GLORY OF ARIZONA

Jack & Peter Wilson

◆ ◆ ◆

'The day before yesterday I was on a UFO for seven hours,' were almost the first words Jack Wilson spoke to Ronald K. Siegel, on the telephone. Wilson had sought out Siegel, a professor at the University of California at Los Angeles and an expert on hallucinations, as he had heard him talk about UFOs on the radio. Siegel arranged to meet Wilson in Los Angeles later that same day and hear his story.

Wilson was an ex-Navy man, 52 years old, and now living in San Diego. He wanted to talk about an experience he had had while driving to California after visiting relatives in Florida.

After an all-night drive he had reached the Arizona border. Stopping just long enough to refuel his car and buy bottles of water to see him across the state, he continued on across a lonely high desert landscape ringed with distant mountains. After a time, he heard a strange 'mechanical' noise coming from the rear of the car, so he stopped and got out to inspect the vehicle. As Wilson stepped onto the shoulder of the road, he felt dizzy and faint, and was aware of a blinding light in the sky.

'That's when I saw it,' he said. 'That's when I saw the little man.'

The creature was humanoid, no more than 1–1.2m (3–4ft) in height. It was wearing a gray, seamless suit and seemed to be inside some kind of force field. It appeared 'blurry', and 'a halo of glowing lights' surrounded its head.

Alarmed, Wilson backed his way into the car, with the small being apparently following him at a distance. Suddenly, he found he was paralyzed, and his body began to feel very light. He started to float, and was drawn upward toward the bright light. As he approached, he saw it was a craft – a 'god-damn gen-u-wine UFO'.

The next thing Wilson knew, he was inside the UFO, floating down a long corridor that was 'honey-combed' with bright metal panels on its walls. There were intricate geometric designs carved on the panels. 'That must have been the cargo bay of their ship,' he concluded.

Wilson finally found himself in a room that somehow reminded him of a hospital operating room. Several gray-suited figures gathered around him. He thought they must have touched his head with something, because then he saw stars like those he had seen once when he was knocked out in a fight.

'That's when…they drained me,' Wilson whispered emotionally. On the verge of tears, he explained what he meant: 'They took…my memories. They took my fuckin' memories!' He knew this had happened because there was a TV-like screen in the room, and he watched disconnected images from his past flash across it as the beings drained his brain. He remembered seeing himself as a boy, fishing with his father, and a ship he served on in the Navy, as well as scenes from his visit in Florida.

In the final image he was sitting in his car beside the highway in Arizona. He seems to have merged with the image, and then found himself awake and physically present in his vehicle. The UFO had gone. Seven hours of 'missing time' had passed since encountering 'the little man'.

Professor Siegel was well aware how many abduction stories had developed from dreams, and he was also aware that people with no prior knowledge of UFO lore were capable of generating plausible, but

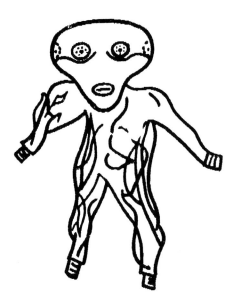

Entity drawn by a hypnotic subject with no previous knowledge of UFO abductions. Note the resemblance to the Gray frequently reported by 'real' abductees.

imagined, abduction accounts under hypnosis. His first thought was that the man had experienced a complex and vivid dream. He suggested as much to Jack Wilson.

'Friend, it was no dream', Wilson said authoritatively. 'My son Peter, was with me. They drained him, too.'

Next day, Siegel took the detailed medical and personal histories of Jack Wilson and his 24-year-old son. They seemed to contain nothing unusual. Wilson agreed to undergo a full physical examination, which included blood and urine tests to see, among other things, if there were traces of any anesthetic that might have been used on him inside the UFO. Siegel explained that he would need to check the car and speak with Peter, and Wilson agreed to this. So while Wilson went for his examination, Siegel had the car checked by mechanics to see if there had been any unusual electrical or other faults, which are sometimes reported to occur during close encounters with UFOs. There was nothing amiss.

◆

there was a TV-like screen in the room, and he watched disconnected images from his past flash across it as the beings drained his brain

◆

Nor did the vehicle show any signs of exterior damage.

Siegel interviewed Wilson again in depth, closely studying his facial expressions and eye movements. If the eyes shift to the left while a person is talking, it may indicate that the speaker is imaginative or prone to fantasize, while shifts to the right indicate that the person has good recall and is speaking directly from memory. Siegel was sure Wilson was being truthful. He described the exact route he and his son had taken in their car, and precisely where and when they had stopped. His words tallied with marks on a map Siegel had found in the car. Wilson said he did not believe in the paranormal, and had never read a book on UFOs or seen any of the popular films on the subject, such as *Close Encounters of the Third Kind*.

The physical and psychological tests showed Jack Wilson took no drugs besides tobacco and caffeine, that he wasn't particularly imaginative or creative, had few daydreams and rarely had nightmares. His blood and urine checked out as normal. There were no unusual marks on his body. He had been 'calm and easygoing' during all his medical tests, even watching the hypodermics going into his arm and the tubes filling with blood. Siegel 'got the chills, just listening to this', for it demonstrated that the fear Wilson had shown when the aliens examined him aboard the UFO was not his normal reaction to such procedures. It suggested that the stolid ex-Navy man was telling the truth about his abduction.

Siegel flew to San Diego and interviewed Peter Wilson. He had a slightly different story to tell. Both men had heard the odd mechanical noise from the rear of the car, both had got out, and both had been startled by the bizarre little gray man. They had then both got back into the car, and talked over what they had seen. From this 'second opinion' and other material he had gathered, Siegel was able to piece together an explanation for Jack Wilson's apparent abduction.

enough to what their mothers reported for Chamberlain to write that 'children's birth memories appeared to be real rather than fantasy.' ('Reliability of birth memory: Observations from mother and child pairs in hypnosis.' Journal of the American Academy of Medical Hypnoanalysts.)

We have to assume that the hypnotists involved were scrupulously careful not to lead their subjects. We can, however, be sure that all three papers at least have the virtue of dealing with indubitably real events in the real world. But if, like Sandow, we want to move beyond the debate over whether or not hypnosis is intrinsically reliable, we first have to acknowledge that abductions don't enjoy that accepted status. Sandow does not quibble over that, but he seemingly fails to recognize that the real issue is not hypnosis, but the nature of memory.

David Chamberlain's investigation of birth memories cited above is 'hard to believe' only in the sense that anyone thought the experiment worth doing. Experience tells us that most children have heard an account of their birth at some time in their lives; and the more unusual a birth is, the more likely it is to become part of family legend. A routine childbirth can surely be reconstructed from general knowledge.

The same problem arises with abductees. As we shall see in the following chapters, abduction accounts have precedents in structure and in detail in folklore, and in by no means rare psychological states. They may even have their roots in the organization of the human brain. A consciously recalled abduction may be no more than a memory of an experience in an altered state of consciousness. The memory itself can be shaped by both personal and cultural factors, and can certainly be altered by persuasive investigators. This has been shown time and again in analyses of accusations of child sex abuse, and the related phenomenon of ritual satanic abuse.

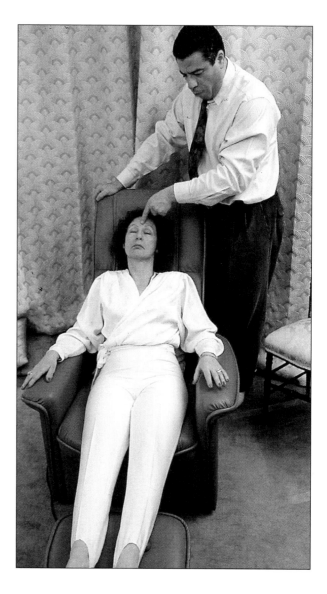

Skeptics accept that hypnosis can refresh memories of actual events, but point out that the technique can also easily create false memories if the hypnotist is biased or unskilled, and the subject is anxious to win approval.

The literalist school of abduction researchers appears too to be unaware of psychologists' heavy doubts about the existence or even possibility of actual repressed memories. Harvard psychiatrists Drs Harrison Pope and James Hudson, for example, have made a massive search of the literature for evidence of genuinely repressed memories of childhood sexual abuse – and found none. Numerous scientific studies have concluded that human memory is not a fixed, immovable record of experience that can be buried, retrieved and replayed at will: it is a *reconstruction* of events, and the building blocks of memory are mutable, susceptible to social and psychological pressure, and unreliable. Confabulation, in short, is not exclusive to the hypnotic state.

The experience of Jack and Peter Wilson on a lonely desert highway near the New Mexico-Arizona border (see feature on page 86) illustrates how special circumstances, little-known natural phenomena, and nothing more than conversation between two people who respect each other can conspire to create an 'abduction' – and a multiple-witness one at that. Had Jack Wilson presented his story to a ufologist inclined to credit the reality of abductions, the case would surely now be a classic in the literature. Instead, he told it to Dr Ronald Siegel, an expert in altered states of consciousness. Siegel ran a thorough medical and psychological inventory on Wilson, made some enquiries of his own, and was ready to present his conclusions.

Siegel showed Jack Wilson the results of his medical examinations. He had a clean bill of health. His only quirks were a tendency to become faint and dizzy when suddenly standing up after being seated for long periods, and slight photophobia, or sensitivity to bright light. Siegel then explained why he believed that the impression of an abduction had been produced by a mixture of objective events and mental states.

Wilson and his son had shared the driving on the long trip from Florida, and neither had slept very well on the journey. At the time they were abducted, they had been on the road non-stop for 30 hours. When Wilson first heard the strange noise from the rear of his car, he himself had been at the wheel for 11 hours. When he pulled up, the car was facing away from the early morning Sun. Siegel had discovered from the weather bureau that at that location the Sun had risen two hours previously, and that there was a slight mist. When Wilson stepped out of the car he felt suddenly dizzy. He then looked back to the rear of the vehicle to check for the cause of the mechanical noise, and was blinded by the glare of the Sun shining at a low angle through the mist. Reacting to his photosensitivity, he involuntarily turned away, and so was now facing west, toward the 'antisolar position', the point in space directly opposite the Sun. This was where he saw the little gray man.

The antisolar point was directly in front of Wilson, situated on the ground at the head of his own shadow. What Wilson saw was a 'glory'. When a shadow falls on droplets of moisture, such as dew, a cloud, or a mist, the 'glory' appears to the observer as a glow of light around the upper part of the shadow. This occurs because the tiny drops of moisture act as lenses or prisms to refract the Sun's rays. Peter had jumped out of the car when his father had appeared to faint, and as he grabbed the older man from behind he too saw the gray figure, with its glow and blurred edges – in fact, his own shadow. When they

> ◆
>
> **when his father had appeared to faint, and as he grabbed the older man from behind he too saw the gray figure, with its glow and blurred edges**
>
> ◆

More than one abductee has described having a close encounter with aliens while driving at night.
Psychologists know that traveling on long, straight, empty roads can produce a condition of 'highway
hypnosis' – an altered state of consciousness that may generate hallucinations.

got back in the car, the two men discussed the figure, Peter recalled, until, eventually, they both drifted into sleep.

Siegel explains that 'super-tired' people often get particularly vivid flashes of visual imagery as they slip from waking into sleep – the condition known as the 'hypnogogic state'. Elements of memory combine to form snatches of fresh and fantastic scenes, and sometimes odd sounds are fleetingly heard. This is the 'germinal stuff of dreams', says Siegel. Hypnogogic images characteristically take the form of abstract, geometrical patterns called 'entoptics': tunnels, spirals, cobwebs, and checkerboard designs. Produced by little-understood processes in the visual cortex of the brain, they are common to all human beings, and to trance states both natural and drug-induced.

Flashes of light often appear too, and in the mind's eye these combine with the geometric forms to transform by association into the passing image of a flame or a bright reflection, or some object or scene from memory. As the person drifts through the hypnogogic state toward sleep itself, a general loss of conscious control of the muscles sets in. This physical and mental condition is not dissimilar to the highly suggestible state a person enters when hypnotized.

Knowing these things, Siegel suggested that while Wilson and his son were drowsily discussing strange beings and UFOs, Wilson drifted into the hypnogogic state and saw what is known as the Isakower phenomenon, one of the universal entoptic forms appearing as an illuminated circle or similar roundish shape that grows bigger, and so appears to be approaching. 'Isakower,' Siegel told Wilson in passing, 'claimed the image was rooted in the memory of the mother's breast as it approached the infant's mouth.'

It is all in the mind of the beholder, Siegel explained. A drowsy person in the hypnogogic state is 'just as open to suggestions' as someone in an hypnotic trance. Wilson's sight of his own strangely glowing shadow had already set him up to think of aliens and abductions.

As the glowing lozenge of light grew larger, Wilson felt as if he was floating along a tunnel toward it. His fading consciousness linked the Isakower light to the glare he had seen outside the car, and turned it into the image of a UFO. He *dreamed* of gray beings, which were mixed with flashbacks from the Florida trip and other scenes from memory. Peter also recalled falling asleep and dreaming of floating inside a hallway and seeing the gray figure. When the two men awoke, Siegel surmised, they traded accounts of their dreams, smoothing out their disjointed nature and between them constructing a finished abduction narrative. It is possible too that both men had fragmentary lucid dreams – a state of consciousness in which mental imagery is so vivid that it appears absolutely real, while the dreamer's mind retains a sense of being awake.

'By the time [the Wilsons] arrived in Los Angeles,' Siegel says, 'the fleeting images of the dream had coalesced into a solid abduction story.'

Siegel next laid out before a rather glum Jack Wilson dozens of drawings by Alvin Lawson's 'imaginary abductees'. They showed long corridors, little gray men, geometric patterns, TV screens with scenes from the 'abductees'' past and medical examinations. They perfectly matched the pictures Wilson himself had drawn. Jack Wilson was less than happy with this prosaic explanation. Siegel ascribed this to

> ◆
>
> **His fading consciousness linked the Isakower light to the glare he had seen outside the car, and turned it into the image of a UFO**
>
> ◆

ROUTE 17 TO ALPHA CENTAURI

Harry Joe Turner

◆ ◆ ◆

Footprint of an astronaut on the Moon, photographed during the first manned mission in July 1969. Ten years later, aliens took Harry Joe Turner to see the real thing.

At 11.15 p.m. on 28 August 1979, Harry Joe Turner was thundering down Route 17, 3km (2 miles) outside Warrenton, Virginia, USA. He was driving a 1974 Kenilworth 18-wheeler, hauling a load of mustard and tomato ketchup from Winchester to Fredericksburg, and intermittently listening to chatter on the CB radio.

First, the radio 'started acting up'. Next, a mysterious noise filled the cab, getting louder and louder. 'I cupped my hand around my ears 'cause I couldn't stand it. It was a screech,' he said later. 'Then something grabbed me on the left side at a pressure point on my shoulder. It was like a bionic grip.'

Bright lights shone in the rear-view mirrors, something dark shot over the cab, then two loud thumps, and the truck's lights and engine failed. The big rig continued to sail on at over 110 km/h (70 mph). Turner now saw what was grasping him: a dark figure was standing just outside the cab door. Then it opened the door. Harry Joe grabbed a .32 automatic and pumped eight shots into the entity – without effect. He screamed: 'My God! I can't kill the thing!' and blacked out.

When he came to, he was in the passenger seat of his cab, and the truck was parked outside the warehouse he had been heading for in Fredericksburg. His watch said 11.17, but the warehouse clock showed 3 a.m. According to the odometer, he had traveled only 27km (17 miles), whereas his whole journey was 130km (80 miles) by road. In an even weirder twist, he later found that the Kenilworth had consumed 518 liters (114gal) of diesel. Inside the cab, his belongings had been scattered about, though nothing had been stolen. Outside, he found his tools lying on the ground, while the truck's CB radio antenna had been sheared off short, and the AM/FM antenna had been partly burned away. The vehicle was covered in a 'filmy substance'.

By the time Turner was on his way home to Winchester, his eyes had become so sensitive to light that they hurt; and he became so confused that at one point he got lost. He told a company manager at Winchester what had happened to him, then went to bed to rest before starting a fresh journey to

Pennsylvania that evening. When he climbed into his cab at 9 p.m., he passed out. He was taken to the Winchester hospital, where it was found he had a broken blood vessel in his left eye.

Once Harry Joe was home again, he began to recall what had happened to him when he blacked out on the highway. He and his truck together had been lifted into a UFO, where he saw pale, humanoid figures who had webbed hands and spoke in squeaky voices 'like a tape recorder played backward fast'. They were wearing white shirts and pants, and caps that covered their ears and foreheads. When they took the caps off, he saw each had a series of numbers on its forehead. Some, he learned, had 'bionic' body parts that were replacements for damaged limbs. The aliens were cold to the touch, just like a dead person.

Apparently the creatures did speak very fast, for when one – unmarked by numbers – slowed down his speech, Turner could understand what he was saying. He was called Alpha La Zoo Loo, and questioned Turner closely about his truck. Turner also said the aliens operated on him, putting an implant into the left side of his chest that would let them control that side of his body.

After this, the aliens took Harry Joe on a joyride through space. He was shown the first footprint of astronaut Neil Armstrong on the Moon, then taken to a planet 2.5 light years beyond Alpha Centauri to see futuristic domed cities. The landscape, however, was devastated, as if by nuclear war. Turner had no recollection of the return trip.

After his encounter Turner was plagued by physical and psychological problems, including unprovoked panic attacks and bouts of intense anxiety; doctors considered that his physical symptoms were caused by his mental state. This was clearly fragile. On 3 September, after downing a huge dose of Valium, he hightailed across several counties in his mother's car, attracting a sizable convoy of pursuing police cars. Harry Joe explained that he had thought the aliens were after him. After a visit to the scene of his abduction he returned with his truck and himself both soaking wet – because, he said, the aliens had sterilized them both. On another occasion he was seen having a fight with an invisible entity, which he explained was an alien. Several times at his house the 'bonic grip' was put on him again.

Turner became deeply religious – attending church, which he had never done before, and studying the Bible for a clue to the meaning of his experience. On one occasion he got lost at a shopping mall; whoever actually rescued him, Turner identified the man as Jesus.

Opinions of Harry Joe's encounter and its aftermath were divided. His minister avowed that 'I have no doubt he is convinced this really happened'. The manager of the terminal from which he trucked goods, however, could not verify Turner's claims about his fuel consumption or anomalous mileage readings, caught Turner telling lies on other matters, and became skeptical. Other workmates maintained Turner had concocted the story because he wanted to be 'bigger than he really is'. Harry Joe also had a reputation as a spinner of tall tales, although some acquaintances said he had 'never taken a story this far' before. The Chicago-based Center for UFO Studies arranged for a materials testing laboratory to analyse the damage to his radio antennae. The CB aerial appeared to have been cut with a hacksaw, and the other had apparently been charred by heat from a single source, such as a blowtorch.

◆

When they took the caps off, he saw each had a series of numbers on its forehead. Some, he learned, had 'bionic' body parts that were replacements for damaged limbs

◆

◆

Philip Klass's dismissive remark that they are 'little nobodies who want to be on TV' is ill-considered and, to many, gratuitously insulting

◆

disappointment: Wilson, he thought, wanted the abduction to be real because the attention would make him feel important, and possibly, famous.

In Wilson's case, this may have been true. And undoubtedly some abductees do relish the limelight (although not all admit it). The prospect of fame has been offered as one reason for suspecting that Harry Joe Turner (see feature on page 92) was being less than truthful about his alleged abduction. The curious aspect of this is that ufologists, not skeptics, have relegated Turner's case to the 'hoax' file, although his behavior suggests he was spontaneously reacting to a series of genuine and terrifying experiences, even if actual aliens may not have been their ultimate cause. Certainly his claims are no more outlandish than many others that ufologists have accepted without question. With this case in mind, skeptics are justified in wondering just how rigorous and consistent ufologists' standards are when it comes to deciding what they will or will not accept as evidence for abductions.

Whatever the assessment of the Turner case, most abductees want no more attention than is necessary to be reassured that they are not crazy, and to give them some emotional and social support in the face of a distressing and often incomprehensible experience. Philip Klass's dismissive remark that they are 'little nobodies who want to be on TV' is ill-considered and, to many, gratuitously insulting. Klass seems to dismiss the possibility that the abduction experience may occur anywhere but on the hypnotist's couch, and be real and frightening, even if it may not be an objective physical event.

Klass's convictions have occasionally led him astray. His proposed solution to the Travis Walton case (see Chapter Two) is probably his most glaring lapse. Klass theorized that Mike Rogers, the employer of the logging crew to which Walton belonged, was desperate to get out of his contract with the Forest Service because he was losing money on it. Rogers was inspired by the NBC-TV movie *The UFO Incident* (a dramatization of Betty and Barney Hill's abduction, aired two weeks before Walton disappeared) to create an abduction story that would allow him to break the contract, on the grounds that his loggers were too terrified to return to the site of the encounter. And Walton, allegedly a UFO buff from a family known for practical joking, knew enough of the necessary lore to pull off the part of the victim. According to Klass, the rest of the crew were duly recruited to the plan, and Travis hid out at his mother's house for five days after the story broke. Unfortunately, the Forest Service officials who administered the Rogers contract have called Klass's hypothetical plot 'absurd' – and Rogers in fact made no mention of the Walton abduction in his dealings over the contract.

Klass, and other skeptics, are on much stronger ground when they criticize the abductionists' refusal to entertain alternative explanations for abduction reports, whether those accounts are derived from hypnosis or from direct experience.

Abduction proponents become especially irritable when skeptics suggest that abductee narratives are influenced by science fiction or other aspects of popular culture. In *Secret Life*, David Jacobs maintains that no science-fiction movie 'has been released with themes or events similar to abduction accounts'. He adds, in magisterial style: 'Many abductees are not science fiction fans. They do not see science fiction movies or

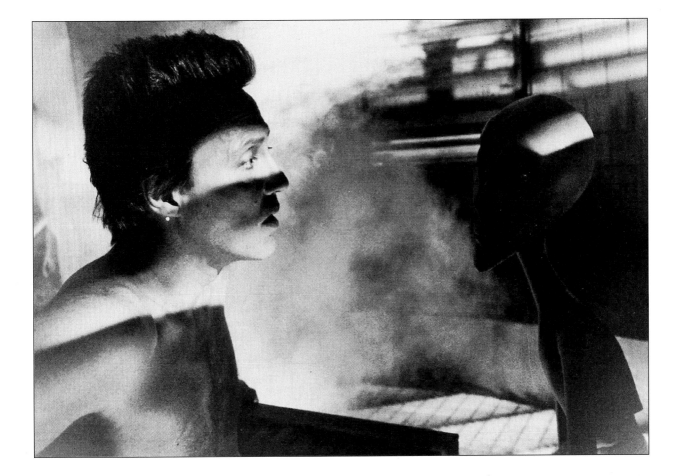

Christopher Walken plays Whitley Strieber in the movie Communion, *based on the bestselling book.*

television shows. They do not read science fiction literature. They are not involved with the world of science fiction at any level.' Even without enquiring how Jacobs acquired this universal knowledge, his position won't stand up to examination.

Since such major audience-pullers on TV as *The UFO Incident* (1975), portraying the Hills' 1961 abduction (and repeatedly shown since), the appearance of almost archetypal Grays in *Close Encounters of the Third Kind* (1977), the space-napping of Fallon in a 1987 episode of *The Colbys* soap opera, and the mini-series *The Intruders* (1992), based on Budd Hopkins's book of that title, let alone the massively promoted books and films of Whitley Strieber's *Communion* and of Travis Walton's 1975 experience in *Fire in the Sky* (1993), there can hardly be a citizen left in the West who does not now have *some* idea of what is supposed to happen next if, one dark and lonely night, they see a diminutive Gray hovering by their bedside or a strange craft swooping down on their pick-up on an empty road out in the country.

It is important to remember that one does not have to have seen these movies to be aware of salient details and so to be influenced by them: in taverns, workplaces and at home people regale one another with retellings and discussions, more or less accurate, of what they have seen and read.

A scene from Stephen Spielberg's 1977 movie Close Encounters of the Third Kind, *which introduced the spindly Gray and the idea of spacenaping to a worldwide audience.*

This second-hand process may well explain the sudden, and among ufologists controversial, appearance of weird wraparound eyes in alien lore with the publication of the Hills' abduction in 1966.

Martin Kottmeyer has an exhaustive knowledge of science-fiction films and TV shows, and is a self-confessed 'bad film buff'. In his essay 'The Eyes That Spoke' (published in *REALL News,* 1994), he points out that Barney Hill first described and drew the aliens' wraparound eyes during a hypnosis session with Dr Simon on 22 February 1964. 'The Bellero Shield', an episode of the science-fiction series *The Outer Limits*, was first broadcast on 10 February 1964, and featured aliens with wraparound eyes. This, says Kottmeyer, appears to be the only instance of spacemen with anything approaching the Grays' weird eyes in science fiction up to that date.

Not only that: in the *same* hypnosis session, Kottmeyer observes, Barney Hill mentions a truly bizarre aspect of 'his' aliens that we noted in Chapter One: 'They won't talk to me. Only the eyes are talking to me. I – I – I – I don't understand that. Oh – the eyes don't have a body. They're just

Alien witnessed by a British abductee who prefers to remain anonymous. The creature has unusual dress and facial markings. Images of aliens are less consistent than 'believers' tend to maintain.

eyes.... The eyes are telling me, "Don't be afraid." ... All I see are these eyes.' In 'The Bellero Shield', one of the fictional aliens explains: 'I cannot read your mind. I cannot even understand your language. I analyse your eyes. In all the universes, all who have eyes, have eyes that speak....' Remarks Kottmeyer: 'By any measure, the case for influence here is not just satisfactory, it is exemplary.'

In *High Strangeness* (1996), UFO encyclopedist Jerome Clark grudgingly concedes: 'This is a point, but not much of one', then reveals that Betty Hill has said she had 'never heard of' *The Outer Limits,* that she and Barney were hardly ever at home nights to watch TV, and that the program wouldn't have interested them anyway. She has confirmed this to me, too. Betty's interests are actually rather more intellectual than one might guess from the ufological literature – at the age of 65, for example, she took a university course in anthropology. And it is as reasonable to believe that her recall is accurate as it is to point out that few of us could say with much certainty what TV programs we did or didn't see 35 years ago.

On the other hand, I don't watch *Star Trek* on TV, but I'm occasionally surprised at how much I've absorbed about the series from reading and idle discourse. Barney could easily have picked up details as striking as the new-fangled alien wraparound eyes that spoke from friends or colleagues who *had* seen the show. And by this time, months into recalling his abduction with Dr Simon, he would hardly find such a conversation tedious. The links are so specific that it hardly seems likely that Barney's account and the airing of 'The Bellero Shield' are joined by mere coincidence. The same may be said of Kottmeyer's analysis of *Invaders From Mars*, a 1953 movie that contains many correspondences with the Hills' abduction, even down to the aliens' 'Jimmy Durante schnozzles' that Betty dreamed of soon after her abduction.

Others have gone further back than Kottmeyer in disinterring precedents for abduction reports as a whole. For instance, French philosopher Bertrand Méheust's *Science-fiction et Soucoupes Volantes*

> ◆
>
> **The links are so specific that it hardly seems likely that Barney's account and the airing of 'The Bellero Shield' are joined by mere coincidence**
>
> ◆

In an illustration from a 1935 Amazing Stories *magazine, humans are abducted by aliens who bear some likeness to those reported today. Such images were rife in science fiction from the 1920s onward. The bald, bug-eyed alien is a modern imaginative archetype.*

('Science Fiction and Flying Saucers', 1978) – a brilliant study unfortunately still not translated into English – reveals that virtually every aspect of ufology's aliens was foreshadowed in British, American and French science fiction from as early as 1904 to the 1940s. Here we have flying saucers, large-headed aliens from dying planets, missing time, and even entire abduction scenarios. We shall be looking very closely at the legendary historical precedents for abductions in the following chapters.

Keith Thompson is a moderate skeptic who has shown how closely the development of ufology has paralleled the antics of some of the more unruly pagan (especially Greek) gods. In *Angels and Aliens: UFOs and the Mythic Imagination* (1991), Thompson draws attention to an aspect of the Hill case that abductionists prefer not to acknowledge: its status as a *mythical* first. One consequence of this eminence is that 'ufologists continue to return to the Hill sighting report as the unspoken prototype for the world of events and images known by the phrase "alien abduction." …Hopkins confirmed the primordial necessity of the Hill case when he said [in *Missing Time*] that he adopted it as a model and primary reference point for his research with abductees.' Implicitly David Jacobs adheres to this creed. In *Secret Life* he reveals the narrowness of his vision of the problems that abductions present: 'I had no ground rules or signposts except Hopkins' work,' he says, describing how he set about his initial research.

The hallowed standing of the Hill case is 'unspoken' only in the sense that among ufologists it is rare to admit its mythic nature. Certainly, it is tantamount to sacrilege to question its reality. If the Hill case is deprived of its authenticity, virtually every other abduction account crumbles to nothing as a literal, physical event. Not only must it

be defended for itself, therefore – it has to be defended as an *unprecedented* event. Hence the ferocity with which the abductionists reject any suggestion that the phenomenon has any forebears in science fiction – or links to myth, folklore, religion or esoteric (but not pathological) psychological states. Hopkins has denounced the exploration of such themes as 'stewpot thinking' and 'an obstacle to science'. 'Science?' skeptic John Harney has ejaculated. 'What do the activities and ludicrous speculations of Hopkins and the other abduction enthusiasts have to do with science?' John Mack, as we have seen, has abandoned scientific thinking altogether rather than confront such difficulties.

It is possible to argue that many of those who report being abducted, and are uncontaminated by hypnosis, are describing genuine experiences, however these may ultimately be interpreted. Skeptics find it harder to acquit the literalist abduction investigators of charges of self-delusion. This tendency is particularly apparent in their claims to have accumulated physical evidence of abductions. These fall under three general headings: alleged alien implants; alien-induced pregnancies; and scars, wounds and other unexplained marks on abductees' bodies.

It can safely be said that no alleged implant has yet proved to be anything other than everyday organic material – cotton fibers and the like – that has wormed its way under the skin and become encysted there. As for self-delusion, the most visible 'implant' collector in the USA, Derrel Sims of the Houston [Texas] UFO Network, also claims among other achievements to have waged intergalactic

> ◆
>
> **many of those who report being abducted, and are uncontaminated by hypnosis, are describing genuine experiences**
>
> ◆

♦

**Hopkins and
Jacobs persist in
claiming at
public confer-
ences that these
anomalous
pregnancies
occur on a
continuing
basis**

♦

battle – successfully, of course – with an evil alien named Mondoz. Those who have had objects extracted from their bodies at his behest have yet to hear the results of any of the scientific tests he has promised them. Hopkins, Jacobs and Mack have all mentioned subjects who have had implants, but none has produced any medical records to justify their claims. The X-ray of New York abductee Linda Cortile showing an odd object in her nose was taken by a member of her family, and in any case is not *proof* of alien intervention: she could, quite simply, have stuck it there herself.

The same problem arises with alien-induced pregnancies. Even when one woman claimed to have been pregnant yet, on examination, her hymen was found to be intact, no medical record was shown in evidence. Nor, surprisingly, have any such cases been reported in the medical literature. Reporting to the Abduction Study Conference held in Cambridge, Massachusetts, USA, in 1992, John G. Miller MD admitted no cases of 'missing embryos' had been found, but joined the ranks of the self-deluders by concluding: 'I still think it is possible that a verifiable case can be found. I think that we have not yet looked hard enough.' Despite Miller's and others' findings, it is a matter of record that Hopkins and Jacobs persist in claiming at public conferences that these anomalous pregnancies occur on a continuing basis.

The 'scoop marks', vaguely resembling punch biopsy wounds, and other marks that some abductees have found on their bodies pose a trickier problem. Some could be self-inflicted, but it is obviously difficult to prove this either way. Some

*Derrel Sims (standing), self-styled 'alien hunter',
claims that rigorous scientific tests are performed
on the 'alien implants' he has collected,
but donors of the anomalous objects have yet to
be shown any results.*

are genuinely mysterious (see the instance of John Velez's wife, discussed in Chapter Four). Some may be produced psychosomatically, just as religious zealots spontaneously produce stigmata (the wounds of Christ) on their bodies. Keith Thompson also reminds us how potent the power of mind over body can be, with these examples, all of them documented in medical literature:

In the process of being treated for sleep-walking, an army officer exhibits deep indentations resembling rope marks on his arms. These appear as he painfully relives an earlier episode during which he is roped to his bed to inhibit his somnambulism.

Diagnosed as schizophrenic, a man who expresses a great desire to give birth begins to feel something moving in his stomach.... During the next three weeks his abdomen becomes more and more distended and he gains sixteen pounds [7.25kg] without altering his diet.

A group of experimental subjects, told what to expect from a certain drug, is able to produce not only that exact effect when given a dummy pill, but also the side effects of the drugs they think they are taking.

A man diagnosed with multiple personality disorder is found to be allergic to citrus juices in all but one of his personalities. He remains free of rashes and other symptoms so long as that one personality retains executive control.

In the light of cases such as these, and given the amount of suggestion from within and without that is involved in the average ufological abduction investigation, the appearance of physical symptoms and 'proofs' on abductees' bodies should surprise no one. The standard skeptical question is still worth asking: is there anyone who, if he or she looks hard enough, cannot find a scar somewhere on their skin that they can't explain? Finally, we should return to the place we started – the hardline skeptic's view: 'Since UFOs don't exist, abductions can't occur.' Not even astronomers and cosmologists agree on how likely it is that extra-terrestrial intelligence exists in the Universe, let alone whether the ETIs would develop a scientific and technological culture *and* have the cultural bias that would inspire them to explore among the stars *and* be so determined to do so that they would expend the resources to overcome all the practical and theoretical problems that face would-be spacefarers.

However, we might remember that on Earth, only one culture (Western European Christendom) has undergone the upheaval that we call the Renaissance, out of which modern science eventually emerged. Humanity itself exists at all only because somewhat earlier – some 65 million years ago – the Earth suffered a cataclysm that wiped out the dinosaurs, which were then the dominant form of animal life. That allowed a tiny shrew-like creature to move out of its ecological niche and evolve into the range of mammalian life we know today. But there was no guarantee that would happen.

In 'Alien Dreamtime' (*The Anomalist*, 1995), psychologist and UFO skeptic Professor Robert A. Baker cites authoritative biologists who have concluded that intelligent human life is an evolutionary *accident*, and there is no reason to suppose that any equivalent *must* have evolved anywhere else, given the remarkably slim chance that it would evolve here. The astounding variety of now-extinct creatures that were fossilized in the Burgess Shale in British Columbia, Canada, some 570 million years ago, says Baker refutes

the anthropomorphic idea that [biological] diversity increased with time....the evolutionary pattern shows rapid diversification followed by decimation with perhaps as few as five per cent [of species] surviving....

Stephen Jay Gould not only concurs, but points out that if we were to replay life's tape there is no reason whatsoever to assume that our particular type of self-conscious being would ever be expected to appear again.... Coffey sums up quite succinctly our anthropomorphic fallacy. 'The evolutionary conclusion that humanoid intelligence elsewhere is improbable,' he says, '[arises] because of the deep understanding that evolution has no real goal other than adapting creatures to specific local environments.

Neither we, nor our mode of intelligence, are the high point of evolution. The pathways of evolution are too circuitous for that ever to be the case.'

'It is also high time we realized,' emphasizes Baker, 'that all our scenarios of extra-terrestrial life...are all *nothing but projections of ourselves.*'

We can step still further back, from the chance advent of intelligent life on Earth to the peculiar, possibly unique circumstances of our planet. In his

Aerial view of a Meteor Crater, Arizona, some 200m (650ft) deep and 800m (half a mile) deep. Random impacts by objects from outer space, random genetic mutations and the equally random formation of the planets in our Solar System have all contributed to the development of human life. Given so many chance events, can we be certain that we are not, indeed, alone in the Universe?

essay 'Cosmic Dancers on History's Stage?' (*The Anomalist*, 1997), Mike Davis explores this notion. For life of any kind to emerge on a planet, he observes, it must be the right size and mass to be at almost exactly the distance from its star that the Earth is from the Sun (the margin of error is about one per cent). That planet also requires a large enough moon to help create tides and seasons, which biologists insist are vital to evolutionary 'progress'. Another, super-massive, gas giant planet (in our case Jupiter) is required further out from the star to attract most of the destructive rain of 'planetesimals' – comets, asteroids and other itinerant junk that would otherwise wreck a planetary biosphere. Those galactic gypsies that do get through, scientists are now recognizing, have profound consequences for the life that does evolve on the planet. It also seems very likely that most of Earth's water has resulted from cometary impacts, for instance.

A scientific consensus is now emerging that the chances that another solar system like ours has emerged elsewhere is infinitesimally small. Australian cosmochemist Stuart Ross Taylor has written: 'If large impacts of planetesimals are a characteristic feature of the final stages of planetary accretion, then the details of the individual impacts become to some extent free parameters.' In other words, not just Earth, but all our planetary neighbors are the product of chaos, and are possibly unique. Mike Davis adds: 'Even in its most general features, then, the present solar system cannot be theoretically "deduced" from…the state of the original solar nebula.' From this it follows that humanity – or intelligent life anywhere – is neither predictable nor presumable.

Impatience with the anthropomorphic extraterrestrial hypothesis and the intellectual laziness of 'researchers' who blind themselves to alternative explanations for abductions leads Robert Baker to a furious denunciation:

Whether intentional or not, the entire alien abduction scenario is an elaborately staged hoax, a production dumped upon the American scene by a naïve and credulous group of sensationalistic zealots and misguided psychotherapists who should know better. Acting in the name of altruism and aided and abetted by an enthusiastic and uncritical media, these alarmists have not only created a full-blown neurosis in many people…but they have also raised the anxiety level of an already beleaguered and overstressed populace. Acting in the name of beneficence and good citizenship, they have succeeded in doing considerable harm and have, in the process, not only managed to discredit science and medicine, but psychology and psychiatry as well. Such alien productions disguised in the name of alien abductions are, indeed, as Philip Klass aptly phrased it some years ago, 'a dangerous game,' a game that no one who is truly concerned about the welfare of others would ever want to play.

With those words in our ears, it behoves us to turn to constructive criticism of the abduction experience, to explore what, besides intrusive and probably non-existent Grays, may be behind it.

> ◆
> **In other words, not just Earth, but all our planetary neighbors are the product of chaos, and are possibly unique**
> ◆

CHAPTER 4

TWIXT HEAVEN AND EARTH

A Middle Way Between Believers and Skeptics

◆ ◆ ◆

Opposite: A bolt of lightning strikes a mountain outside Tuscon, Arizona. Some analysts have suggested that natural electromagnetic activity is responsible for some UFO sightings, and may trigger some abduction experiences.

The difference between those who believe in the idea that alien abductions are actual, physical events and those they label 'skeptics' and 'debunkers' is not quite as stark as the 'believers' would sometimes suggest.

Skeptics might agree that it's extremely unlikely that UFOs and their alien occupants are extra-terrestrial craft. They would reject other exotic notions too, such as that aliens are interdimensional or extra-dimensional beings, able to ignore or bypass the laws of nature as we understand them. And few, if any, skeptics would put any faith in testimony acquired through hypnosis.

But not all skeptics would suggest that the experience of being abducted can be pigeonholed as a fiction created by a tribe of self-deluders, hoaxers, liars, attention-seekers, and inadequates of various other kinds – all of whom have fallen into the clutches of incompetent investigators with indefensible beliefs. No doubt many abduction stories do arise in this way, and deserve debunking because of it. But people also exist who, without benefit of hypnosis, say they have undergone events as strange and traumatic as any reported in a state of trance. There is no need to doubt the honesty or sincerity of these witnesses, just because it is hard to take their accounts literally. And, without becoming entangled in dubious presumptions about otherworldly visitors, a number of skeptics have pondered on how such apparently genuine experiences could arise in the first place, and discussed why they match probably confabulated ones so closely.

In August 1975, Los Angeles UFO investigator Ann Druffel received a phone call from a mellow-voiced, 43-year-old woman, Sara Shaw (pseudonym). She explained she had been watching a Channel 11 TV series about UFOs, and it had 'started me thinking'. She had decided to try to solve the mystery of a period of missing time that had occurred to her 22 years previously and had bothered her ever since. Druffel took the case on, and about three years later she invited parapsychologist D. Scott Rogo to participate in the still-continuing investigation.

To begin with, there was little enough to go on. Just before 2 a.m. on 22 March 1953, Sara Shaw was awoken by a glow of bluish light outside the isolated cabin she shared with her then partner, Jan Whitley (pseudonym), in Tujunga Canyon, north of Los Angeles, California, USA. All the natural sounds of the night had ceased. Sara kneeled on her pillows and peered out of the window. She could not see the source of the light, which was swinging back and forth somewhere to the left of the window. She wondered if a gang of bikers that had passed earlier in the evening had come back, trouble on their minds. Jan, by now awake, got out of bed and put on a robe from the closet. Sara glanced at the clock, and then 'a strange giddiness, a sense of loss and confusion overcame her.'

The next thing she knew she was no longer kneeling at the window, but seated on the bed. The time was now 4.20 a.m. But Jan seemed not to have moved from where she was standing by the closet. The air seemed hard to breathe. Fearing their butane heater was leaking fumes, the two terrified women rushed into the kitchen to check it. Nothing was wrong there, but their pet cat and dog were crouched under the stove, and strangely quiet. Gathering

Swiss psychotherapist Carl G. Jung, whose ideas on UFOs profoundly influenced thinking about abduction experiences in the 1970s.

the animals, Sara and Jan ran for their car. Outside, Jan thought she saw 'a vaporous something superimposed – or standing against – the dark green leaves' of a bush at the side of the garage. 'The apparition distinctly showed the head and shoulders of a long-haired personage,' wrote Druffel and Rogo, 'but the features were dim, composed only of light and shadow.' Jan and Sara drove off to take refuge with Jan's foster-parents, who lived in a nearby city.

The ensuing investigation revealed a complex trail of abductions that involved Jan and several of her friends and later partners, which need not concern us here. Jan had no recall, consciously or under hypnosis, of actually being abducted in March 1953, but Scott Rogo was to draw some fascinating conclusions from Sara's accounts of what happened during the period of missing time. His interpretation of the Tujunga Canyon event drew on several sources.

In 1975 ufologists and journalists of the paranormal Jerome Clark and Loren Coleman published *The Unidentified*, in which they declared their belief that the UFO mystery 'is primarily subjective and its content primarily symbolic'. Physical traces reportedly left by UFOs, they considered, were 'psychokinetically generated byproducts of those unconscious processes which shape a culture's vision of the other world. Existing only temporarily, they are at best only quasi-physical.' This idea harks back to a hint dropped in 1959 by psychologist Carl Gustav Jung in his book *Flying Saucers*. Almost as an aside Jung suggested that while UFOs were a 'visionary rumor', a symbol of wholeness and spiritual health that had appeared to an alienated and dangerously divided world, the need that created them might be so powerful that they took on some kind of physical reality.

Clark was later to reject the ideas he first formulated in *The Unidentified*: he is now 'absolutely agnostic' about the reality of abductions, and believes that the extra-terrestrial hypothesis (ETH) provides a satisfactory explanation for the UFO phenomenon. Perhaps somewhat to his discomfort, however, his thinking of the 1970s has remained influential, especially among European 'psychosocial' ufologists. They may not accept the idea that UFOs are psychokinetic constructs; but they do regard UFOs as far more symbolic than real, and believe unraveling the meanings of individual UFO experiences is more fruitful than arguing over their genuineness (which, in any case, they largely dismiss). After 1975, in light of the Travis Walton case (see Chapter Two), Clark considered some abductions could be actual physical events, and in 1978 he and Scott Rogo co-authored *Earth's Secret Inhabitants*, which reflected this change.

In Clark's adjusted hypothesis – on which Scott Rogo was to elaborate – a force, intelligence or supermind, which for convenience they called 'The Phenomenon', is at large in the Universe and creates physical responses to human emotional or spiritual needs. 'We went on,' Scott Rogo wrote, 'to speculate that UFOs come into existence through our very belief in them. In other words, they are symbols hidden deep within our own minds that become reflected in The Phenomenon, which physically creates them and projects them into our

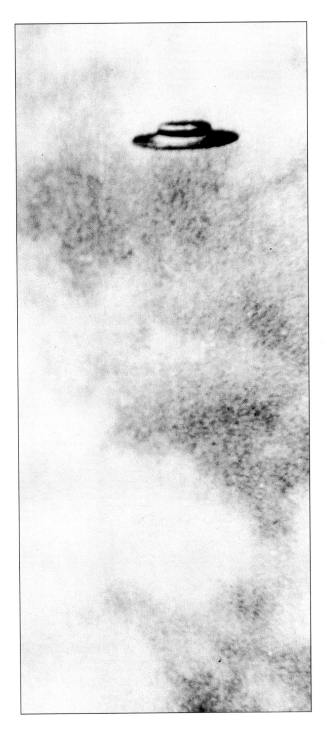

UFO pictured over the Marde Plata, Argentina, in April 1971. 'New ufologists' of the 1970s speculated that such anomalous objects might be created by psychic energy generated by human emtional and spiritual needs.

world accordingly.' Scott Rogo applied this idea specifically to abductions:

UFO abductions occur when the witness is in a state of psychological need, and when the unconscious mind needs to impart an important message to the conscious mind.... [The supermind] structures this information as part of the abduction scenario and presents it to the witness in objectified form. The supermind does all this by relying upon a prototypical experience, which it then individually molds to best communicate a vital message in symbolic form to the witness.

This is the reason why so many abduction reports seem to share many common characteristics.... I think we can go a step further [than Clark and Coleman] and suggest that UFO abductions are sometimes structured around [not archetypal but] individual symbols in the witness's mind.

Scott Rogo noted that in 1953 Jan Whitley and Sara Shaw were lesbian partners. Sara had been brought up by her mother to regard sex as taboo and 'rather distasteful'. 'By living with Jan, cut off from men,' says Scott Rogo, 'she did not have to worry about her mother's approval, which made it psychologically less threatening.' But Sara left Jan not long after the abduction experience, and then married a quadriplegic – an act that Scott Rogo sees as 'a last attempt to deny her sexuality' – whom she divorced; she was later married again, this time to a man in entirely good health.

In view of those biographical details, what happened to Sara, according to her account under hypnosis, is significant. She and Jan were separated in the alien craft, although Sara could see what was happening to Jan. Sara – floating over, not lying on a table – saw Jan fight the aliens as they tried to undress her. 'She doesn't have a bra on, and it really bothers her. She's so big that it bothers her to have anyone see her.... None of them seem to have breasts.' The aliens then added to the insult by feeling Jan's breasts. (During this episode Sara observed that the aliens were all tall, at least 1.7m [5ft 7in] in height, and dressed in one-piece black body stockings that covered everything but their faces.) Sara was examined by male entities while the females stood back and, once she realized no harm would come to her, she was surprised to find the experience both interesting and enjoyable – 'kind of fun', as she put it. Scott Rogo comments:

To one familiar with dream symbols and psychoanalytic thought, an interpretation of the story is obvious. At some deep level Sara must have realized that her companionship with Jan was not fulfilling, and that personal satisfaction would come only when she entered into a healthy heterosexual relationship. This concern is reflected in the sudden appearance of the aliens in her room who symbolically rape her, but [to her surprise, one might emphasize] leave her with a sense of enjoyment and fulfillment.

Jan, on the other hand, struggles against this male intrusion – demonstrating her resistance to any threat to her relationship with Sara, as Scott Rogo points out. But her response also indicates her lack of sexual interest in men, as well as an uncomplicated, instinctive rage at being violated. Sara's response too fits with a recognition, at some level of consciousness, that male attentions may be alarming, but may not be as horrible as she had been led to imagine.

After her first hypnotic regression, it's worth noting, Sara said: 'I feel like I'm conjuring the whole thing up.... I wouldn't be surprised but that I could create it. But yet, it was very different from patterns of anything I've ever created before in that I hadn't had to search for it. I fell into it.'

Readers would be correct in thinking that I have selected that last remark for quotation because I suspect that Sara did indeed 'conjure the whole thing up'. Clark, Coleman and Scott Rogo's notions, that either the human mind or a supernormal supermind can transmute an idea into physical reality, bite the dust by one of the simplest rules of science: it won't do to explain one group of perplexing phenomena (UFOs and abductions) as a function of another set of equally unknown and unproven mechanisms (psychokinesis, supermind).

As a psychological interpretation, Scott Rogo's thesis is quite plausible, but it has major logical flaws. If Sara Shaw's unconscious was so anxious to communicate this message to her conscious, what was the point of burying its information in a period of missing time (and therefore a blanked-out part of her mind) to which she had no access? Even at a symbolic level this abduction makes sense only if the supermind could somehow foresee that she would eventually be hypnotized. True, she was hypnotized – but not till more than 20 years after the abduction had taken place, by which time she had long resolved the problems that the event dramatizes. All of which points to the imaginative or dream-making faculty set free by hypnosis as the source of the imagery – relevant as it was to the period to which she was regressed.

John Velez indicates where a giant UFO hovered over a Brooklyn street immediately before his apparent abduction in August 1979.

Either the abduction phenomenon is real, and can be accounted for within the terms of scientific knowledge, or it is not physically real at all. I have discussed in Chapter Three why the ETH is unsatisfactory, and how some abduction 'cases' have been created out of extremely mundane materials. But clearly we still have to resolve the paradox that abduction experiences can both seem utterly real and yet have no material content or objective basis.

In other words, from the way Sara Shaw's 'hypnotically refreshed' memory was designed to reveal the true nature of her sexual preferences, we can see that the abduction scenario can serve as a framework for dramatizing powerful, personal psychological material. But what could have triggered the initial sighting and led to the period of missing time? And why is it that her account so closely resembles other abduction narratives that do not derive from hypnosis? The same queries could be raised about the experiences of John Velez (see feature on page 112).

There are many potential answers to those questions. Here I want to consider two. Both recog-

An 'earthlight' photographed at Hessdalen, Norway. Proximity to these enigmatic lights may induce hallucinations that may later be interpreted as abductions.

nize the reality of the experience and the integrity of the witness, but avoid the pitfalls of skepticism and schemes that explain one unknown in terms of another, and make ufology just another undisciplined, self-referential branch of the paranormal. The two approaches described here call on many established scientific disciplines, and can be tested in scientific terms.

First, let us consider what strictly earthbound event could trigger an abduction experience. Even if many abductees' experiences can be reduced to an hypnotically induced dramatic projection of (real) personal, medical or social tensions or problems, there may be an objective component in some cases. It could be that the otherworldly, nightmarish experiences are triggered by close contact with an energetic object such as an earth-light. These UFOs, it is claimed, are exotic but natural luminous phenomena, probably a kind of luminous plasma, produced by processes occurring within the Earth – perhaps meteorological, atmospheric, or tectonic-geological activity, or perhaps a combination of such mechanisms.

From humble beginnings in the 1960s and 1970s, the study of these enigmatic lights has developed into a dynamic research program. Its puzzles are real enough to have piqued the professional curiosity of conventional scientists. Earthlights remain an anomaly, but they enjoy a good deal more scientific authenticity than psychokinesis or 'superminds'.

In 1983 Michael Persinger, a neuroscientist and geologist at Laurentian University in Sudbury, Ontario, Canada, described a number of possible effects an earthlight could have on the body, brain and mind of a witness. The consequences depended on the distance from the light phenomenon, and were calculated from clinical observations of the effects of electromagnetism on human physiology.

At a range beyond the influence of the energy fields associated with an earthlight, a person will simply see a strange light. Closer in, the observer will notice the lightform's colors, shape, internal fluctuations, and so on. As the light moves closer, or is approached, the witness enters the electromagnetic fields believed to be associated with the phenomenon. The first effects to be noticed would include tingling sensations, goose bumps, hair raising, and an oppressive feeling on the chest. Closer to the light phenomenon and deeper into the field, brain function is increasingly affected, and the observer is likely to enter an altered state of consciousness. Hallucinatory material is released into waking awareness. The closer the encounter, the deeper will be the modifications of consciousness, vision and memory. Witnesses may find themselves in the grip of uncontrollable terror or even religious awe.

If the electrical aspects of the electromagnetic field predominate, localized effects on neck and thighs would be felt; if the magnetic components are dominant, then the waist and genital area would be especially affected. Sensations in these parts of the body would readily be incorporated into the witness's mental imagery. We have all experienced this to a lesser extent in deep sleep, for instance, when external sounds such as a door banging or an alarm bell going off, or bodily discomfort such as thirst or a stomach ache, become woven into what we are dreaming. If the

Clarke Hathaway's The Mouth That Ate The World *- based on visions he had in 1970 and 1971 of future cataclysmic changes in Oregon and northern California.*

AMBUSHED IN BROOKLYN

John Velez

◆ ◆ ◆

*John Velez outside the house on 62nd Street, Brooklyn, New York,
where he was living in August 1979. Walking home in the early
hours, he was confronted by a gigantic UFO; his next memory was
of waking covered in blood and bruises. Hypnosis revealed an
abduction had occurred during a period of 'missing time'.*

John Velez is a native New Yorker and has always lived in the city. When still in his teens he became a highly successful professional drummer; his encounters with drugs on the music scene led to his working for 10 years as a counselor in the Phoenix House rehabilitation program. He then spent 16 years in the printing industry and, as that 'downsized', turned to freelance graphic design in the 1990s.

John Velez has conscious memories of encounters with alien beings that go back to his earliest years, and has had numerous UFO sightings.

As a child, he saw spheres and shafts of light dancing in his bedroom; aged five, he saw a 'silver circle' hanging over his head in an East Side park; when he was eight, he woke up one night to find himself being carried across his bedroom by what he now recognizes as aliens. He believes his wife and son have also been abducted. The most dramatic of his own encounters took place in late August 1979, when he was living on 62nd Street in Brooklyn.

That night Velez had gone out to dinner with friends. His wife Margie was ill, and stayed home with their two children, then aged four and two. Velez walked the eight blocks home from his evening out, and at about 1.30 a.m. was about to turn into 62nd Street when, beyond a factory on the corner, there appeared a light 'the size of a small moving van' floating about 10-12m (30-40ft) above the roofs of three tall, red-brick apartment buildings in his street. The light was the shape of a football. 'I got scared, and I started running like a schoolgirl,' Velez recalls. 'The feeling I had in my chest was that I was going to get mugged, that I was going to get hurt on the way home.'

Velez remembers getting near to his house, 'and then the next second, it's daylight, and I'm sitting bolt upright in bed. It's seven o'clock in the morning. And I've got blood all over me, on my pillow and on my teeshirt, and my eye hurts. I go to the dresser and look in the mirror and my eye is out here, very red and swollen, and the white of the eye is completely red.' Velez thought he had been mugged and beaten - the blood was all from his nose - but his wallet, money and other valuables were still in his pants and vest. He cleaned himself up, and woke his wife, who was shocked at his injuries. They went to the emergency room at the nearby Lutheran Memorial Hospital. The attending doctor prescribed basic remedies, but seemed unusually interested in whether Velez had had any nose surgery. He assured the doctor he had not. Curiously, the doctor found no evidence that the eye injury had been caused by an impact, such as a punch.

There were other incidents after that, but in 1993 Velez read Budd Hopkins's *Missing Time*, but he became so disturbed by it that he gave up. The book revealed too many parallels with his own experience, and the notion that he might have been abducted by aliens was deeply distressing. Nonetheless, he contacted Budd Hopkins and, over two years, in four or five sessions of regressive hypnosis, Velez recalled what had happened that night in 1979:

> *I was about 20ft [6m] from my house, and three of these fucking gray things with big black eyes came out - they didn't walk out, they floated out - from behind the hedge around my house, right in front of me. And I stopped. It felt like somebody had sucked the air off the Earth. I was gasping to breathe. What's buzzing in my head is: What is that? What is that? I thought they were skinned cats. I'm trying to make sense in my head of what my eyes are showing me. I can't move. All I want to do is run, and I can't.*
>
> *Then, the next sensation. All that fear, all that terror, just washes away. And I'm thinking: Oh, I know you. Everything's okay. I look off to my right, and above my neighbor's house, there's the UFO, with this red light on top going round like on an ice cream truck. Then two of the little guys come floating over toward me, and each one very gently takes an arm, and they turn me. We get hit with, like, a theater spotlight. I take two steps forward and - airborne. We're floating up, and I'm getting off on it, I'm enjoying it. It's like being Peter Pan or something.*
>
> *There are no doors in this thing up above. We're moving very slowly, but my instinct is to put my hands up because my head's gonna hit this thing. We're about four, five feet [1.5m] away. A black line appears, then it opens. There's a black square in front of me. We go through this. I can't see anything in there, but my clothes are being pulled offa me. That switches very rapidly - I'm on a table now. There's about six or eight of these fucking things in the room. The one behind me puts his hand on my forehead and talks to me the way I used to talk to my kids when they were upset. 'It's okay. We have to do it. You'll be fine. Nobody's going to hurt you.'*

A larger entity than the others, like a praying mantis, approached. It held a very slim 'wand', which it thrust up Velez's nose and penetrated the bone. Then there was a blinding flash as one of the other beings probed Velez's eye - it felt to him as if it was being pulled out of his head. At that point Velez

> *sank into abject terror. After [Budd] had calmed me, he asked me what transpired next. I jumped right to the end of the abduction where I am being gently tucked into my bed by several of the little gray buggers. He kept trying to take me back to the...eye procedure, but it was like staring at a blank wall...whatever it was must have been pretty hard for me to take, or that I was rendered unconscious...It's all speculation as to why I can't remember. I did remember clearly how it all ended, but absolutely nothing of that 'missing time' within missing time!*

witness and the light draw still closer together, the person may lose consciousness, with partial or complete amnesia on coming round. Even closer contact could result in burning, hair loss, and radiation sickness. (All these effects have been found on some claimed close encounter witnesses.) An extremely close encounter could result in death by electrocution or, as Persinger puts it, by 'carbonization'.

The parts of the brain most likely to be affected by electromagnetic fields are the temporal lobes and amygdala, as they are particularly electrically sensitive; that is why seizures are most often associated with them. The amygdala and the

Neurologist and geologist Dr Michael Persinger, pictured in 1987. Dr Persinger suggests that natural phenomena may affect electrical activity in the brains of certain vulnerable individuals in a way that creates exotic hallucinations, including abduction fantasies.

hippocampus are beneath the temporal cortex. The amygdala is associated with emotional feelings, while alterations in the functioning of the hippocampus can change or modify memory and release dreams into the waking state.

All human brains register somewhere on a scale of temporal lobe sensitivity. Those at one extreme, 'temporal lobe sensitives', are the most likely to undergo transpersonal – mystical or otherworldly – experiences, as well as to suffer epileptic seizures. Temporal lobe epilepsy occurs because of tiny but chronic electrical seizures within the temporal cortex. A sufferer will report dreamy states, hearing voices, seeing apparitions and feeling compulsions; periods of missing time can occur.

In clinical experiments, small currents have been induced in the tissues of the hippocampus and amygdala. The subjects report scenes or apparitions, and experience alterations in their perceptions of time and space, as well as out-of-body experiences, feelings of unreality, *déjà-vu*, and memory blanks. Meaningful auditory messages may seem to emanate from the subject's environment. Even brief stimulation can cause hours of alteration in the brain's information processing.

The biochemical and electrical alterations in these sensitive brain tissues can be caused by a number of circumstances, such as electrochemical effects within the brain itself resulting from a person's medical condition, behavior patterns, psycho-spiritual exercises, taking certain drugs, or exposure to external electromagnetic fields, whether natural or artificial. When electrical disturbance within the temporal cortex has happened once or a few times, cells within the tissues become 'primed', so that people become prone to entering altered mind states with the minimum of stimulation from whatever external or internal source.

The power of Satan, as visualized by Norman Harrison. He received this and other equally disturbing visions of worldly corruption through what he believed was telepathic communication with aliens, who had calculated 'via strict mathematical extrapolative calculus' that human society was in 'catastrophic decline'. Investigator Nigel Watson suspected Harrison was mildly schizophrenic.

Since the late 1980s, Persinger has been running a series of experiments to test the effects of magnetic fields on the temporal cortex. The subject is placed in a soundproof chamber and is specially fitted with a helmet containing computer-controlled electrodes that direct magnetic 'vortices' to the temporal lobes with great precision. Some people see visions – of, say, a figure from the iconography of their religious beliefs (a person's expectations and beliefs have a profound effect on the content of visionary material, however caused), or even ghosts or demons. One participant said that the acoustic chamber ought to be exorcised as it was haunted by the Devil himself! But most simply have a powerful feeling of a 'presence'. 'After several sessions,' Persinger told journalist Ian Cotton, 'it took little to trigger the mystical state of mind.'

In the early days of the experiments, Persinger formed two groups of subjects who had never experienced a close encounter with a UFO. One group used the magnetic helmet, while the other group, acting as a control, did not. Both groups were told to imagine that they were emerging from woods and could see a light in the sky. Persinger set up a pulsing electric light in the laboratory and asked his subjects to free-associate. Those having their brains magnetically massaged disgorged images full of standard UFO abduction scenes – 'from gray-skinned, slit-mouthed aliens to blue beams of light to horrific reports of medical probes', reported ufologist and journalist Dennis Stacy. Such imagery was far richer in those exposed to the magnetic field than in those who were not.

But what about the real thing? Is there any evidence that this sort of brain-effect could be occurring during some actual UFO sightings?

As a matter of fact there is. A wave of lights had been reported throughout the 1970s in the Yakima Indian Reservation, Washington State, USA, and especially between 1973 and 1974. Firewardens in lookout posts saw red-orange and yellow-orange lightballs floating within the reservation over various locations, among them Goat Rocks. These were quite large, though 'ping-pong balls' of light were also seen bounding along Toppenish Ridge and Satus Peak. Columns and flares of lights were also seen, as were white lights with smaller, multi-colored lights apparently connected to them. Some lights took complex forms, and some displayed luminous protrusions or 'horns'.

Analysis of these events carried out by Persinger and American geologist John Derr showed that 78 per cent of the reported phenomena were lights seen in the night sky. They were seen most often near the ridges that cut across the reservation – each riddled with geological faulting and therefore tectonic stresses – and around Satus Peak, which is in the general area of a surface rupture and is where one of the stronger earthquakes in the region occurred during the 13 years covered by the study. Lights were frequently seen in the seven months preceding the biggest earthquake of that 13-year period, in June and July 1975. Regional seismic activity also increased at the times in 1972 and 1976 when most sightings were reported.

And, consistent with Persinger's theory and his experimental results, it was not merely weird lights that were reported. As well as hearing poltergeist-like gravel-crunching around their remote lookout posts, the reservation's firewardens also described 'happy little voices singing', a woman screaming,

> ◆
>
> **One participant said that the acoustic chamber ought to be exorcised as it was haunted by the Devil himself!**
>
> ◆

Paul Devereux, photographed on a hunt for earthlights in the northern Australian outback in 1995.
The expedition succeeded in recording a number of anomalous lights and simultaneous
geomagnetic disturbances, as predicted by the earthlight hypothesis.

someone 'hollering'. There were no mundane explanations for any of these. In addition there were reports of strong, repulsive odors (olfactory hallucinations can occur as well as visual and auditory ones), and in one case the fleeting appearance of a 2.1m- (7ft-) tall, wild-looking humanoid.

There was an interesting reported close encounter between an earthlight and a group of people traveling across the reservation one night in the midst of the wave of sightings. Their car broke down and they saw a light in the distance, and getting closer. No one recalls what happened next – when they later recovered, they all were suffering from amnesia. One man in the group,

however, did recall a sensation of floating out of his body and glimpsing the others standing stock-still as if in trance. It is easy to imagine this witness, with the right predisposition and in the hands of certain investigators, producing a full-blown abduction narrative under hypnosis, which would include seeing his companions 'switched off' while the aliens went about their work.

Indeed it is possible to interpret at least two particularly well-known abduction experiences as the product of encounters with earthlights.

In Debbie Tomey's account (see Chapter Two), it is noteworthy that the aliens and the spaceships appeared only in hypnotically derived imagery. If

UNDER THE SKIN

Pat Parrinello

❖ ❖ ❖

Pat Parrinello, in front of the stretch of Texas pasture over which he has seen and videotaped UFOs. While never claiming to be an abductee, Parrinello recounts many related experiences.

Pat Parrinello works today as the manager of an apartment building in a small town about 80km (50 miles) south of Houston, Texas, USA. When he was six years old, living near Minden, Louisiana, he had a very strange experience one night on the family farm. 'I don't know if this comes from a dream, or if this really happened,' he says. 'But there seems to be evidence it wasn't a dream.'

As he tells the story: 'One night I had one of them sudden paralyzing feelings, and suddenly started to move involuntarily. I got up out of bed, went out the back door of the farmhouse, went right around behind the house, over the barbed wire fence and out into the field. It was a special field. My daddy planted sweet potatoes on it.

'I'm walking down the field, and all around these lights are moving in the sky. At that age I wasn't thinking about UFOs, or flying saucers or anything – I didn't know what an airplane was yet, not really. Then this round thing came down right in front of me. Seemed to be a metallic sphere, about yea high' – he gestures, showing how the sphere was about 60cm (2ft) in diameter.

'For some reason I wasn't afraid of it. Then it started to spin. I suddenly got scared, and that's when I was able to break this thing a little bit, and as I turned around to run, it seemed like the damn thing exploded and got ahold of my hand right here.' He remembers no more of the incident, but he woke up the next morning 'sick as a dog. Bleedin', and pukin'.'

'After that, it seemed like I was an alien. Wherever I went, very few people would have anything to do with me. And I developed incredible sensitivities.' One was a painful sensitivity to light; another was an ability to hear very high-frequency sounds, well beyond the usual range of human hearing: 'I could hear all the way up to probably 25 KHz. Traffic lights, buggy alarms, anything operating by ultra-sound, they drove me up the wall. Writing tablets, low grade paper, newspaper – just touch it, it would set my teeth right on edge. I couldn't write with a pencil because of the noise it made. It affected my school work, everything. First grade in school – I was a perfect student. Second year in school, I was a total mess. When I was trying to get in the Navy, it showed up in all these tests they give you.'

Parrinello wonders if his childhood experience may also have created or enhanced a power of precognition. He found he had an extraordinary talent for anticipating what people were about to say, for example – even names they were about to mention. But there were more concrete premonitions.

When he was 18, he bought a plane – a 1946 Erlon Ercoupe – and started to take flying lessons. One day, exchanging 'hangar talk' with other pilots at the airstrip, 'I had this daylight idea. And I said "Wouldn't it be funny if somebody hijacked a plane and it landed down here at Lake Jackson?" And everybody laughed. Two days later I was coming through Brazoria, past an airport there – that no longer exists – and I looked across, and there's a 707 right there on the runway. Hijacker. Hijacked the airplane out of Houston. Pilot convinced him he was out of fuel and had to make an emergency landing. Came down right there in Brazoria.'

When he was working for a local hydroblasting company, Parrinello was sent to 'scope out' an old well with a broken pump on a property – that is, find out what waterlines ran from the well. He had had an odd, very vivid dream the night before: 'There was this rattlesnake coming up to me…and then I'm sitting there, holding this rattlesnake and he's looking at me. Next day, tracing these pipes out, I noticed this faucet sticking up just across the barbed wire fence. So naturally I started moving it, to see which direction the pipe runs, see if it goes over toward the well. I suddenly remembered that dream. I looked down at my feet, and there, dead asleep, was this great big rattlesnake. I jumped backwards about 10 feet [3m].'

On another occasion he was convinced the car he was driving was on fire. 'I was coming back from leaving my mother at the bus station. I got this sensation of fire in the car. I was feeling the floorboards, sniffing. This sensation's telling me, there's a fire, there's a fire. Five minutes later the car ahead of me broke out in flames underneath.'

In 1971, on holiday with his parents in Punto Fijo, Venezuela, the car he was driving was hit in the left side by another, traveling at high speed. X-rays showed the bones in his left elbow were cracked – but also a revealed a small triangular object buried in his hand. The Venezuelan doctor said it was a cyst, and nothing to worry about. In 1984, Parrinello tried out a miniature metal detector that he came across in a flea market – and it reacted to his 'cyst'. He began to wonder if it was a fragment from the apparent explosion of the sphere he had encountered as a child. 'But how the hell did it get in there without leaving any scar, or what have you?' he asks.

In the mid-1990s, Houston investigator Derrel Sims persuaded podiatrist Dr Roger Leir to extract possible 'implants' from a number of people who, Sims believed, were abductees. On 19 August 1995, Dr Leir operated on Pat Parrinello. According to Dr Leir, the object – whatever it was – connected to nerve tissue and to bones in the hand.

Parrinello does not know where the object is now. Sims retained it for a while among a collection he shows of alleged implants and eventually sent it to the National Institute for Discovery Science (NIDS), a private organization dedicated to investigating various aspects of the paranormal. NIDS told Parrinello the object wasn't metallic, but didn't supply him with any details of any tests they may have run on it.

Parrinello has never himself claimed to be an abductee, and calls himself '75 per cent skeptical' about abductions. Asked if he would consider whether something like a lucid dream was responsible for his encounter at the age of six, he says: 'I'd buy that.' But his experiences (including two striking UFO encounters) and the seemingly anomalous object that was once buried in his hand leave him wondering.

Debbie's brain functions had been affected by energy fields associated with the ball of light that she and her mother saw, then such confabulation, let alone partial amnesia, would be a typical consequence. That something of the kind did happen is supported by the discovery, made by earthlights and consciousness researcher Paul Devereux, that a geological faultline runs beneath the Tomey household in Copley Woods.

The hypnotic regression merely probed the period of amnesia and the peripheral periods of disturbed memory. The 'set and setting' of the sessions with a well-known researcher (Budd Hopkins) could well have simply organized, or dressed up, Debbie's memories of hallucinatory imagery into an abduction narrative. Talking with abductees in both Britain and the United States, Paul Devereux has found them prepared to entertain an 'altered-states' explanation for their experiences. As one said to him: 'The UFO abduction explanation was the only one I knew about.' Other abductees have expressed to me a similar willingness to consider alternative explanations for their experiences – see, for instance, Pat Parrinello's comment in the feature on page 118.

Cognitive science now understands that memory is not like some video library or photo album from which objective, stored snapshots of the past are retrieved, but is mediated by electrical configurations within brain cells that *reconstruct* memorial images. While these memories are real to the person concerned, they do not necessarily reflect anything that objectively happened. In Debbie Tomey's case, we see a hybrid of traditional

> ◆
>
> **science now understands that memory is not like some video library or photo album from which objective, stored snapshots of the past are retrieved**
>
> ◆

fairy changeling themes and modern UFO lore, perhaps spiced with imagery expressing her response to living in a modern technological society with all its pressures, fears and alienating aspects. The context of extra-terrestrial abduction had been powerfully supplied by Hopkins himself, not least through Debbie Tomey's prior reading of his book *Missing Time*. In another culture or time, Debbie's memories might have featured demons and spirits.

Travis Walton's story (see Chapter Two) has been denounced as a transparent hoax and simultaneously held up as one of very few genuine abduction narratives. But it could be that the real answer exists between these extremes. Walton's description of his encounter with the UFO is consistent with electric shock caused by close proximity to a glowing plasma. This in turn would have caused a brief initial mental blackout and seizures within Walton's temporal cortex, with concomitant hallucinations, partial amnesia, mental confusion and further blackout periods. As one of the reporters at the time was later to suggest: 'He had seen something out there in the woods, some kind of an eerie light that had triggered a powerful hallucination that might recur at any time.'

Could Travis Walton have wandered about disoriented for five days in the woods, alternately hallucinating and lapsing into unconsciousness, oblivious to hunger and night-time cold? Lack of food would not have been a problem, but he would have had to huddle in survivable warmth overnight, and to have taken water in some form – dew off leaves, a stream, or whatever. Could anyone have maintained such an instinctive behavior pattern while in traumatized, confused, trance and semi-trance states? The answer is yes; it is known that people can perform quite complex tasks such

Frames from a video of an apparent UFO shot on the evening of 14 November 1996 by Pat Parrinello. It was also seen by several other witnesses.

as driving a vehicle for quite long periods while in an unconscious, entranced state. But what exactly happened to Travis Walton must remain an open question.

Jerome Clark emphasizes Walton's description of entities that later dominated abductees' accounts. This does not mean there was any physical objectivity in Walton's abduction account, nor that fetus-like extra-terrestrials took a sudden fancy to our planet in the mid-1970s. The recurring image of the alien with large head and enormous black eyes might well be a product of deeply ingrained cultural and psychic factors (discussed in Chapter Five).

To return to where we began this chapter: it is at least conceivable that the consciously recalled episode of a mysterious light, missing time, consequent hallucination and irrational panic that spurred the long investigation into the alleged abductions of Sara Shaw, Jan Whitley and her friends, was triggered by an encounter with an earthlight.

British researcher Albert Budden has also examined in detail a range of close encounter cases in the light of the effects of electromagnetism on the mind. He wrote in 1994:

Such high-strangeness encounters occur in locations where the environmental electromagnetic fields are elevated.... The encounters can take the form of vivid hallucinatory visions induced by the effects of electrical fields on the brain and are 'symptoms' of a syndrome called 'Electrical Hypersensitivity and Multiple Allergy'. This condition, which is the subject of university and clinical research, is caused by prolonged exposure to electromagnetic fields induced by such environmental hot spot sources as radio/TV transmitting antennae, radar, radio-cab offices, telecommunications towers, electrical sub-stations, pylons, etc.

My own research has shown that individuals who experience these bizarre high-strangeness encounters have usually had a major electrical event in their formative years which acts as an initiation for electrical hypersensitivity in later life. This event may have been proximity to a lightning strike, ball lightning, geological light phenomena (i.e. 'earth lights'), major electrocution, and so on.

Budden is suggesting here that the typical close-encounter witness has had a 'priming' experience that has sensitized his or her temporal cortex, and needs relatively little stimulus to enter an altered state of consciousness. (Budden might have added that some people are in any case 'temporal lobe sensitives' simply because of their neurophysiological make-up.)

One of many cases Budden has reviewed is known to British ufologists as the 'Quantock Horror'. In 1988, the witness, Tony Burfield, was taking photographs on the Quantock hills in Somerset, south-west England, when he saw an object flying toward him. It flew directly over him and was huge, blocking out the light of the Sun. It was a very complex object with 'bat-like' wings. He took several photographs, including one that he said showed an entity standing on the rim of the craft. (Budden saw one of Burfield's photographs, and it showed little more than a black dot, which the investigator felt looked like a hang glider.)

Burfield had an allergic sensitivity to aspects of his home environment, and used to go for walks on the Quantocks to make himself feel better. But after his encounter Burfield developed serious problems, such as an inability to eat solid foods, extreme sensitivity to electrical equipment, and a constant metallic taste in his mouth. He suffered memory loss, and became oversensitive to light, so that even car headlights at night caused him pain and blinded him with after-images. He also saw fleeting hallucinations of 'little men' in his house. These often shot at him, he said, with painful rays.

Budden discovered that Burfield lived close to a row of high-tension electricity pylons, and suggested that his hallucinatory imagery was actually his subconscious articulating the effects of the strong electromagnetic fields on his home. Budden further pointed out that the metallic taste Burfield complained of was typically caused by the effect of an electrical field on the mercury-tin amalgam of tooth fillings.

It also transpired that the encounter itself took place between two intersecting rows of pylons carrying high-tension cables, and Burfield revealed that he had had 'a big electrical accident' in the past. Budden concluded that the witness had been made electrically hypersensitive with multiple allergies as a result of his initial accident and, later, his highly charged home environment. His experiences were, in effect, symptoms of his condition. These had perhaps been brought to a crisis by the location of the 'encounter'.

Critics have questioned some of Budden's interpretations of his data and some of his generalizations, it should be said. Nonetheless the core of his argument, that electromagnetic pollution produces hallucinogenic effects, which reflect the percipient's circumstances, is powerful. The case of Kathy, reviewed in Chapter One, whose experiences were brought to a frizzling halt by a massive electric shock, certainly supports the notion that electromagnetic effects are somehow entangled in the roots of some abduction experiences. (As it happens, Kathy today does have

Pylons carrying high-tension electricity supplies can, according to some researchers, help to create allergies to electromagnetism. These in turn may cause hallucinations.

disastrous effects on electronic hardware. Her friends won't let her near their computers, and she reckons she needs to replace major components of her own computer system about once every six months or thereabouts.)

And it is not surprising that in the radically 'alien' environment of an hallucinatory 'other-world', personal difficulties, including allergic reactions to electromagnetic pollution, are then dramatized through our culture's most accessible – not to say ubiquitous – personification of an other world: the Gray alien who worms his way in everywhere floating through the walls of your house, invading and stealing your mind, and robbing you of the future, which is represented by children.

The second candidate for a mundane cause of abduction experiences is the internally generated vision, as distinct from one induced by external, introduced or environmental agents such as electromagnetism, drugs, or regimens of physical and mental exercises. The usual term for these visions is, of course, 'hallucinations'. The word itself is part of the ancient armory of die-hard skeptics, and in that context the insinuation that some UFO witnesses and rather more claimed abductees are slightly crazy is rarely very far away. This is unfortunate, partly because the clinical use of the word 'hallucination' doesn't carry these connotations, and the literature on hallucinations is bursting with perfectly sane, if distressed, people, some of whom are suffering organic (biochemical) malfunctions, but not psychosis.

It is unfortunate too because I am myself convinced that the vast majority of those who have had *bona fide* abduction experiences, which have not been spawned by amateur hypnotists with leading questions to ask and private agendas to fulfill, are not mentally disturbed. The word 'hallucination' is used here in a neutral, clinical, dictionary sense: to mean no more

Ufologist Jenny Randles has noted connections between abductions and altered states of consciousness.

> ◆
>
> **hallucinatory tendencies that are not rooted in personality disorders do not show up in the standard psychological profiling tests**
>
> ◆

than an apparent perception of external objects or events that are not actually present. The key to an hallucinatory experience is that it wouldn't be an hallucination if it didn't seem real. And hallucinatory tendencies that are not rooted in personality disorders do not show up in the standard psychological profiling tests.

In her 1995 book *Star Children*, British ufologist Jenny Randles retails case after case of abductees – and others, including herself – who have played with balls of light as children. Abductee Linda Cortile (see Chapter Two) has recounted how she has had a nocturnal 'encounter' with a ball of light, and 'always' glimpses inexplicable things

out of the corner of my eyes. But only when I'm at home watching TV. I've always thought, somehow, that the TV screen might've been reflecting lights through the corner of my right eye because of the prescription glasses I wear to watch TV. So, on a whole, what you are saying, is that what I thought to be reflections, might in fact be things that no one else can see. I can only see these things through the corner of my eye. But as soon I turn my head quickly to the right, there isn't anything there.

As Professor Ronald K. Siegel points out in *Fire In The Brain* (1992), both these manifestations – seeing balls of light and 'things' on the periphery of vision – can be symptoms of a minor or incipient neurological disorder. They may also be hypnogogic (pre-sleep) or hypnopompic (post-sleep) visions. The simplest available explanation for these is that the brain functions that control sleep, associated muscular states and dream imagery kick in or continue to exert their control even while separate functions, appropriate for being awake, are in operation.

Hypnogogic and hypnopompic hallucinations can also arise during activities that themselves induce a trance-like state through demanding little body movement and fixed focus of the eyes – such as watching TV or, more commonly, driving at night, with little visible beyond the pool of light cast by headlamps. The latter is a classic circumstance for setting the scene for an abduction experience.

More terrifying are the hallucinations known as 'night terrors', which can involve the senses of smell, pressure and touch. Here again the body and brain are in a contradictory state, simultaneously in sleeping and waking modes; but the muscular paralysis, necessary to prevent us wrecking our beds and infuriating our partners while we dream, remains in place. Ronald Siegel describes his own hair-raising experience of this state. He felt pinned to his bed by a weight on his chest, while a 'murky presence', which gave off a 'dusty odor' approached his bed. Then it loomed over him and whispered in his ear, the words 'expelled from a mouth foul with tobacco' and sounding 'almost like English spoken backward'. Then the presence straddled his body, 'folding itself along the curve of my back.... There was a texture of sexual intoxication and terror in the room.' Siegel began to lose consciousness, then the voice stopped and he sensed the 'intruder' moving slowly from the room.

Siegel concluded that he had actually been the victim of two unnerving sleep-related phenomena: sleep paralysis and a hypnopompic hallucination. And he makes the crucial point here (as throughout his book) that the perceived form of any hallucination is built from 'images, thoughts, fantasies, memories, and dreams', and they are 'the only building blocks necessary for the construction of the final perception'.

All these 'mental creations' have at least two major components: social and cultural material that is accessible to – even if not shared by – everyone, and items of peculiar, idiosyncratic significance to the individual. By combining and emphasizing different aspects of both elements, a basic framework like the abduction scenario can be tailored to suit any individual set of preoccupations, while retaining a validity that is universal within a given culture. The case of Betty Andreasson (see Chapter One) offers one instance of such a bespoke rendition of the basic story; Sara Shaw's case offers another.

While Siegel modestly chose not to attempt to interpret his own experience in print, he clearly did not find himself slipping into the opening scenes of an abduction. So the question remains as to why some people who slip into these twilight zones of consciousness find themselves interacting with aliens, and others do not. This question becomes all the more puzzling when one considers the case of David Howard (see feature on page 126, and below), whose experiences with alien entities had no hallucinatory stimulus.

With these known psychological phenomena in mind, we might look at the experiences of New

> ◆
>
> **Hypnogogic and hypnopompic hallucinations can also arise during activities that themselves induce a trance-like state**
>
> ◆

PERCHANCE TO DREAM

David Howard

◆ ◆ ◆

Toward the end of 1983, David Howard, a 39-year-old manager for a chemical supplies company in Devon, England, was lying in bed next to his wife when he was flooded with a brilliant white light, so bright 'it went through me.' He felt himself being picked up and carried. Whatever was holding him put him into a sitting position and tipped him backward through his bedroom wall. There was a 'hissing, crackling' sound as he passed through.

He then found himself alone, floating through a 'square' tunnel that glowed brightly around him as he passed along it, and twisted and turned so much he could not see very far ahead of him. He next found himself lying, unable to move, and naked except for a cloth that partly covered him, on a table in a room that 'seemed misty'. Close up to his face he could see two large black blobs in a bluish background: he soon realized that the weird blobs were the eyes of a creature with bluish-gray skin, and he screamed in terror. Then he heard a gentle voice say inside his head: 'Don't be afraid. We're not here to hurt you.' It sounded 'so soothing you couldn't help but relax'.

As Howard's surroundings came into focus and his examination continued he saw that he was being attended by two entities about 1.2m (4ft) tall. They were wearing tight-fitting blue suits with pointed collars and black markings. He observed that they did not have buttocks like humans, but 'a solid bit that sticks out at the back' above the point where the legs joined the torso. Their eyes had lids top and bottom that, when closed, 'met in the middle'. Also present were four smaller beings (about 15cm [6in] shorter than the others) dressed entirely in black, who never spoke, even among themselves. Howard noticed they had three long fingers and a long thumb on each hand. A seventh entity, entirely unclothed, stood nearby; it was very thin and had bronze-colored skin. He learned later that these creatures could render themselves invisible, and were used by the taller entities as spies, observers or 'watchers'.

As the voice in Howard's head continued to soothe him, clamps of some kind were put on his legs. He did not see what was done to his legs, but it was painful. Meanwhile probes were put on his sides, then he was turned over and something was done at the back of his head. He demanded to know what was happening. In a tinny voice, speaking badly pronounced and rather limited English, the first entity explained that they were putting a 'tracer' on him – imprinting it on a single brain cell, so 'we will always know where you are'.

'You're treating me like an animal,' protested Howard.

'Well, you are an animal,' said the entity. When it spoke, Howard noticed that the movements of its lips did not match the English syllables he heard.

David Howard encountered this being many times thereafter until late in 1996, and they became friends. His name sounded something like Zaorddiklayclicclick, which Howard shortened to 'Jordeye'; his companion was called Gowrrodwen. They lived on the planet Dut, in the double-star system of Seetar–Mytar. Their eyes and faces never showed emotion; Howard says that he felt their emotions rather than saw them. Their eyes also acted as ears, and over a wider range of frequencies than ours, while the ear-

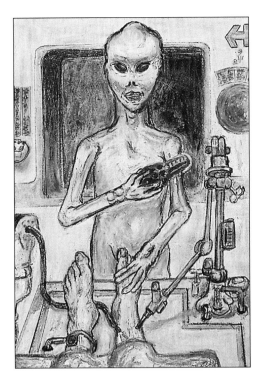

David Howard's first impression of 'Jordeye', the alien abductor with whom he later struck up a close and fascinating friendship.

like organs they did have were used mainly to maintain their balance. He always knew when they were coming, because of their extremely pungent smell. As he described it: 'Imagine the aroma of an abattoir mixed with warm beer, and you've got something like it.'

The Seetar–Mytar system has several inhabited planets, which are host to several races of beings besides the Dutions. During later experiences Howard visited Jordeye's home village and toured Dut with him. On these occasions he was obliged to wear a thin, rubbery blue suit with a hood and mask ('a bit like a gas mask') whose eyepieces had dark lenses. The suit fitted him 'like a skin', but he did not find this embarrassing. He assumed (but was never specifically told) that this garb helped him deal with the Dution atmosphere. He always arrived on Dut at night, when it was usually pouring with rain. A curious feature of life on Dut, he says, is the complete absence of children.

Howard also visited another planet in the system, Marjon (pronounced Mayrjjon). The planet is largely desert, and the people live near the coasts; the oceans there are a reddish pink. The inhabitants, he says, 'have their origins on Dut. They are a very gentle people, yet most of the male population are recruited into a service [that requires] fighting, even giving their lives in the protection of peace among other peoples.'

Other peoples in the system included Cys (from Cylo), the smaller silent ones who assisted at Howard's initial abduction; the Cygetts, who wear no clothes and can become invisible; Arians - very like the 'Nordics' described by other abductees, whom Howard saw only acting as engineers; and Marmens. Howard came upon only two of these, in rather unusual circumstances.

Some time after his encounters began he read an account of Antonio Villas Boas' experience (see Chapter One), and during a later abduction demanded facetiously why similar pleasures were denied to him. 'Because you can't make sex,' Jordeye replied. It turned out he had this impression because the aliens had detected that Howard had had a vasectomy some years before. This misunderstanding corrected, Howard was then 'bundled' into a room that contained soft white drapes and furnishings and two 'very female' creatures with 'somewhat catlike' faces whose 'very human' bodies were covered in extremely short, reddish-beige fur. 'What they did to me was unbelievable,' he says. Apart from demonstrating remarkable inventiveness in the sexual arts, they had an extraordinary physical attribute: 'The vagina extended out like a tube, and just grabbed me in there.'

David Howard suffers from narcolepsy, a sleep disorder that makes people fall straight into dreaming sleep several times a day. The episodes can last a few seconds, or for hours. All his alien encounters and abductions have occurred while he is asleep. 'You could very easily think these things occurred outside my head,' he says. 'But, really, they were inside my head.'

Yorker John Velez. As with Debbie Tomey, specific details of Velez's 1979 experience (see feature on pages 112-13) emerged only under hypnosis. He himself is ambivalent about that hypnotically retrieved information. He says he doesn't trust 'that questionable stuff' and that he keeps it 'in a B folder' or 'on a back burner', and says emphatically: 'My attitude toward my own experience has been to really cut it up. I can't accept this at face value. You got to really knock me over with some proof before you get me to buy this.' And he welcomes any investigative approach that may help to explain it.

At the same time, he is convinced that abductions are physically real; for him, no other explanation can account for all the inexplicable events that have befallen him and his family, especially the mysterious nosebleed and bruised eye that occurred in 1979. All these incidents may have prosaic solutions, but Velez feels that taken together they are related and at very least point to the likelihood of alien interventions.

One Saturday morning in about 1980, when Velez's son Jamie was four or five years old, John woke him in time for breakfast. 'Daddy, what were all the lights in here last night?' was the first thing the little boy said. 'The Sun was in the window and then it came inside the house.' John reassured him it was a dream, but Jamie insisted that he had been awake, and that when the light came into the house it made him fall asleep. Hypnogogic hallucination or prelude to an abduction?

One morning, roughly 10 years later, Jamie was deeply upset to discover a 7.5-9cm (3-3.5in) 'surgical' scar on each knee and insisted they had not been there the day before and couldn't explain them. Intermittent pains in his knees (the family pediatrician suspected arthritis) that he had had since childhood ceased after this. A coincidence,

John Velez's depiction of an alien that –
he recalled under hypnosis – abducted him in summer
1992 from a motel room in Pensacola, Florida.
To his surprise the entity greeted him in
old-fashioned, formal Spanish.

possibly, but so far the cause of the scars remains unexplained.

In 1992 John's wife awoke one morning to find a bizarre indentation in the flesh of one thigh, as if someone had tightened a tourniquet about the width of a belt around it, and left it for hours. Within this mark was an oval impression as if a spoon had been pressed against the flesh. Velez has good reason to know that the mark was not there the previous night, and the family doctor said he had seen nothing like it in his life. The indentation took some 18 months to fade away. The only explanation that has been offered the couple came from Budd Hopkins who, says John, has photographs of very similar marks on two other women. Hopkins says they were bound during abductions, while struggling to keep the aliens from examining their genitals. (Mrs Velez says only that if she has been abducted, she doesn't have time to think about it; it would be too disturbing.)

What alerted me to the possibility that an hallucinogenic process of some kind lay behind John Velez's experience was a number of scenes that he related from his childhood. At night, balls of light would float in his bedroom; later on, even into adulthood, shafts of light would come through the window, from a very bright exterior source, although in one house the window faced onto a narrow

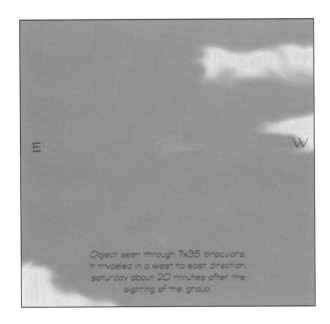

UFO photographed by John Velez as it flew from west to east over his home in Queens, New York, in the summer of 1997. Besides his close encounters, Velez has spotted numerous 'daylight disks' while skywatching.

passageway between buildings. These are, classic hypnogogic and hypnopompic hallucinations.

Velez also saw, or at least sensed, entities present on some occasions. When he was eight years old, he 'woke up one night floating through my living room being carried by little people.... And the shock of finding myself there, in the dark, and up in the air – I was afraid to breathe, much less move. And then I felt the little hands holding me up, like cannibals carrying away the missionary, you know? Panic, pure terror, like I've never felt at any other time in my life, came from the pit of my stomach like a wave. And then, everything just goes black. But I know, I *know*, I was really awake.'

On another occasion in his childhood, a human and several 'dwarfs' came through the wall of his room, talking, and then retreated back through it. As an adult in 1981, he bolted upright in bed one night and saw the room full of aliens. One was rummaging through a chest of drawers; on the other side of the bed, three aliens were staring intently into his wife's face. Three more carried John through his apartment and outside – where it was freezing cold. When he began screaming and biting, one tapped him with a kind of wand, and everything went blank.

These could possibly be instances of 'false awakening', an impression of waking up within a dream, which can seem absolutely genuine. More likely, they are hypnogogic hallucinations: Velez was awake, but dream material was intruding onto his waking state. And here, one has to remember that the hallmark of an hallucination is that it does seem absolutely real. Velez's conviction that this

◆

Hopkins says they were bound during abductions, while struggling to keep the aliens from examining their genitals

◆

experience was an objective event cannot be taken at face value, especially in light of the probable source of his other experiences.

None of which explains his nosebleed and bruised eye following his 1979 UFO sighting, or indeed the sighting itself. But psychological processes may explain a little-known aspect of some abductions investigated by Budd Hopkins, including those of John Velez. More than 30 of Hopkins's subjects, including John, have drawn what they remember of examples of alien script. These are, according to those who have seen them, virtually identical, down to individual characters and what may be construed as 'words'. Hopkins keeps these to himself, because he does not want to contaminate potential subjects any further than popular culture does already, and he believes the scripts give him a means to authenticate the accounts he hears. John Velez broke down in tears when he saw how his example exactly matched the others in Hopkins' collection, because they seemed to confirm the actuality of his experience.

I have seen some of this script, which is very simple in form, being built up of lines, arcs, and dots. I speculate that it may be derived from 'entoptic' visions – geometric forms that appear before the eyes in altered states of consciousness (of which hypnotic trance is one) but are exaggerated forms of 'floaters' – cell débris – and light effects within the eye. Just as hallucinations are built up from simple mental materials, entoptic patterns could form the mental building blocks from which the appearance of 'writing' is constructed – with the stimulus, the idea of writing itself, and the stringing together of the entoptic shapes, coming from the context of the scene being discussed under hypnosis.

Whatever the ultimate source of John Velez's experiences, it is often said that the consistency of

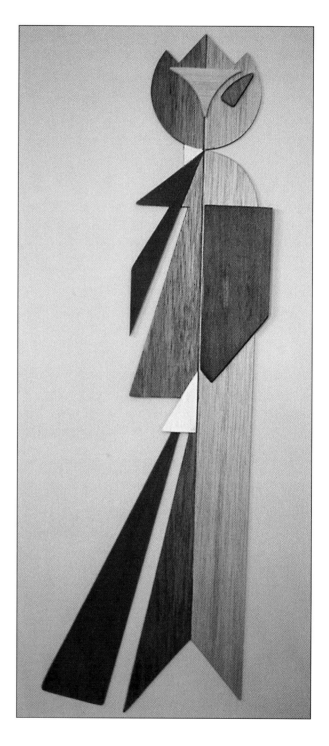

Made of contrasting woods, with some painted surfaces, this abstract representation of an alien encounter hangs in John Velez's home. Most of the abductees interviewed for this book showed striking artistic talent.

accounts from one abductee to another supports the proposition that abductions are objectively real events. The content of David Howard's astonishing narcoleptic dreams undermines this argument and saves the reader from a tedious exposition of its weakness in logic.

David Howard has had two major periods of narcolepsy in his life, one from his late teens until his mid twenties, and the other beginning when he was about 38, in late 1982. Prior to that, in February 1982, he and a workmate had a very close sighting of a gigantic UFO near Plymouth, Devon, UK. Apart from social gossip and seeing *Close Encounters of the Third Kind* and *Star Wars* when they were released (in 1977), he had no specific acquaintance with UFOs or abductions. Howard's narcoleptic dreams are extremely vivid, like lucid dreams – which seem entirely real to the dreamer, all of whose senses become fully engaged in an apparently solid, three-dimensional environment. Unlike standard dreams, which tend to fade rapidly in the memory, David Howard's are as memorable as everyday life.

Howard does not have the lucid dreamer's full capacity to manipulate his dream world, but he has traveled about his neighborhood and even into outer space in an out-of-the-body state within his dreams. He has also suffered from hypnopompic visions: 'If I woke up suddenly, figures from my dreams would come out with me, and carry on what they were doing in my bedroom. It was very confusing. I'd just have to wait for one or the other to go away before I knew where I really was.'

Such control as he had over his entirely realistic dream realm ended in late 1983 when, immediately on going into a narcoleptic trance, he found himself undergoing a classic abduction in his sleep. During this his legs were clamped; and

when he woke up they had bruises on them. Over a dozen years' dreaming David came to know his captors, their star system and their planets well. He was also 'abducted' and examined many times, despite this convivial relationship. Besides constant contact with the alien he called 'Jordeye', he became friends with another entity named Karactcaq, one of the planet Marjon's warrior class; in the course of 18 months in his company David witnessed military exercises, rescue missions, and battles, including Karactcaq's final, fatal combat.

In his dreams at this period, David would go to sleep on Earth, and instantly 'wake up' on Marjon. After going through the dream-events of a Marjon day, he would bed down there, go to sleep, and at once wake up in bed at home. So realistic were his dreams that he became confused about which of the two 'worlds' he inhabited was the real one. Physically, as his family will attest, he remained firmly on Earth.

Dreams and visions may be fulfillments of wishes; they can also be understood as the unconscious mind's means of sorting through (and sorting out) existential problems. That David Howard has had experiences that are identical to those of abductees 'taken' while they were – more or less – awake is an unambiguous indication that all honestly reported abductions have a psychological basis.

But why are so many details in these experiences identical? How did John Velez see Grays as a child in 1956, when they were barely known even to ufologists? Why do abductions always follow the same order of events?

> ◆
>
> **Besides constant contact with the alien he called 'Jordeye', he became friends with another entity named Karactcaq, one of the planet Marjon's warrior class**
>
> ◆

CHAPTER 5

THROUGH THE LOOKING GLASS

The Roots of a Modern Myth

◆ ◆ ◆

Opposite: Clarke Hathaway's rendition of the Mantis Woman who abducted him in October 1994. Her appearance was preceded by a UFO landing and then lights floating like balls of cotton in the air.

The celebrated anthropologist Joseph Campbell once remarked: 'The latest incarnation of Oedipus, the continued romance of Beauty and the Beast, stands this afternoon on the corner of Forty-Second Street and Fifth Avenue, waiting for the traffic light to change.'

Campbell's point was twofold. Ancient myths live on in modern guise – that is an easy enough insight to accept. But Campbell was also saying – more poignantly – that myths are really neither ancient nor modern, but timeless: they are intrinsic to the way we cope with the human condition. They set out our collective wisdom, and our dilemmas, in dramatic, narrative form. Living in an ostensibly post-religious, rational, technologico-scientific era, we tend to forget these truths. We don't just look *back* at the pre-scientific past: often unwittingly, we look *down* on it, too. And so we fail to recognize the value of the mythical way of dealing with the world, and fail to identify our own myths for what

they are. To recognize myths today we may have to look rather hard, and be prepared to find them in unexpected places. Such as right under our noses, on an everyday intersection in Manhattan.

UFO encounters and alien abductions in particular can be interpreted as a modern mythology, albeit an incomplete one. Two things follow from that.

First, the structure of the myth will dictate the nature of the abduction experience, and that alone would account for the many similarities found in abduction reports. It will also account for the way abduction researchers draw order out of confusion, and publish tidy chronicles that are actually based on chaotic raw material. To anyone who has compared the transcripts of the hypnotic sessions to the received story, the Myrna Hansen case (see Chapter One) is an excellent example of this transformation at work.

Similarly one finds that researcher Budd Hopkins, presumably in the interests of a neat

PREY OF THE MANTIS

CLARKE HATHAWAY

◆ ◆ ◆

Clarke Hathaway,
artist and abductee.

In August 1990, Clarke Hathaway and a group of friends spent a weekend at an isolated cabin in a meadow near Pulga, California, USA. Around midnight on the first night there, Clarke left the cabin to sleep in his camper van. Before long, he dozed off. Then:

'I was awakened by a loud high-pitched drone that quickly faded. Raising up onto one elbow, I looked out windows in the back of the van. Directly to the east I noticed a very bright blue-white light, somewhat smaller than a dime held at arm's length, off in the distance.'

Clarke was startled to notice that the light was coming closer, and expanding. He wondered fleetingly, 'What is a helicopter doing up here?' As he watched and listened for the chop of the rotors, the light reached 'the size of a silver dollar', then seemed to pause, changed into a rounded oval, then once again began to grow rapidly.

'"Oh no!" I thought. "It's coming down into the clearing." I still heard no rotor chop, and must have closed my eyes. That's all I consciously remember.'

Under hypnosis with Dr Richard Boylan, Clarke recalled what happened next:

In just a moment, my inner eyelids were illuminated, and I struggled to open my eyes. The inside of the van was lit up brighter than daylight. Immediately before my face were fluorescent cotton balls of neon red, green, yellow and blue popping on and off. Beyond these down the meadow was an arc-like light that I couldn't look directly into. It dissipated off to the left. Within this misty light, three shadowy figures began to materialize. One stood at least a head above the others. This figure detached itself from the others and, to my horror, began to approach very rapidly.

It had a large domed head. The lower portion of the face tapered sharply in, and flowed into a long thin neck and narrow, sharply sloping shoulders. Askew, and seeming not to be moving, long, very thin arms with bulging pod-like endings were angled down and away from the shoulders. Suddenly, its face appeared at the window, tilted to the side and looking upward at me. I saw it grasp the window sill in the door. Curling over the edge were three mauve fingers, the middle one half again as long as the others. I had a sense of cautious, mischievous humor emanating from the thing.

The being abruptly twisted to its left while raising up and moving forward in one fluid motion. I realized that it had done all of this through the glass, the bed, as well as the steel body of the van itself – as if they were of water. It gently but firmly gripped my upper arms. Huge, glossy black eyes, which filled close to a third of its face, stared into mine. I desperately tried to wrench my way free but was totally unable to move. Overcome with terror, I sensed that it was going to take me out the way it had come in. As it moved backward, pulling me forward, I thought I was going to be slammed into the back of the van. We emerged outside before the thought had ended. My eyes rolled down to see the ground rushing backward beneath my dangling feet. Looking up again, I could see that we were entering the outer haze of light and the other two figures were becoming more distinct.

I closed my eyes against the now too-bright light. When I opened them, we were in a hallway that curved to the left. Gripping my upper left arm, the being led me a short way down the hall to an open doorway to the right. Ushered into the room, I was urged toward what looked like a table, which was waist high. The recessed top looked to be fashioned from a light blue metal, and had a mirror finish. As we approached this table, I got the distinct feeling it was alive!

Swiveling, the Mantis – as I think of it – gripped both upper arms and, seemingly without effort, lifted me onto the table. Rather than being cold and hard as it appeared, the top gave way, providing support to the contours of my body. A soothing warmth surrounded me, tension flowed out of my body, and my consciousness began to drift.

Clarke was suddenly jerked back to awareness as he felt other presences entering the room. One seemed to pass something over but above his body. Then he drifted off again.

Clarke came round to find himself alone with the Mantis, which he now felt was female. The Mantis led him into the hallway and on into another, larger room. Then:

My attention was riveted on the face of an obviously human female who stood, naked, on a low, sculptured platform against the wall directly across from me. Rigid, with heels together, arms loosely hanging by her sides, she stared straight ahead. Her eyes didn't seem to be seeing anything at all. They did not move, nor did her eyelids blink.

She had wavy light-brown hair with a slight reddish tone, cascading down to frame her face and disappear behind her shoulders. I had the feeling I knew this woman although, with a start, I realized that I could not see her face. It was a blur. Only her eyes were clear to me. My concentration was interrupted by a mental image of caressing her to the point of arousal.

'No!' I thought. 'But, you must,' came the meaning from the Mantis. 'No,' I thought again. 'Why must I?' The next impression took me aback. 'You made the commitment,' it declared. I thought: 'I don't remember any commitment.'

At this, the Mantis took Clarke back to the original room, and left him there. Moving to the opening, Clarke found he could not step through it. Then the Mantis returned with the woman. 'You must! came the meaning, with a feeling of impatience. No!...I don't do that, I thought. The woman moved forward. My back came up against the table and I could once again feel its pulse. Why? came the impression from the Mantis. You committed.'

The Mantis moved forward quickly and gripped Clarke's right upper arm as the woman came forward and lightly put her finger tips on his chest. Her mouth became clear in a big smile. Clarke tried to twist away but could not move. 'Her fingers traced a trail down my skin, across my stomach – '

At this point in the hypnosis session, Clarke snapped out of trance. For medical reasons, he has not explored his experience further under hypnosis.

narrative and a coherent argument, decided not to include in his book *Intruders* details of Debbie Tomey's tendencies to hallucination and her family's history of poltergeist attacks (see Chapter Two). But this is how myths are made. The bits that don't fit are simply ignored. It's unlikely that the experience reported by Clarke Hathaway (see feature on page 134) would ever have made it into the Hopkins canon.

Second, if myths are at bottom timeless, eternal reflections of the human predicament, we should be able to find, in the myths and legends of earlier cultures and surviving traditional, pre-industrial societies, the equivalents of the UFO-alien-abduction stories of modern times. We shouldn't expect those older stories to describe sophisticated medical examinations and technologically advanced aerial transports, because myths dress themselves in the costume of their time.

For example, in the ancient Greek myth, Oedipus was traveling on foot when he met his father at a crossroads and, not recognizing him, killed him. In a modern version he might be called Eddie Pass, drive a Lincoln, and shoot his father in a fit of road rage; or even meet and murder him while changing planes at London's Heathrow Airport. But it would still be the same myth, bearing the same meaning. So where in modern abduction accounts we find the medical/gynecological examination, in older myths we might expect to find physical examinations or interrogations, perhaps even tortures. We should also expect to find a somewhat prurient interest in sexual matters.

At the same time we should not expect too

> anomalous experiences may also force us 'to grapple with the Shadow – the dark challenging corridors we have to pass through at the frontiers of the soul'

close an accord between the ancient and the modern, and should beware of interpreting whatever we find too simplistically or directly. In *Frontiers of the Soul* (1992), Michael Grosso notes how visionary beings and occasions may carry symbolic meaning:

A black dog with red eyes or a winged headless man that assaults us on a lonely road is frightening. Yet in a way such visions are merely histrionic gestures that allude to the far greater horrors of actual existence: death squads, serial killers, organized armies and their technologies of murder. Likewise, the vision of [the Virgin] Mary is glorious to contemplate, but its deeper significance is the potential for divine compassion that lies within us. The angel that rescues us is also the angel within, our own potential to transcend the possible, our own existential option to be angels to one another....

Alien encounters evoke images of higher worlds, higher intelligences. An image of a higher intelligence at large disposed to help us in our daily lives might provide the stimulus we need to dare things we might otherwise feel too intimidated to accept. The gods in the Homeric epics seem to work that way....

But, as Dr Grosso says, anomalous experiences may also force us 'to grapple with the Shadow – the dark challenging corridors we have to pass through at the frontiers of the soul. Clearly, not all alien realities are unqualified in their benignity.' Even so, confronting the Shadow, which is 'the side of ourselves we dare not look at', may be revealing,

Dominique Ingres' painting of Oedipus answering the riddle of the Sphinx. Many universal themes are reflected in the ancient Greek myth of Oedipus, from the nature of child-parent relationships to the inescapability of fate. Alien abductions may not be physically real events, but they clearly hold a fascination and an appeal for many people in the Western world. Is that because they too are mythic events - dramatizing deeply rooted human problems?

even healing: 'Terrifying, disorienting experiences may hurt and damage us, but when we are attacked by alien forces, our inner resources are more likely to be awakened [and] meeting them can be a way to enlarge our self-understanding.'

The warning implicit in Dr Grosso's examples is that we shouldn't look for limited and limiting one-to-one symbolic meanings in mythical figures or scenes. Myths are often ambiguous, bearing more than one interpretation, and sometimes conflicting ones. In the Oedipus myth, for example, as an infant Oedipus is cast out to die on a mountainside because it has been prophesied that he will one day kill his father, the King of Thebes. Rescued by a shepherd, he grows to manhood, kills his father - not knowing who he is, ironically - over a trivial disagreement, solves the riddle posed by the monstrous Sphinx that is besieging Thebes, and as a reward is given the hand of Jocasta, the widowed queen of the city. She, of course, is his mother. On discovering the truth, Oedipus blinds himself.

Sigmund Freud, the founder of psychoanalysis, believed that this drama reflected the unconscious wish of small boys to usurp their fathers in their mothers' affections, and there is probably some truth in that. But it is not the only meaning of the story, which from a broader perspective can be interpreted as also being 'about' the futility of Oedipus's father (or anyone) attempting to avoid his destiny, and the horrible consequences that ensue when one does. These two interpretations hardly exhaust the significances of the Oedipus myth.

> ◆
>
> **The Greek myths are full of strange otherworldly beings from the sky – the gods – who descend on hapless mortals, rape or seduce them**
>
> ◆

We can expect to find that the UFO abduction myth, if it is a myth, is equally specific and general, and thus ambiguous – even contradictory – in its meanings. As hinted by Dr Grosso, an alien encounter can both offer a positive stimulus to expand our capabilities, and be a reflection of destructive aspects of ourselves that we do not care to contemplate openly. This apparent contradiction can be resolved: by accepting our hidden 'dark' side, we may be able to free ourselves of its surreptitious, limiting influence.

By analogy, to see abductions as mythic experiences is to enable ourselves to step out of the quagmire of the unending ufological debates over the reality or otherwise of any particular abduction claim. Whether physically real or not, abduction experiences still tell us truths about ourselves, and 'speak to our condition'.

First, then, let's see how ancient myths and folklore contain images, scenes and even characters that we find consistently repeated in abduction scenario narratives.

The Greek myths are full of strange otherworldly beings from the sky - the gods - who descend on hapless mortals, rape or seduce them, and so procreate hybrid children. Zeus almost made a habit of this, and even supplied screen memories to cover his lubricious exploits. To Leda, he appeared as a swan, and the child of that union was Helen, over whom the Trojan war was fought. To Danae, he appeared as a shower of gold, and fathered Perseus, who slew the Gorgon Medusa and with her severed head turned the king and courtiers of Seriphos to stone. Still more venerable stories of sky beings breeding with humans are found in Sumerian texts - the world's oldest-known written records, dating back over 5000 years, while the myths themselves are probably thousands of years older. Scholars have good reason

Formula hæc Leda est, cignus fit Iuppiter illam   Ex illo gemini pollux, cum castore fratres

to believe that Sumerian themes found their way into ancient Greek culture.

In *Alien Identities* (1993), Dr Richard L. Thompson draws attention to many parallels between abduction stories and the interaction between human beings and the gods of the Sanskrit Vedic sagas of northern India. In one incident in the epic called the *Mahabharata*, King Duryodhana – who has just embarked on a slow suicide, deliberately fasting to death – is transported to the nether world (which in Hindu

The ancient Greek god Zeus appears to Leda in the shape of a swan in order to rape her. Abduction accounts contain the same motif of all-powerful, sky-dwelling predators.

mythology is in the heavens, but is reached by entering the Earth) by Krtya, a 'wondrous woman with a gaping mouth', who is in fact a demonic being. She takes him to the Danavas, 'gruesome denizens of the netherworld who had been defeated by the gods', who explain that he should not kill himself because it would spoil their own plans. His birth on Earth was part of their cosmic strategy, and he owes his strength and invincibility in battle to their 'manipulations'. They promise Duryodhana their support, which includes

STOLEN BY LITTLE PEOPLE

ANNE JEFFERIES
and
THE LADY OF BALMACHIE

◆ ◆ ◆

Contemporary illustration of Anne Jefferies in the company of the fairies who abducted her from her home in St Teath, Cornwall, England in 1645. Her story, which was backed by contemporary documents, including a report to the Bishop of Gloucester, bears a remarkable similarity to alien abduction accounts.

In 1645, in the midst of the English Civil War, teenager Anne Jefferies was abducted from her home in St Teath, Cornwall, England – not by aliens, but by fairies. Her story is backed by contemporary documents. One is a report to the Bishop of Gloucester from the son of the family for whom she worked. Her story, and the much older Scottish legend of the Lady of Balmachie that follows it here, show unmistakable parallels with alien abduction accounts.

Anne was a servant in the Pitt family household in St Teath. Although illiterate, she was a clever, inquisitive and resourceful girl. One day she fell into a fit while knitting in an arbor just outside the garden gate. She was ill for some time afterward, and when she was fully recovered she said she had not had a fit, but had been carried off by the fairies.

The first she knew of their presence was a rustling in the leaves near the arbor where she sitting. She thought her sweetheart was teasing her, and took no notice. The branches rustled again, and she heard a suppressed laugh. Irritated, she called out: 'You may stay there till the cuney grows on the gate ere I'll come to thee.' This was answered by a tinkling sound and a musical laugh, which alarmed her because it was definitely not her sweetheart's voice. But she stayed where she was, and before long heard the garden gate open and close softly. Then six little men appeared in front of her. They were dressed in green; their leader had a red feather in his cap. All had very bright eyes.

Anne was fascinated by fairy lore and had often said she wanted to meet the local 'piskies'. The leader spoke to her 'lovingly', and she put her hand down to him. He jumped into her palm. She lifted him onto her lap. He then climbed up her bosom and began to smother her neck in kisses. According to folklorist Katherine Briggs's account, Anne was 'perfectly charmed' with the little man's attentions and 'sat there in ecstasy until he called his five companions and they swarmed up her skirts and dress and began to kiss her chin and cheeks and lips'. Then, one put his hand over her eyes.

She felt a 'sharp pricking', and everything went black before her eyes. She was then lifted into the air and 'carried she knew not where'. When she was set down on solid ground again, a voice said 'Tear! Tear!' She found she could see again: she was now in 'a gorgeous fairyland'. There were temples and palaces of gold and silver, and hundreds of beautifully dressed people strolling in gardens, dancing, or sitting at their ease. Anne too was now finely dressed. Most remarkably, the piskies were now of normal human height. Anne was courted by all six of her abductors, but especially by their leader. He and she managed to steal away from the group and, it seems, were actually making love when the five others, with an angry crowd in tow, burst in on them. Anne's lover 'drew his sword to protect her, but he was wounded and fell at her feet'. The fairy who had originally 'blinded' her then put his hands over her eyes again, and she was 'whirled up into the air with a great humming'. She came round to find herself 'lying on the floor of the arbor surrounded by anxious friends'.

Although Anne Jefferies never returned to fairyland, the piskies apparently kept her supplied with food, for she gave up eating at the Pitt family table. She developed powers of healing and prophecy, and was jailed in 1646 by a Puritan judge for foretelling the victory of the King in the Civil War. During her years in prison, too, she was never seen to eat. After the end of the war she was released, and later married a laborer.

In the 1690s Moses Pitt sent a friend to interview Anne Jefferies for the report he was preparing for the Bishop of Gloucester. Like many a modern abductee, she refused to co-operate. Asked why, 'she replied, that if she should discover it to you, that you would make books or ballads of it; and she said she would not have her name spread about the country in books or ballads of such things, if she might have five hundred pounds of it.' Fear of ridicule, and perhaps of another spell in prison, kept her silent.

Katherine Briggs notes of 'Anne's delusion' that 'not fifty years after the first performance of *A Midsummer Night's Dream*, we have an illiterate country girl building up a courtly Fairyland of diminutive fairies with all the minuteness and amorousness of [those] in Shakespeare, Drayton and Herrick. It is clear that the poets built on a real country tradition.'

In *Folklore and Legends, Scotland* (1889) folklorist W.W. Gibbings tells how the Lady of Balmachie fell ill, just before her husband the Laird set out on his horse for Dundee. Returning in the twilight, he came upon a troop of fairies carrying a litter, on which was a human. The Laird drew his sword and demanded in the name of God that they release their captive, at which the fairies vanished. He then discovered that the prisoner was none other than his own wife, dressed in her bedclothes. He quickly carried her home, saw to her needs, and marched into his chamber, where a fairy changeling, looking just like his real wife, lay apparently ill in bed. Pretending to make her more comfortable, the Laird ordered the fire to be built up, and then threw the impostor into the roaring flames. From which, says Gibbings, 'she bounced like a sky-rocket, and went through the ceiling, and out at the roof of the house, leaving a hole in the slates.'

While this neat resolution has its comic side, the really interesting aspect of this ancient folk story is the Lady of Balmachie's description of her abduction, which follows a pattern that will sound distinctly familiar to modern ears:

> *some time after sunset, the nurse having left her for the purpose of preparing a little caudle [a sweet, spiced gruel], a multitude of elves came in at the window, thronging like bees from a hive. They filled the room, and having lifted her from the bed, carried her through the window, after which she recollected nothing further, till she saw her husband standing over her....*

using mind control to help vanquish his enemies, in a coming battle, and Krtya returns him to where she found him. After she has gone, Duryodhana thinks the whole episode has been a dream.

Dr Thompson comments that this story has a number of features 'also seen in UFO abduction accounts' and lists eight:

> *1. A strange being takes Duryodhana bodily to another location, where he has a meeting with other strange beings.*
> *2. Mystical or higher-dimensional transport is used.*
> *3. The strange beings have human form, but look 'gruesome'. Certainly they are aliens.*
> *4. These beings have been guiding Duryodhana's life from the very beginning.*
> *5. They designed his body so that he would be nearly impervious to weapons. Thus they apparently engaged in genetic manipulations, or something similar.*
> *6. The aliens were planning to manipulate human beings through mind control.*
> *7. After his interview, Duryodhana was returned to the spot where he was taken, and after setting him down, his captor disappeared.*
> *8. After the experience, it seemed to be a dream.*

This is not the complete abduction scenario (there is no examination phase, for example), but it certainly echoes many of the scenes and themes reported by abductees and noted by investigtors.

One of the more remarkable aspects of the gods described in the *Mahabharata*, is their aerial mode of transport, the *vimanas*, which in many respects resemble witnesses' descriptions of UFOs. They are, for example, capable of interdimensional travel, defy gravity, and frequently appear more spacious on the outside than their external dimensions suggest. They also come in all shapes and sizes.

Encounters with otherworldly beings, but especially gods, frequently begin with extraordinary light phenomena. For examples from the Hebrew Bible and New Testament alone: Moses was confronted by a burning bush; Ezekiel saw an astonishing atmospheric display that he took to be a vision of God; the shepherds at Bethlehem saw that 'glory shone around' when an angel appeared to them; Saul of Tarsus was transfixed on the road to Damascus by a beam of light (an experience also reported by Joseph Smith, founder of the Mormon religion). In each case, messages of divine (otherworldly) origin and cosmic import were delivered to amazed and humbled human beings.

In Western folklore, there are also more malev-

An angel appears to shepherds to announce the birth of Christ. Reports of visionary experiences, like abduction accounts, typically begin with strange light phenomena. Each culture interprets such events in its own way.

olent entities whose activities echo those of today's aliens. Fairies are generally smaller than human beings, are frequently referred to in old songs and stories as 'gray', are capable of flight, live in an Otherworld that is reached through entrances to round or saucer-shaped mounds in the earth, and steal human children (sometimes replacing them with sickly ones of their own), and abduct handsome or beautiful adults. Folklorist Dr Katherine Briggs observes of this:

> *Women, however, are in much more danger of capture by the fairies than men. Nursing mothers are in great demand to suckle fairy babies (for the quality of fairy milk seems to be poor), and the time between childbirth and churching is one of great danger. There are many stories of precautions successfully taken, or of the attempted rescue of wives from the power of the fairies.*

Fairies steal a human baby, in an illustration from Wirt Sikes's 1880 survey of British goblins. The theme reappears in some female abductees' claims that they have been used as breeding machines by aliens.

As has been said of the Grays, the fairies are reputed to be a dying race, which the bloodline of abducted humans helps to regenerate. Dr Briggs remarks that 'perhaps the chief motive' for the fairies' capture of mortals was 'to inject the dwindling stock with fresh blood and human vigour'.

Once in the fairies' clutches, it is extremely difficult to escape. The way out is usually found at liminal zones such as fords, bridges or crossroads, and the worst and best of times are the equinoxes, Hallowe'en, May Eve and New Year's Eve, when the risk of abduction is at its height, but escape from the Otherworld is easiest. Aliens habitually abduct people from the liminal zones of the modern world – on the highway between one physical location and another (that is, 'nowhere'), from trailer parks

on the edges of towns, and especially in the limbo between wakefulness and sleep. The fairies also favor this last 'twilight zone' for taking captives, as well as liminal mental states such as epileptic fits (see feature on page 140) and spiritual lacunae, as observed above, between childbirth and the ritual purification of mothers at 'churching'.

In connection with abductions, anthropologist Steve Mizrach has observed how another fringe group – this time human – has been credited with the ability to pass between two worlds – and by flying: witches. Many of those accused of being witches during the Great Witch Hunt of the 15th to 17th centuries in Europe and America were midwives. Apart from having a profession inseparable from birth and (in those days) death, it seems

> **The proof-mark
> of congress
> with the Devil
> was the
> so-called
> 'witches' teat',
> usually found
> between the anus
> and the vulva**

quite likely that they had a darker function as abortionists. Apart from their clear medico-gynecological associations, they straddled two worlds in the most fundamental way. As witches, they did the same: traveling through the air to fornicate with Satan, lesser demons, and incubi. It was not unknown for these women's children – the alleged offspring of these hideous unions – to be thrown onto the burning pyre when their mothers were put to death.

The proof-mark of congress with the Devil was the so-called 'witches' teat', usually found between the anus and the vulva (although any mole,

*A witch in the shape of her animal familar surprises
Satan in a sexually suggestive manner. Witches'
confessions were so consistent that any one seemed to
confirm the others – as with abduction accounts today.*

anywhere, would pass muster for most accusers). The devil's mark was discovered by stripping the accused women naked and examining them all over in the presence of many witnesses, while inquisitors fired what must have seemed irrelevant and surreal questions at them. Scholar James Pontolillo notes that 'particular attention was paid to the private parts of female suspects: the tearing of breasts with hot pincers and the insertion of heated iron spikes into body cavities were favored methods of securing desired confessions.' Pontolillo considers that the Great Witch Hunt (and, to a lesser extent, the fairy tradition) and today's abduction scenario express a terror and hatred of women that is longstanding in Western culture:

> *The ancient misogynist view of women as hypersexual beings with generally corrupt tendencies that was rampant in the Church at this time led to a unique and one-sided interpretation of fornication with demons. Succubi preyed on innocent men, while incubi tended to the insatiable carnal appetites of willing women; the feminine aspect was both the aggressor and the guilty party in every instance of demonic intercourse. These ideas found ultimate expression in the medieval iconography depicting Woman and her dreaded genitalia as the essence of pure Evil. Images of the Devil as a gruesome, muscular female with flames spouting from 'his' vagina or possessing a toothed vagina with which to indiscriminately devour men were common.*

The modern UFO myth has translated the witchfinders' 'medical' and moral inquisitions, and the attitudes that inspired them, back into the Otherworld, and made the crazy single-mindedness of the obsessed torturers part of the alien character. This is not surprising, for that is where it belongs in yet another, and vastly more ancient, otherworldly narrative tradition, that of the shamanic trance journey. Shamanism is the world's oldest visionary religion.

It has been pointed out many times how the experience of shamans in trance directly parallels the abduction scenario as it was understood before the notions of an alien 'breeding program' and hybrid children were introduced. French philosopher and teacher Bertrand Méheust was among the first to note these parallels in his 1987 essay 'Abductions and Religious Folklore'. He also cited legends and folktales from African, New World, Australian and Siberian sources that tell essentially the same story. A person, usually alone in a remote or dangerous location, is abducted by monsters, gods or demons and removed to an otherworldly, often underground, cavern; they may be tortured or even dismembered, or their internal organs are removed and replaced with fresh ones; substances (sometimes crystals) are inserted in their heads or arms; secret wisdom is imparted; and on their return they recall little or nothing of the experience. Méheust comments:

> *a timeless structure [lies] behind the variations...described in contemporary abductions....But...most of these motifs have been 'resemantised' [i.e. given a new meaning and a fresh context]. The ball of light which sometimes descends on the chosen one, becomes a glowing spaceship. The amnesia is attributed to a deliberate action on the part of the abductors, anxious to efface all traces of their mysterious activity. The crystals implanted beneath the skin [which traditionally confer healing powers or invulnerability to evil spirits] have been replaced by electronic gadgets intended for mental monitoring. Ritual surgery becomes a medical examination; the initiatory cavern, a laboratory or operating theatre; even the tortures which formerly prepared the transfiguration of the subject are now inflicted by sadistic or superhuman experimenters. The stigmata or other physical marks are interpreted as the result of surgery or radiation. The celestial journey of the shamans becomes the interplanetary excursion on board a spaceship.*

Tibetan shaman Nyima Dhondup pictured in 1989 in a state of trance. The shaman's spiritual journey and the standard abduction scenario are strikingly similar.

> ◆
>
> **they may be tortured or even dismembered, or their internal organs are removed and replaced with fresh ones**
>
> ◆

We might note additional equivalences. In fairy abductions and shamanic journeys what Dr Jacques Vallée calls 'relativized time' – when minutes or hours spent in the Otherworld turn out to be days or even years in Earthly time – is echoed in 'missing time' episodes in abduction stories. In a similar inversion, whereas fairies once abducted nursing mothers to foster fairy children, or stole human children, leaving a 'changeling' behind, in today's alien encounters we find surrogate motherhood foisted on female abductees, who become pregnant temporarily and later 'bond' with hybrid children. The fairies' and the gods' underground cavern has now become a labyrinthine 'underground alien base' as described, for instance, by Myrna Hansen. In the UFO mythology these subterranean haunts are allegedly found either on other planets or in what are felt to be half-magical, half-alien 'other worlds' on Earth – personified in the USA by American Indian reservations and in the UK by forbidden regions such as military training areas. The motif of 'twilight zones', ill-defined locations, times of day or year, and social, psychological or spiritual conditions recurs throughout ufology.

Each culture has its own variations on these themes; ours has lately crystallized into UFO abduction narratives. This public, mythologized version of the shaman's private spiritual journey is a technological variant of what Méheust calls 'a permanence of certain elements in the universal language of the imagination', and he concludes that its stage-properties are technological rather than overtly religious because we are 'the first civilization to construct a social life without any reference to the sacred'. Or, as one abductee put it to me: 'Science has destroyed religion, and put nothing back in its place.'

Abductee Chris McLachlan has pointed out an even broader cross-cultural sweep that embraces many of the motifs described above and the abduction scenario as well: the hero myth. McLachlan is fascinated by the 'alien underground base' theme and notes that in hero myths

the underground journey is a metaphor for the self turning its attention inwards, and the realization of its own, terrifying depths. The journey of the hero is a pilgrimage to self-mastery and spiritual wholeness.... Part of the heroic quest is to risk the death of the self as it is understood in order to gain a deeper and richer understanding of that self. Along the way, one must gain mastery of one's inner demons.... Heracles had to subdue the hound of Hades and bring it back to the surface, i.e. confront and subdue his savage self and integrate it with his consciousness.... The images, if one cares to read all the stories, are repetitive and consistent. It is not surprising to me, then, that [abductees'] experiences should be couched in terms of torment by demonic figures and threat of death.

The essential structure of the hero myth is the journey into the Otherworld, virtual death, and metaphorical rebirth (spiritual renewal). In the Christian religion and in certain ufological circles, this ancient mythic pattern is presented as literal fact. In both one is explicitly invited to believe the story literally, or to lose one's soul, damned as heathen or as debunkers.

Accepting that risk, I should like to draw attention to just one among the many strands that appear in both the ancient or traditional forms of this myth and the abduction scenario, and that is a preoccupation with birth, rebirth, and procreation. It is there in the *Mahabharata*, in the Greek myths, in the fairy and witchcraft legends, the shamanic tradition, and has become the focus, for the most vocal ufological researchers, of the abduction scenario.

The significance of this theme will be clearer once we have explored why these accounts – especially alien abduction narratives – are so consistent from one to the other. For it is a central tenet of the abduction researchers' (if not always the abductees') faith that abductions must be real events, because, they stoutly maintain, the reports agree so closely from one victim to another.

In fact, the conventional wisdom as to what happens when someone is snatched by the aliens has taken some time to settle into its present form. The structural template remains the Betty and Barney Hill account of 1961 (see Chapter One). But ufologists conveniently overlook all the aspects of today's Grays that do not appear in the Hills' testimony – their hairlessness, their all-black

eyes, their taciturn aloofness, and their frequent nudity, let alone their infamous 'breeding program'.

It has taken three or four books and 20 years for Betty Andreasson Luca's initially unique account (see Chapter One) to match the received version of alien encounters promulgated by Budd Hopkins, David Jacobs and John Mack; and details of Mrs Luca's encounters coincided with those found by these researchers only after they had, so to speak, shown the way.

Other abductees, we've seen in earlier chapters, had widely differing versions of the phenomenon to report. Thomas 'Ed' Bullard found that of the 270 cases he analysed in 1987, some 104, or 38 percent (nearly 4 in 10), did not follow the 'correct' order of events that he discovered in the other accounts. Yet the consistency of reports – after weeding out hoaxes, confabulations, etc. – was the reason he maintained they may represent real experiences. In scientific experiments, the convention is that the results are invalid if more than just one in 20 tests deviates from the norm.

Abduction proponents also rarely, if ever, cite the work of Dr Edith Fiore, whose subjects (described in her 1989 book *Encounters*) provide unique details of the 'medical' phase of their experiences. One is laid on her side and her buttocks pried apart for a rectal 'examination' with a narrow probe, but there was no ritual genital inspection; another was examined only by machine, and perfunctorily; two sisters claimed to have had chronic yeast infections cured by having their uteruses swabbed out and a curative gel applied 'deeply by hand' – routines directly contrary to medical wisdom and

> ◆
>
> **it is a central tenet of the abduction researchers' (if not always the abductees') faith that abductions must be real events**
>
> ◆

practice. Indeed there is quite a wide variation in the descriptions of gynecological techniques, including the implantation and removal of fetuses and/or ova, that Jacobs's and Hopkins's subjects provide. And, as James Portolillo has pointed out, they are strangely entangled with sexual material and activities that in real life would be 'unnecessary for, and guaranteed to hinder, any seriously intended gynecological procedure'.

The dismissal of awkward differences and contradictions in matters of 'small' details (even though the consistency of these details ought to be deemed crucial in validating the reality of the events as described), and even whole bodies of research, is a feature of the current set of assumptions about abductions. The reincarnations, dual identities, psychic talents and apocalyptic fears of Dr John Mack's subjects seem likely to be ignored by the abductionist establishment in much the same way as Dr Fiore's wayward findings have been. This leads one to suspect that the received version of the phenomenon is more a construct of certain investigators' (pre)conceptions and the influence they can command over their subjects and over their public, than it is the product of conclusions drawn impartially from all the evidence to hand. This selectivity appears to occur even when researchers confine their 'evidence' to what can be found within the bounds of ufology itself.

Yet many abductees, the specialist audience of UFO enthusiasts and, in the USA at least, a large segment of the general public, do seem to have accepted the Hopkins–Jacobs version of the abduction scenario, with its grotesque little

> ◆
> **The dismissal of awkward differences and contradictions in matters of 'small' details...is a feature of the current set of assumptions about abductions**
> ◆

Grays, 'breeding program' and associated terrors. Leading questions by amateur hypnotists, media influences, and the information exchange and pressure to conformity that reportedly characterize abductee support groups all, no doubt, play some part in refining and bringing uniformity to individual narratives. But the widespread acceptance of these stories suggests that their appeal is very deeply rooted.

Jung's concept of the 'collective unconscious', which abounds with archetypal images and symbols that are said to be inherited, has been cited by many psychosocial ufologists as the ultimate storehouse from which an abduction narrative is supplied. While the idea is attractive, Jung lacked the means to indicate the physical (and therefore inheritable) basis of the collective unconscious, and it remains no more than a concept. However, neurologist Michael Persinger's conviction that malfunctions - organic or induced - in the temporal lobes of the brain were the driving force behind the abduction experience put some scientific gloss on Jung's abstraction for those who wanted to see it. Persinger recognized that the awareness of particular parts and functions of the body is located in specific areas of the brain; if stimulated at the same time as the temporal lobes, certain combinations of physical sensations and basic mental imagery would be inevitable. The distinctive details of the experience - a shamanic spirit journey, a visit to Fairyland, a vision of the Virgin Mary, or a spacenapping - would be filled in by the individual according to background, knowledge and circumstances.

Some have gone further and implied that given the right stimulus the brain will generate quite specific images. Terence McKenna, a major authority on hallucinogens, has described the effects of

Artist's impression of the abduction of Carlos Alberto Diaz from Bahia Blanca, Argentina, in January 1975. Although judged a hoax, the witness's story is consistent with an experience in an altered state of consciousness.

ingesting the psychotropic chemical N,N-dimethyl-tryptamine (DMT). This substance is naturally present in the body, works directly on the language centers of the brain and, like adrenalin, may be 'dumped' in huge quantities given the right stimulus. According to McKenna, DMT brings one into a dialogue with 'Something-or-Other', in a 'somehow insulated' place that seems entirely real although it is extremely strange. One also 'meets entities', which McKenna describes as 'self-transforming machine elves', 'dynamically contorting topological modules', 'tryptamine munchkins', and 'fractal elves'. 'These beings,' he says, 'are like fractal reflections of some previously hidden and suddenly autonomous part of one's own psyche.'

Clearly there is much still to be done in establishing whether or not at least some of the components of abduction imagery are somehow inherent in the human brain and its chemistry, and in discov-

ering what triggers and organizes them. But, unlike the anecdotal evidence on which ufologists base their large claims about alien activities, Persinger's and McKenna's hypotheses are truly scientific, for they can be tested and either confirmed or shown to be false.

Even if parts of the abduction experience are potentially present in everyone's physical make-up, one can hardly ignore the cultural dimension in considering how an account of an alien encounter is organized. Or rather, dramatized, for all of us have a playwright hidden in us, who emerges most often as the author of our dreams. Human beings love to tell, or listen to, a good story.

The skeptical literature is full of instances of comics, books, films and TV material that contain scenes and details of consciously fictional abductions and that preceded the emergence of the 'real' phenomenon (some examples were reviewed in Chapter Three). The argument usually runs that such-and-such an abductee borrowed various details of their account from these sources – and if the abductee did not, he or she was led, perhaps unconsciously, by an investigator who did know the material. In some cases the relationship is clear-cut, but in few is it actually proven. I suggest that the existence of a direct cause-and-effect link does not have to be proven, because the process of creating an abduction narrative takes place at a much deeper level.

In his 1987 study, Thomas 'Ed' Bullard concluded that the consistency of events, and the uniform order in which they occurred, in 270 abduction accounts indicated that they represented real experiences. In a classic article, 'Entirely Unpredisposed' (published in *Magonia*,

◆

The skeptical literature is full of instances of comics, books, films and TV material that contain scenes of consciously fictional abductions

◆

CIRCUMSTANTIAL EVIDENCE

SUE MCLAREN

◆ ◆ ◆

Canadian postal worker, Sue McLaren, who saw a huge, dark UFO that blotted out the stars one night in October 1994. Thereafter, dreams of Gray aliens and recollections of many curious events in her life, including a brief, mysterious pregnancy, led her to suspect that she was an abductee.

At around 10.10 p.m. on a Friday in late October 1994, postal worker Mrs Sue McLaren left her daughter Candy's house in a suburb of Toronto, Ontario, Canada, to catch a bus home. Waiting at the bus stop, she had a sense of foreboding, 'as if someone was there but I couldn't see them'. At the same time there was the sound of leaves 'swishing', although no leaves were on the ground. Then she heard 'what sounded somewhat like a helicopter, but not like a helicopter, a kind of whooshing sound'. Looking up, she saw a huge, vague, dark shape blotting out the stars. The UFO carried no lights and was moving very slowly. She looked around to see if there were any other witnesses, but there was 'not a soul around, no cars, no animals, nothing'.

Then a dog appeared, a big, reddish dog that came up to her and made an odd 'yowp!' kind of cry. The dog came so close to Sue that she backed off until it had her pinned against the bus stop. She stayed there, increasingly frightened, for about 15 minutes, until the bus finally arrived. Strangely, during this time, no people or traffic came along the normally busy street.

About five minutes after getting on the bus and sitting opposite the driver, Mrs McLaren saw a particularly bright 'star' very low in the sky, which suddenly raced across the heavens. When she was almost home another brilliant 'star' appeared in the west, and suddenly flew over the bus, but did not reappear on the other side. 'I'm sure the driver saw it too. After it flew over she turned and looked at me, but she didn't say anything.' Once home, Sue went to sleep with the lights on. She remembers dreaming of 'three Grays, the middle one slightly taller than the others. I have no idea what they were trying to convey to me.' One night shortly afterward, 'I was startled awake by something like a cold finger touching my back.'

These curious events set Sue McLaren off on a program of reading about UFOs and abductions. After recalling several curious events in her life, and after another, daylight UFO sighting, she came to wonder if she too may be an abductee.

As a child – she had a very happy childhood – she would often wake up in the morning to find her night-dress strewn in some odd corner of her bedroom, and with no recall of taking it off. In 1974, in her twenties, she thinks, she had a brief, mysterious pregnancy. Normally regular as clockwork, she missed two periods, and a urine test showed positive. A second test was negative, and 'that very next day I became quite aware that I certainly was not pregnant.'

In August 1995 she became suddenly obsessed with a musician, the vocalist with a rock band. Several of the band's songs have themes connected with abductions, although the singer does not publicly claim any unusual experiences. Sue believes that in some way he is forwarding the aliens' plans, which reflect a concern for ecology and the environment.

In April 1996 she went to stay with her daughter Caroline at a Holiday Inn in Los Angeles for a brief break. One night, she went to bed at about 10.30 but tossed and turned, unable to sleep. 'I remember being in a semi-comatose state.... I then got a sort of message in my head that "they will be here soon". This happened 'twice. The next thing I knew [there was] a picture of my hand and a Gray's almost touching. His arm I remember was pencil thin, and his fingers were very long but rounded at the tips. My first thought was how much I wanted to hug him, and then I felt all this love and affection coming back to me, emanating from him. He had the kindest, warmest eyes. Very black, and very very large – I will never forget those eyes.'

When the hour beeper went off on her watch, she thought it was about midnight, or 1 a.m. at the latest. Still unable to sleep, after 'another five minutes' she got up to get a drink and discovered that the time was actually 3.43 a.m. 'I know I did not go to sleep,' she says, and regards this experience as an episode of missing time.

On one occasion after this, before going to sleep, Sue McLaren asked the aliens for a sign of their presence – a small cut. She dreamed of being with 'familiar people' on a spacecraft. Next morning she found a fresh cut on the outside of her thumb, but wonders: 'Could I have done this by myself?' She next asked to see the aliens' spacecraft, and dreamed she was on a ship being given a guided tour. The dream ended when 'my daughter Candy came up to me and said "Mom, come on, we're all ready to go." I asked where Jenny, my youngest daughter, was and Candy said, "She's waiting in the bubble." The dream seemed to take all night.'

At about 10.40 a.m. on 11 August 1996, Sue was walking home after accompanying one of her daughters to a friend's house. About 200m (660ft) away, off to the left, over the roof of a school near her home, she saw a pair of bright blue-white lights about 150m (500ft) in the air, slowly heading southwest. She thought them strange, but figured they were aircraft landing lights. A few moments later she turned onto her street, and looked over her shoulder to see the lights now heading low over the rooftops toward her. No structure was visible: just the lights. Feeling uneasy, she walked on and, just after she rounded a bend in her street, she turned again to see the UFO change direction, following the curve of the road. It did not bank like an aircraft: the lights remained horizontal and equally in plain sight when they changed direction. The thing was also entirely silent. Sue ran the rest of the way home. After a minute or so she stepped into her back yard to see where it had gone. The lights – looking exactly as they had when the UFO was flying toward her – were now traveling west, away from her.

From about this time Sue began waking at 3.30 a.m. at weekends with panic attacks. These and several other odd nocturnal events added to her suspicion that she is an abductee. Her attitude wavers from 'I don't expect anyone to believe it – I might be totally wrong' to a total conviction that she has been abducted by aliens. From the way she has assembled her evidence, one feels she would rather be considered an abductee.

◆

'I remember being in a semi-comatose state.... I then got a sort of message in my head that "they will be here soon"'

◆

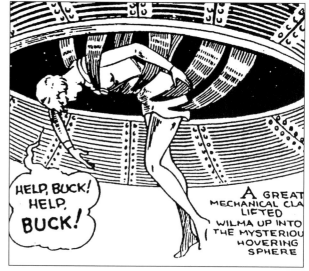

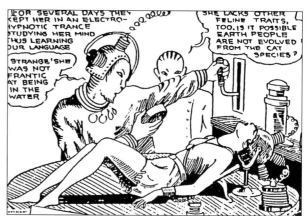

A Buck Rogers cartoon of 1930 conforms more closely to the standard abduction scenario than most allegedly real abductees' stories. The fictional cartoon reveals the instinctively dramatic nature of abduction.

1990), Martin Kottmeyer reproduces a 1930 Buck Rogers strip cartoon that, he points out with quiet satisfaction, contains more of Bullard's eight basic abduction events – that is, capture, examination, conference, tour, otherworldly journey, theophany, return, aftermath – and in the 'correct' order, than all but one allegedly 'real' account cited in Bullard's own study. As Kottmeyer remarks, 'it must be granted that a long-forgotten cartoon is not a credible influence on present-day abduction [stories].' He goes on to argue that 'real' abduction accounts and this fictional one in particular are so similar because both follow an 'intuitive ordering principle subconsciously acquired from drama.... To put it simply, Bullard's correct order is the right way to tell a story.' Kottmeyer explains:

A relabelling of Bullard's elements should make the logic clearer:

1. *character introduced,*
2. *peril and conflict,*
3. *explanation and insight,*
4. *good will and attempt to impress,*
5. *excitement,*
6. *climax,*
7. *closure,*
8. *sequel.*

Examination, as the peril, is the downer part of the story and would ruin a happy ending if sequenced late. Even in deviant

cases the examination is never put near the end. Pragmatically, putting theophany before examination might instill trust in the abductee and make testing go better. Dramaturgically, however, such an order would be stupid since it ruins the intensity of the peril and spoils the joy of the ending and the sense of closure.

Faceless terror makes for more primordial fear. Dramatically it would be unwise to reduce the alienness before the peril by conferring with the aliens or [having] them host a tour. It is also bad behaviourism to place aversive stimuli after sending one's signal - the message and information in the conference, tour and theophany.

The otherworldly journey is a form of excitement and can appear any place between the capture and climax.

The claim, made by all leading abduction proponents, that science fiction plays no part in abduction stories, can now be seen to be untrue at the most fundamental level. By chance, I discovered that it is not true at more superficial levels either. In a New Hampshire bookstore in April 1997 I picked up a used copy of Frank Herbert's *The Heaven Makers*, first published in 1968, when virtually the only abduction report in circulation was Betty and Barney Hill's. Herbert's story features an abduction of a human woman by dwarfish, large-headed, big-eyed immortal aliens who have discovered that they can cross-breed with humans. Some of these hybrids are living on Earth, 'passing' as ordinary people. The aliens, whose mothership is hidden under an ocean, can make themselves invisible to and control the minds of all but a few 'immune' humans. They have manipulated human history from the beginning and broadcast it to their fellows throughout the galaxy as drama, to help them relieve the terminal boredom of eternal life. By the end of the novel, there are distinct hints that some humans at least are in league with the aliens, some of whom have learned the advantages of mortality. A significant number of these themes crops up throughout ufology, and in the late 1980s were developed to a paranoid extreme by a loose-knit group now known as the Darksiders.

Taking Martin Kottmeyer's sharp observation one stage further, I would suggest that *The Heaven Makers* shows that, provided with a few essential materials and an instinct for storytelling, the human imagination will make something similar of them. Exactly what it makes of them will vary from age to age. One era may treat them lightly. Another – as I believe is the case with alien encounters – will use them as a far-reaching, reflective metaphor for its

own predicament. If a sense of that predicament is widespread, the story will be much the same in both structure and details: as the 18th-century playwright Count Carlo Gozzi discovered and the critic Georges Polti later demonstrated, only about 36 dramatic situations – plots – have ever been represented in world fiction. The central metaphor will also express both general and individual circumstances. The abduction scenario can reach so deeply into the psyche that some people actually seem to want to be identified with it (see feature on page 150), despite the high risk of ridicule that 'coming out' entails.

To some extent this explains why abduction stories, whether from real experience or generated under hypnosis, or whether concerning aliens, fairies, demons or spiritual journeys, are so similar in themselves and combine and recombine the same dramatic ingredients.

The dramatic imagination and its limitations don't account for some of the most striking details about aliens and abductions, however. Why has our portrait of the aliens stabilized in the image of the Gray, with its oversized head and huge black eyes, atrophied body, and heartless demeanor? And why are the Grays so fascinated by sexual matters? Why are they so closely associated with death?

It is automatically assumed by scientists, science-fiction writers and ufologists that any extra-terrestrial race that has the technology and the stamina to reach Earth from elsewhere among the stars will be enormously 'more advanced' than ourselves. It is quite often also assumed that the only practical way these visitors will be able to get here will involve faster-than-light travel. In other words, they will have been clever enough to outwit the laws of nature as we understand them. In effect, they can perform miracles; theirs is a magical technology. From the earliest days of science fiction, as well as in encounter reports in ufology, aliens from space have been depicted with bulging brain-cases to signify their vastly superior intelligence.

Reports of their bizarre black eyes probably derive directly from the cover art of Whitley Strieber's 1987 book *Communion*, but that does not reduce their mythic significance or power. The image instantly proclaims two things: the aliens are all-seeing, and at the same time they are unreadable, inscrutable, for they show no emotion and reveal no thought processes. These qualities are not unrelated to the aliens' miraculous scientific knowledge. They are the attributes of gods. It

Alien being from the 1954 movie This Island Earth. *The bulging headed, large-eyed alien was a cultural ikon long before abductions were first reported.*

should be no particular surprise to anyone that a new conception of a deity should be surrounded, in the modern world, by technological trappings. A whole thesis can be written on the parallels between meeting the aliens and the aliens' conduct, and the emotional and intellectual world of the Judæo-Christian religious tradition. But unlike the traditional image of God as loving and benevolent, the Grays display fiendish properties too.

This ambiguity is reflected in that impersonal – even deathly – gray skin. Grays are not so much neither black nor white, as *both* black *and* white. Their blurred identity is, furthermore, accessible only from liminal states of being, and often by people in ill-defined social conditions or rôles – people who are in some sense outsiders, and who resist categorization. To many in such indeterminate positions, there is much to be gained from this state, not least a sense of freedom and self-determination. But in a highly politicized, status-conscious and conformist society, there is a major drawback. A central feature of living near, or across, culturally defined boundaries is powerlessness: socially and politically, either one is invisible, or one can safely be ignored. It is clear that a sense of powerlessness is central to the abduction experience. It is also the defining characteristic of nightmares. Martin Kottmeyer has drawn attention to psychologist Ernest Hartmann's finding that the people most prone to nightmares have 'boundary deficits' – they are less likely than most of us to make rigid distinctions between (for example) fantasy and reality, sleep and waking, passion and reason, self and not-self, masculine and feminine. Hartmann found that people with thin boundaries tend to be

> ◆
> **It should be no particular surprise to anyone that a new conception of a deity should be surrounded, in the modern world, by technological trappings**
> ◆

emotionally vulnerable (and consequently wary), slightly paranoid, and prone to daydreaming. They are also seen by others as 'different':

> *They are unusually alert to lights, sounds, and sensations. They tend to have fluid sexual identities. Bisexuals are over-represented in the nightmare sufferers' population, and it is rare to find manly men or womanly women in it.... They are not rule followers.... There is a striking tendency for these people to find their way into fields involving artistic self-expression.... Some develop their empathic tendencies and become therapists. Ordinary blue or white collar jobs are rare.... Boundary deficits also contribute to fluid memories and a fluid time sense.*

In passing, we may note here that one Siberian term for the shaman – the 'soft man' – reflects the frequency with which homosexuals and even hermaphrodites have been initiated into the rôle.

Using psychological profiles of known abductees, Kottmeyer makes a strong case for the generalization that abductees form another 'boundary deficient' group. They are certainly 'different', and aware of it. That many have artistic talents has often been noted, particularly by Jenny Randles, and is liberally demonstrated in the illustrations in this book. Kottmeyer also stressed that boundary deficiency will not show up on standard tests for mental dysfunction, and that it is not 'abnormal'. If we regard myths, like nightmares, as dramatized projections of our deepest concerns, we might also expect that the Grays have equally thin boundaries. And so they do. Their blurring of distinctions is represented symbolically, in concrete images – the

ability to manipulate time, space and memory, to ignore solid barriers like walls, to become invisible, to change shape, to read minds, and so on.

Perhaps the Grays' greatest boundary deficit lies in their incapacity to distinguish between abuse and respect, cruelty and consideration. Grays are capable of *anything*, good or evil. And the favor is returned, in that we can project anything on to them. As we see in the faintly factitious disputations that bubble up constantly among ufologists, there is little agreement among researchers and abductees over the positive or negative intentions and effects of an alien encounter. On an individual level, the significance of an abduction can range from divine revelation (Betty Andreasson's experience) or a sense of expanded personal potential and power ('Kathy') to what many commentators have seen as the expression of the social difficulties of an interracial marriage (Betty and Barney Hill). The existential and emotional nature of abduction experiences is still as various as it ever was, although the positive aspects of the experience remain inadmissible to the most influential researchers in the field, and their followers.

The dominant, 'ufologically correct' version of the abduction myth also exists in a wider social context than its proponents like to acknowledge. It emerged in embryonic form in the early 1980s, at about the same time as the world first learned of AIDS. From its working title, Budd Hopkins's first book could have been mistaken for a study of that disease: it was called *An Invisible Epidemic*. The other great ufological myth that mushroomed into an industry in the 1990s, the Roswell incident of 1947, was also making its debut, with all its paraphernalia of secrecy, conspiracy and cover-up (a concept roundly endorsed by Hopkins). There were two

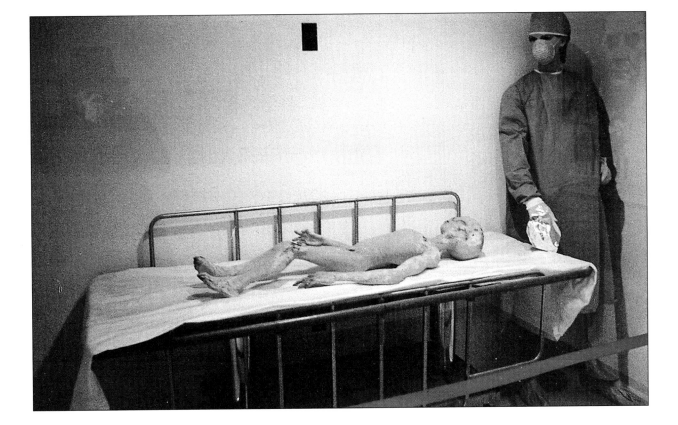

Model of a dead alien, like those said to have been retrieved from a UFO that supposedly crashed near Roswell, New Mexico, in 1947.

underlying, identical messages in the grim news from medical science and in the claims of a long-standing extra-terrestrial alien presence: nothing was as it seemed; and the future was blighted, and uncertain, as never before. And both messages were framed in the language of sex and reproduction.

For the generation born after World War II – to which the overwhelming majority of abductees belong – the discovery of AIDS carried a much more obvious message about sexual habits and assumptions. Free love was not, it had turned out, without its price. The dominant political mood of the era, in the USA and in Europe, also radically restated the doctrine of individual rather than communal responsibility. Especially vocal in condemning the 'moral degeneracy' that had produced AIDS and in decrying 'socialism' in even its mildest forms (such as Medicare) was the Christian fundamentalist right. In the USA this self-appointed 'moral majority' also made a political issue of, and so polarized, the debate about abortion, which was a price that many had paid for sexual freedom. Medical termination of pregnancy had been legal in the USA since 1972, and in the UK since 1967.

In two essays, published in the *Bulletin of Anomalous Experience* (1992) and *Magonia* (1992), Dennis Stacy set out his hypothesis that the Grays were what they looked like: dead human fetuses. He proposed that the abduction experience was a way to expiate guilt over abortions. He first noted that what he called the New Revised

Abduction Scenario, the version promulgated by Budd Hopkins and David Jacobs, differed from the Old Standard Scenario described by 'Ed' Bullard in two crucial respects. Bullard's scenario had no hybrid children and no claimed cases of missing fetuses. Meanwhile, claims for the extent of the abduction phenomenon, said Stacy, did not stand up to simple common sense. If, as some maintained, some 3.7 million Americans had been abducted several times in their lives, the night air would be thick with UFOs: 'The numbers alone are just too staggering,' Stacy wrote, 'conjuring up images of flying saucers stacked like [gigantic heaps of] pancakes over the world's major airports, awaiting hovering and abduction rights from some global air traffic controller.' Therefore, one should seek a terrestrial explanation for the exponential increase in reports of abductions, particularly those featuring hybrid babies and missing fetuses, since the late 1980s.

> ◆
>
> **If, as some maintained, some 3.7 million Americans had been abducted several times in their lives, the night air would be thick with UFOs**
>
> ◆

Stacy remarked that since 1972 in the USA, some 30 million women had had abortions. (In 1993, about 78 million women were of child-bearing age or had been since 1972, which meant that in those 21 years nearly four in 10 women had had abortions. The proportion of the US population thus potentially affected far outstrips even the wildest claims for the number of 'probable' abductees in the USA.) Polls showed that Americans held contradictory opinions on the subject. While 73 percent of Americans supported abortion rights, 77 percent viewed the operation as a form of murder. These figures can only mean that most people managed to endorse both ideas at once. Clearly, this was fertile ground for internal conflict, guilt and shame. Such an

Anti-abortion demonstration, Washington, DC, January 1997. Abduction accounts may be dramatizing tensions and contradictions within individuals and society over this sensitive issue.

incongruity of feelings, I will add, may also be seen as a kind of twilight zone, in which boundary deficits are a source of conflict and pain rather than a wellspring of holistic perception.

Stacy pointed to the many fetus-like physical attributes of the Grays, and suggested that out of powerful emotions they had metaphorically become 'avenging angels' or:

The hybrid baby...is nothing less (or more) than the aborted fetus brought to life. The 'missing' fetus is no longer dead, then, but lives on in a 'heaven' (outer space) from which it can never physically return, perhaps even aboard a 'Mother' ship. And the only way it can be revisited is for the abductee to be 're-abducted'.... Allegorically, [the Grays] represent the souls of all departed, or aborted, fetuses. And the fact that the Grays are now responsible for the 'missing' fetus – both literally and figuratively – absolves the aborter of the original sin, that is, it reduces any guilt attached to abortion per se.... The abduction experience, then, serves a fundamental purpose, namely, the reduction of psychological tension occasioned by guilt.

Stacy pointed out that men may feel as guilty and confused over their rôle in an abortion as women, and members of both sexes could be morally appalled and bewildered without having been directly concerned in an actual abortion. In the new abduction scenario, the victim of the termination becomes the victimizer, punishing the guilty. But, justice having been done and dues paid, the individual is once more free to grow; and this explains what the promoters of the revised abduction scenario prefer to overlook – the abductee's post-abduction rebirth or 'psychological resurrection'. Signs of this include 'an increased appreciation of life, greater self-acceptance, a deeper concern for others, an expanded level of spirituality, and a heightened level of concern with social/planetary issues'. Dennis Stacy's hypothesis is not, either, incompatible with the shamanic process of spiritual rebirth. Indeed, it is a restatement of it, in appropriate contemporary dress.

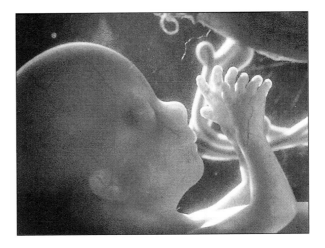

The resemblance between the typical Gray alien and the human fetus is unmistakable. Is it entirely coincidental that abduction reports are so concerned with birth and reproduction, and anxiety over the human future?

I remarked at the beginning of this chapter that myths will bear more than one meaning. The abduction scenario meets that criterion, for it can be interpreted as a religious fable for a godless an anxious age, a hero myth, a shamanic ritual, or the purging of a specific guilt. Any one of these generalized psychodramas may be adopted and varied to fit the peculiar needs of a particular individual's development. One could go so far as to say that the very fact that something as preposterous as abduction accounts can be taken to be the literal truth is an unmistakable sign of their mythic potency. Even if only one of the thousands of abduction reports now on record were revealed to be true, the mythical aspect of abductions would remain, independent of the facts, emotionally and psychologically fruitful. And if it could be proven tomorrow, beyond all shadow of doubt, that no alien has ever abducted a human being, the myth would also survive. True or false, the abduction scenario tells us too much about ourselves to die.

MEANINGS AND REALITIES

Interpreting the Abduction Phenomenon

◆ ◆ ◆

*Opposite: Hiroshima, Japan, after the nuclear strike in August 1945. Prophetic scenes
of terrible destruction feature in many abductees' accounts today.*

A story of being abducted by aliens may possibly have many meanings. The leading abduction researchers say the horrible truth is all too obvious: that aliens are here, now, and doing something incomprehensible with our stolen genes. But in his essay 'The Mythic' (1954), French philosopher and anthropologist Eric Dardel reminds us that: 'Every period declares "its" truth…

*A Ku Klux Klan demonstration in Houston, Texas,
in 1985. Conceivably, abductions may
reflect deep conflicts and concerns over
the future of society.*

Our "truth" of the moment is often only a myth that does not know it is one, and…we make myths every day without knowing it.' In saying this, Dardel is not being dismissive. Myths, he says, are neither true nor false, but rather are *complementary*

to reason. They are 'beyond our logic's horizon', and 'by means of the mythic image, there is an externalization of…the emotion of man as he meets the world.'

The abduction scenario is an affront to both conventional science and our humdrum habitual ways of looking at things. So too are the propositions that a swan, who was really the premier member of a pantheon of gods, once raped a woman.

Yet, on some level, the ancient Greeks believed both far-fetched claims. The abduction phenomenon, although more complex, is hardly any more plausible, yet people believe it. The real question here is why people would *want* to believe it. In short, what deep human concerns does the abduction phenomenon reflect – what does it *mean*?

Some surprising answers have been offered. For example, in her essay 'Alien Abductions and the End of White People' (1993) Annalee Newitz, the co-editor of the Internet journal *Bad Subjects*, suggested that the 'aliens' represented the imperialist tendency in all of us:

> *One might say the alien abduction story is too allegorical to be true. It is as if, hundreds of years later, white people...are having fantasies in which they imagine themselves victims of the same uncontrollable injustices suffered by non-whites for centuries under Western imperialism.... But [as] Jacobs and other UFO researchers like Budd Hopkins point out, people from every racial and class background are being 'abducted'. In fact, the famous Barney and Betty Hill case involved an interracial couple.... If the alien abduction narrative is merely fantasy, then this would seem to indicate that one of our basic fears as human beings is a fear of being colonized. This is not a fear specific to any race, class or nation.*

Anthropologist Steve Mizrach expressed a related, though more tightly focused, idea, in 1994, in the *Bulletin of Anomalous Experience*:

> *The US is currently dealing with the fact that its white majority is decreasing, thus provoking all the debates about 'multicul-*

> *turalism.' White supremacists take to the talkshow airwaves every day to proclaim the dangers of 'race betrayal' by those who 'miscegenate' and 'pollute' the white race. And Budd Hopkins tells us that women – the majority of whom are white and WASP, heartland, middle-America types – are being carried off by aliens to achieve a 'hybridization' of them and us.*

Mizrach was not suggesting the investigators were racist: only that they and their subjects were articulating an unconsciously perceived threat to their cultural identity. (He noted that black nationalists too have conscripted the abduction phenomenon to their own cause, alleging it is part of a genocidal plot.) What Mizrach calls 'race fear' can take appalling forms but, however it is expressed, it manifests a sense of threat to the secure future of a culture and a way of life. Even the most thoughtful people, of any race, may be ambivalent about cultural mixing, without being at all racist. That is, they may welcome the way contact with another culture enriches their own, while being wary, lest their own culture is thereby undermined.

As Mizrach says, abductions have to do with more than just racial tension. I observed in Chapter Five that the fixation on reproduction, birth and death within the abduction phenomenon is a mark of deep anxiety about the future, whether that means the human future or the immediate fate of the individual. Both Newitz's and Mizrach's interpretations confirm that basic principle.

Insofar as the human future is part of the meaning of the abduction myth, perhaps the phenomenon, as the literalists say, does bear directly on humanity's relations with aliens and outer space. Having lifted our eyes to the stars, and having been

◆

one of our basic fears as human beings is a fear of being colonized. This is not a fear specific to any race class or nation

◆

Two drawings by Sue McLaren – created before her encounters with UFOs and alien entities (left) and after. Mrs McLaren believes her skills improved as a result.

drenched in a century of science fiction, we may be pondering through abduction stories on the risks involved in finally setting out to explore outer space. The logic is anthropocentric, but it embraces a respectable emotional truth: 'People on Earth are proverbially unpleasant to foreigners. If *we* – taking all our faults with us – can step among the stars, then maybe so can anyone else out there. And suppose whoever is out there is as barbaric as we are – or even worse? *What monsters might we meet?'*

To repeat: the logic is anthropocentric. What terrifies us most is the most dreadful part of ourselves. These ideas are echoed by some ufolo-

gists' speculation that the aliens may be the future form of humanity, traveling back in time on a kind of genetic mining expedition. Different as it is, Dennis Stacy's 'abortion hypothesis' likewise addresses abduction tales as a meditation on the precariousness of the future, signified by our being haunted by the human potential we have deliberately destroyed. Whichever way we read the myth, it insists on telling us that *we* are the aliens.

Skeptical ufologists Peter Rogerson and Paul Devereux also suggest that the aliens are projections of our social selves – alien-*ated*, dis-*eased* with ourselves and one another – and with the disspirited, impersonal, conformist and uncontrollable elected dictatorship of a society that we – or worse, persons unknown, but uncomfortably like us – have created and, more important, sustain. In his regular column in *Magonia*, Rogerson has written:

> *The 'grays' are surely personifications of 'little gray men' – that stock term of abuse for petty, colourless, hidebound bureaucrats – an apt image of 'only doing my job' cosmic social workers. I would go further, and say that there is being made here an identification between the impersonal forces of mass society and the impersonal forces of wild nature.*

Paul Devereux echoed this, in an unpublished conference paper: 'My guess is that the extra-terrestrial is the image of our own estrangement from our own inner selves and from nature itself.'

I could argue at length and in detail that Rogerson and Devereux are really saying the same thing. The different kinds of unease and dissatisfaction they describe may very well lead to a violent assertion of a religious impulse that is otherwise unappeased in our time. The 20th century has seen previously unimaginable cruelty and destruction, and both religion and humanism have failed to save humanity from its incomprehensible self. And so a frustrated craving for the transcendental has elaborated on technologically otherworldly elements in contemporary culture and combined them with motifs from traditional Western religion to explain, or redeem, the human predicament.

◆

The 20th century has seen previously unimaginable cruelty and destruction and both religion and humanism have failed to save humanity from its incomprehensible self

◆

Of the literalists, John Mack is the most honest about this aspect of the phenomenon – although not as an analyst. I suspect the connection arises from his well-known concerns about nuclear arms and 'the environment' – concerns that, by a mysterious coincidence, his subjects' aliens seem to share. In this, they form an historical link with the fears of nuclear catastrophe expressed by the much-maligned UFO contactees of the 1950s. In his Foreword to David Jacobs's *Secret Life*, Mack writes:

> *Is it possible that…an effort is being made to place the planet under a kind of receivership? This would…arrest the destruction of life and make possible the evolution of consciousness or whatever the anima mundi has in store.… I would merely suggest that if we could allow ourselves to reintroduce the possibility of a higher intelligence into the universe, and experience the numinous mystery of creation, this scenario is consistent with the facts of the abduction phenomenon.*

Mack's 'facts' are not of a kind that are acceptable to the science he so strenuously rejects. But it is certainly not hard to detect apocalyptic elements in the imagery of abductees' 'visions'.

Religious beliefs meet, thematically, with the abduction phenomenon in another way: human powerlessness. Just as we are powerless to control the future, we cannot govern the whims of either gods or the aliens. Both appear to be omnipotent. The time-honored human response to unrestrained power is to propitiate or worship it, while at the same time squirming under its weight. We fear the aliens as much as once we feared the Lord, and on the other hand see them as harbingers of a new

George Adamski's first claim that he had met angelic Venusians. Fictions, hoaxes and 'real' abduction stories may be different but related ways of dealing with the same essential questions about life on Earth.

and enlightened era, as doorways to new technical and spiritual knowledge. John Mack sees them as instigators of an evolution in human consciousness that will somehow integrate objective and subjective perceptions. Yet one reason he gives for believing that abductions really happen is the fear, tears and terror he sees in his subjects as they recall their experiences under hypnosis.

The abduction phenomenon is rife with such paradoxes. Dennis Stacy touches on one aspect of this in his portrayal of the revised abduction scenario as an outlet for internal conflict over the issue of abortion. Many critics have been bemused by Budd Hopkins's assertions that he does not believe the aliens are malevolent, even though he actually describes them performing monstrous acts. Abductees themselves inform us of their rage at being violated, yet may also be overcome by love for their captors. These are too similar to ambivalent human responses to the caprices of the gods to be entirely coincidental.

Is there any measure of reality in the abduction phenomenon? To me, as to Annalee Newitz, full-blown abduction stories seem too allegorical to be true. In his 1977 essay 'Facts, Frauds and Fairytales', John Rimmer, editor of *Magonia,* proposed that in ufology there is no *essential* difference between admitted fictions (i.e. science and fantasy fiction), hoaxes, genuinely unexplained reports, and honestly reported but later explained experiences. Rimmer saw each of these as fueled by the same 'artistic' impulse, subject to the temper and nature of their times. To illustrate his point he compared J.R.R. Tolkien, the creator of Middle Earth, the hobbits and *The Lord of the Rings,* with George Adamski, creator of the contactee movement, 'Nordic' aliens and the *Space Brothers:*

Here a writer of considerable talent [i.e. Tolkien] has created a vast, mythical world in a series of compulsively readable works of avowed fiction. Yet is his achievement so different, except in the manner of its execution, from someone like Adamski, who feeling the same urges for sub-creation produces as potentially great a vision [but]

Javier Perez de Cuellar, pictured here in January 1991 when UN Secretary-General, was allegedly abducted from New York City in 1989. Sr de Cuellar has denied all knowledge of any such incident.

in a series of botched-up, half believed-in hoaxes?... And does it matter too much whether this universally felt [archetype] is expressed in a great work of imaginative fiction; or as a message from a real space-man; or as a lucrative hoax in some paper-back potboiler?

Rimmer answers his own question thus: 'It is certainly the same ore that is being mined, and it is capable of being refined and fashioned into a Fabergé Egg or an old tin can!' With John Rimmer's radically inclusive theory in mind, I should like to make two points.

First, it should be clear from this and every-thing else I have said that abduction narratives created or confabulated under hypnosis are no more true or false than those events experienced by others apparently in full waking consciousness.

The stories come from the same mythopeic, dream-weaving, storytelling source in all of us.

Second, I would admit the extremely remote possibility that extra-terrestrial aliens are here and are conducting rather strange experiments on human beings. The scientific smart money is not on this option, however, and while science is neither perfect nor complete, it is the best tool we have for exploring and explaining the material universe – and so far, it has worked astonishingly well. I might put this another way: even if abductions really were happening as reported, the evidence that ufologists present is unscientific at best, is unsupported most of the time, and at worst is sheer hokum.

We might illustrate the point by briefly survey-ing the flaws in the 'UFO case of the century', the 'abduction' of Linda Cortile from her Manhattan apartment and the subsequent abduction of two security guards and the then Secretary-General of the United Nations, Javier Perez de Cuellar. Budd Hopkins, the investigator and chief proponent of this extraordinary set of allegations, suggests that it is a unique case because it was, he says, indepen-dently witnessed.

The 'abduction' of Linda Cortile itself first emerged only under hypnosis. According to her own account in *MUFON UFO Journal*, all Linda consciously saw was a strange being 'standing at the foot of my bed, staring at me!' Sleep paralysis, a vague hypnogogic vision, and seven months' acquaintance with other abductees' stories then melded into a coherent abduction narrative when she was hypnotized.

Unfortunately, the independent witnesses amount to one person ('Janet Kimball') who now refuses to be questioned further. Another, known as 'Marilyn Kilmer', who was said to be abducted with Linda on another occasion, has since dissociated herself from the case. The security guards do not count as 'independent' witnesses, as they too were allegedly abducted at the same time as Linda. Sr Perez de Cuellar has publicly denied being involved.

Hopkins maintains that the glowing red UFO that carried Mrs Cortile away made itself 'selectively invisible' to avoid detection, and then produces other witnesses from sundry parts of Manhattan to corroborate its appearance.

Equally suspect is the long gap between the otherwise routine abduction of Linda Cortile and the appearance (15 months later) of 'security guards' Dan and Richard with their astonishing side of the story. Linda meanwhile had recalled nothing of their version of events, but did so under later hypnosis. It is in this space of time that, one suspects, any hoaxing involved was hatched. To what extent it then or later involved Mrs Cortile is anyone's guess. What can be said with some certainty is that Dan's and Richard's reasons for not 'going public' with their evidence are fatuous. They maintain that to do so would expose their true identities and create problems for the (unnamed) agency for which they supposedly work. For anyone in authority in that agency, it would be the work of moments to discover who was accompanying Sr Perez de Cuellar on 30 November 1989.

There are many other difficulties with this case, but to examine them all would take hundreds of pages. Meanwhile, Hopkins maintains that if this case is a hoax, two things follow. Linda Cortile and/or her fellow conspirators can only be in it for the money; and that 20 or more people would have to be involved.

Money, however, is not the only incentive to pull a hoax. The notorious MJ-12 papers, which supposedly document a supersecret project to handle débris from crashed flying saucers,

consumed huge amounts of ufological energy when they appeared in public in 1987, and still cause controversy. They have been shown to be fake as conclusively as can be without a signed confession. Hopkins does not accept the analogy. Indeed his standards for what *is* acceptable in logic are difficult to deduce. When I told Hopkins Kathy's story of visiting an alien spacecraft parked within the Sun (see Chapter One), Hopkins exclaimed: 'But that's absurd!' Kathy's claims are certainly remarkable, but no more outrageous than anything in the Linda Cortile case.

And if the 'UFO case of the century' is a hoax, it need not involve more than three outside parties plus Mrs Cortile. They are Dan and Richard, and Janet Kimball. They are all that is required to play the various parts involved, given who saw whom, when and where. Everything else can be accounted for by coincidence, gullibility, rôle-playing, and the products of a wish to please (or string along) a famous investigator. Hopkins has obligingly tied up the putative hoaxers' loose ends, largely through 'confirming' the fictions of the enigmatic Dan and Richard using the fallible medium of hypnosis. Any remaining logical difficulties and inconsistencies he ascribes to the astonishing powers or inscrutable mindset of the aliens.

Hopkins and other leading abductionists have been criticized by many for their reliance on hypnosis, and even more caustically for subjecting very young children to the technique. Some, according to the written accounts, have been as young as two and a half years old. John Harney speaks for common humanity when he writes:

I find it difficult to read such stuff without becoming nauseated. When I was a small child I suffered from nightmares,

David Howard's drawing of a huge UFO that he and a companion saw in February 1982, shortly before his narcoleptic dreams of abductions began. Many 'real' abduction accounts now feature no UFO sighting at all.

but my parents comforted me and reassured me that the monsters in them were not real and that they were only dreams. I believe that most children are treated in this way. Imagine the effects, then, of making it plain to children that not only are the dream-creatures real, but that there is no escape from them. Such an approach hardly seems therapeutic, to put it mildly, but this is the line taken by Hopkins and company. If they can persuade intelligent and more or less sane adults to believe such nonsense, the long-term effects on children hardly bear thinking about.

Perhaps the best people to make this point to researchers are abductees themselves. For the record, all of the abductees I spoke to in researching this book were appalled at the practice of hypnotizing children.

In other respects too they were often less than impressed with the approach of the leading investigators. John Velez (see Chapter Four) has urged those who suspect they may be abductees not to approach abduction researchers. He explained why for this book:

There is a rapidly growing number of folks...who are beginning to remember their abduction experiences. Few have sought the counsel of their personal physicians or a competent mental health professional. Many simply contact the established abductionists (who already have their minds pretty much made up as to what's going on). But the need for abduction experiencers to report to competent professionals is obvious: someone who already has their mind made up is simply not going to render an objective evaluation.

Memory, and the nature and accuracy of it, along with a proper analysis of the validity of material recovered through hypnosis, should be the immediate focus of psychological investigators. The experiencers themselves require proper counselling regardless of their personal belief or disbelief in the reality of the abductions. People are confused, unsettled, and otherwise disturbed when they find themselves confronted by the possibility they have been abducted.

Those I interviewed for this book knew that I planned to make general, and sometimes specific, assessments of the abduction experience as well as of what I am inclined to label the abduction industry. In that case, I felt, they had a right to comment too. With some explanatory background, this is what they had to say after reading the relevant parts of this book. Their words should make one thing clear. Abductees are not easily lumped together for the sake of facile generalizations to which both 'believers' and 'skeptics' are all too often prone.

John Velez may not be impressed with abduction researchers, but he is no defender of skeptics either. He wrote:

Although I myself am convinced of the physical reality of abductions, there are a great many 'psychological' elements and issues involved that beg further inquiry. As an 'experiencer' my only interest is in getting at the underlying truth of these extraordinary events (whatever that 'truth' might eventually turn out to be) and to help recruit the assistance of as many mainstream professionals as possible.

I don't expect to go before the public with my accounts of alien intervention without being willing to substantiate my claims. When the TV science program NOVA asked me to participate in their segment on 'abductions', I consented, and requested time and time again that they perform some of the following tests on the abductees participating.

1. Complete psychological work up and evaluation, utilizing a professional of their choice. (I had already taken a battery of these tests and I knew that I'd come up with a clean bill of mental

heath. But, in all fairness, I thought it proper to afford them the opportunity.)

2. Polygraph examination. I know a polygraph test cannot show the truth of the abductions themselves but I knew it would show that I was not intentionally lying or attempting to perpetrate a fraud or a hoax.

3. I invited NOVA to interview my family members and to conduct whatever testing they may have needed on my home. (Checking for magnetic anomalies, unusual radiation etc. etc.)

4. I also consented to X-rays or CAT scans in order to determine the presence or absence of any 'foreign objects' ('implants') in my body.

You'd think that serious science investigators looking into this admittedly odd subject would leap at such an opportunity. None of the tests that I proposed were ever performed. In fact, what NOVA did was have us analysed 'on air' by 'experts' who had never met us or interviewed us!

There's too much at stake to dismiss our claims so thoughtlessly – or our offers to be subjected to some good old-fashioned empirical testing. We need help and resources, and the finest minds that can be gathered, to begin properly to address the question of the origin of perceived alien intervention into individual human lives.

Clarke Hathaway (see Chapter Five) and his partner Julie Presson have both, and simultaneously, witnessed bizarre entities appearing at the foot of their bed; both believe in reincarnation and the imminence of 'earth changes', which will correspond to 'a change of consciousness in mankind'. Clarke is erudite in occult and philosophical, 'metaphysical' literature. In the 1930s his grandparents were part of contactee Guy Warren Ballard's I AM group, centered on Mount Shasta, California. Of the two, Julie is distinctly the more skeptical about abductions. Clarke wrote:

I feel that in your commentary on mythology you are on a valid path, but would argue that what constitutes reality to one is not the same flavor to another. For myself, I lean heavily in the direction of an astral explanation for most, if not all, these occurrences. In simpler terms I do not feel that these beings are real in a physical, third dimensional sense. This is not to say that in a broader sense they are not real. Far from it! They are real and can exert some influence eventually affecting the life of those who encounter them.

Taking a decidedly Metaphysical view, these experiences must contain some consensus within the group consciousness, otherwise their occurrence would not be so widespread and be so similar. This certainly is not to imply that their incidence constitutes a physical happening. The paranormal aspects of these visitations blatantly point to their occurring on another level.

Many UFO sightings that have taken place over the years can be described in the same way. That is, that not all of the witnesses on the scene see the same thing,

◆

'I would have no patience for anyone who would disbelieve or dissuade me from my own truths'

◆

or see anything at all! The hint therefore is that something indeed valid is occurring, but on another level of perception.

Kathy (see Chapter One), said to me:

I agree with your kind of skepticism. Aside from my experiences, I can only hope that some day there will be an accepted truth to be found in the matter of the UFOs and the alien presence. And, I can assure you that humanity has a duality in its future. There will be those who choose not to accept or change for the future. Then there will be those who will be the great explorers of the rest of the universe. I personally have done my best to see the future, to be a part of it and to see that I am not alone in that kind of future....

I would have no patience for anyone who would disbelieve or dissuade me from my own truths. I have not had the inclination to confirm or deny any of the facts I have learned during my experiences. To me, facts are arbitrary by definition, being true for one person and his experiences and yet, just as not true for other people in the same time and experiences. So, with this in mind, I have not troubled myself about any kind of facts. It keeps things very simplified and easy to manage.

Sue McLaren (see Chapter Five) was the least happy of those I interviewed. She said:

I certainly know what I felt and what I saw. And until someone can come up with a logical explanation for this, I will

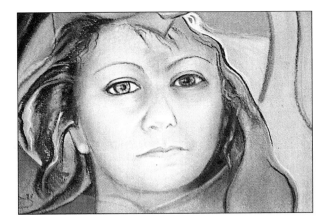

Portrait of hypnotherapist Julie Presson,
partner of abudctee Clarke Hathaway.

continue to believe that abductions do exist. You have made it clear that you do not agree, and you have quoted from numerous books to try to prove your point. But to me the growing number of incidents and the number of people now coming forward to attest to the fact that they have seen something strange or claim to be abducted are not to be ignored.

We cannot all be wrong or hallucinating, or have dream disorders. To date I have not received any reassurance that what I have experienced was not an abduction. Until I am given actual proof that there are no such things as aliens or UFOs or abductions I will continue to believe that they do exist.

I might sum up my own position like this: I am entirely unimpressed by the claims of abduction researchers, and shocked at the emotional damage they may be wreaking on their clientèle, but I cannot deny that the abduction experience may give rise to a profound upheaval.

The literalists' belief in extra-terrestrial intervention is not, in my view, absolutely impossible, but reason and evidence are overwhelmingly against it. Meanwhile, no one has yet assembled a satisfactory, over-arching psychologically based hypothesis that accounts for *all* aspects of the abduction experience. Indeed it may be that we are dealing with a variety of mental and physical phenomena that meet and fructify in some common ground – rather as from the soil sprouts an infinite variety of plants.

Perhaps, it is less disturbing to put a literal construction on the abduction experience than to contemplate even the *possibility* of one's own mental disintegration. And people react in this way because the polarities of the skeptic-versus-believer 'debate' have left the middle ground empty – bereft of uncontentious observations and demonstrations that very weird things can and do occur in, and to, the consciousness of irreproachably sane people. To suggest that the abduction experience may be a 'psychological' phenomenon is emphatically not to impugn the rationality of those involved. And we should be grateful to them, for the mythic insights they provide.

In many ways our present understanding of the abduction phenomenon is like a pre-concert orchestral warm-up that has gone on too long because the conductor is unforgivably late, and the leader of the orchestra hasn't taken his seat either. The brass section and the percussionists keep playing the same few bars over and over. The woodwind is in danger of going out of tune. The cellos are running through some tricky passages that aren't even on the program. The audience is getting restive. A fight is about to break out among the critics, who haven't even paid for their seats.

Where will it all end?

References and Further Reading

References

Adamski, George & Leslie, Desmond. *Flying Saucers Have Landed.* Werner Laurie 1953

Adamski, George. *Inside the Flying Saucers.* Abelard Schuman 1955

Appelle, Stuart. 'The Abduction Experience: A critical evaluation of theory and evidence', *Journal of UFO Studies New Series #6* (1996)

Baker, Robert. *Hidden Memories.* Prometheus 1992

Baker, Robert. 'Alien Dreamtime', *The Anomalist #2* (1995)

Blackmore, Susan. 'Alien Analysis', *UFO Magazine* (UK) May–June 1996

Blackmore, Susan. 'Abduction by Aliens or Sleep Paralysis?' (unpublished MS 1997)

Bloecher, T., Clamar, A., & Hopkins, B. *Final Report on the Psychological Testing of UFO Abductees.* Fund for UFO Research 1985

Bowen, Charles (ed.) *The Humanoids.* Spearman 1969

Bowen, Charles (ed.) *Encounter Cases from Flying Saucer Review.* Signet 1977

Boylan, Richard. *Close Extraterrestrial Encounters.* Wild Flower 1994

Brenneis, C. Brooks. 'Belief and Suggestion in the Recovery of Memories of Childhood Sexual Abuse', *Journal of the American Psychoanalytic Assoc.* Vol 42, #2 (1994)

Briggs, Katherine. *A Dictionary of Fairies.* Allen Lane 1976

Brookesmith, Peter. *UFO: The Complete Sightings Catalogue.* Barnes & Noble (USA), Blandford (UK) 1995

Brookesmith, Peter. *UFO: The Government Files.* Barnes & Noble (USA), Blandford (UK) 1996

Brunvand, Jan Harold. *Readings in American Folklore.* W.W. Norton 1979

Bryan, C.D.B. *Close Encounters of the Fourth Kind.* Wiedenfeld & Nicolson 1995

Budden, Albert. *Allergies and Aliens.* Discovery Times Press 1994

Budden, Albert. *UFOs: Psychic Close Encounters.* Blandford 1995

Bullard, T.E. *UFO Abductions: The measure of a mystery* (2 vols). Fund for UFO Research 1987

Bullard, T.E. *The Sympathetic Ear.* Fund for UFO Research 1995

Burridge, Kenelm. *New Heaven, New Earth.* Blackwell 1971

Clark, Jerome. *UFOs in the 1980s.* Apogee 1990

Clark, Jerome. *The Emergence of a Phenomenon.* Omnigraphics 1992

Clark, Jerome. *High Strangeness.* Omnigraphics 1996

Clark, Jerome & Coleman, Loren. *The Unidentified.* Warner 1975

Collins, Andrew. 'The Aveley Abduction – A New Look', *The Supernaturalist #1* (1981)

Conroy, Ed. *Report on Communion.* William & Morrow 1989

Dardel, Eric. 'The Mythic', *Diogenes #7* (1954)

Davis, Mike. 'Cosmic Dancers on History's Stage', *The Anomalist #5* (1997)

Paul Devereux. 'Beyond Ufology: Meeting with the alien', *New Ufologist #1*

Devereux, Paul & Brookesmith, Peter. *UFOs and Ufology.* Blandford (UK) 1997, Facts on File (USA) 1998

Douglas, Mary. *Purity and Danger.* Routledge & Kegan Paul 1966

Druffel, Ann & Rogo, D. Scott. *The Tujunga Canyon Contacts.* Prentice-Hall 1980

Evans, Hilary. *Visions · Apparitions · Alien Visitors.* Aquarian 1984

Evans, Hilary. *Gods · Spirits · Cosmic Guardians.* Aquarian 1987

Evans, Hilary & Spencer, John. *UFOs 1947–1987.* Fortean Tomes 1987

Evans, Hilary & Stacy, Dennis. *UFO 1947–1997.* John Brown 1997

Evans-Wentz, W.Y. *The Fairy Faith in Celtic Countries.* (1911) Citadel 1994

Fiore, Edith. *Encounters.* Doubleday 1989

Fowler, Raymond. *The Andreasson Affair.* Prentice-Hall 1979

Fowler, Raymond. *The Andreasson Affair – Phase Two.* Prentice-Hall 1982

Fowler, Raymond. *The Watchers.* Bantam 1990

Freud, Sigmund. 'Screen Memories', *Works*, Standard Edition, Vol 3. Hogarth Press 1953

Freud, Sigmund. *The Interpretation of Dreams* (1900). Allen & Unwin 1954

Fuller, John G. *The Interrupted Journey.* Putnam 1966

Gillmor, Daniel S. (ed.) *Scientific Study of Unidentified Flying Objects.* Bantam 1969

Goodbeer, Richard. *The Devil's Dominion: Magic and Religion in early New England.* Cambridge University Press 1992

Gotlib, David. Review of J. Mack, *Abduction* in *Bulletin of Anomalous Experience.* Vol 5 #3 (1994)

Grosso, Michael. *Frontiers of the Soul.* Quest Books 1992

Harney, John. 'He Can Remember It For You Wholesale', *Magonia #59* (1997)

Hendry, Allan. *The UFO Handbook.* Sphere 1980

Herbert, Frank. *The Heaven Makers.* Avon 1968

Hill, Betty. *A common sense approach to UFOs.* Betty Hill 1995

Hopkins, Budd. *Missing Time.* Ballantine 1981

Hopkins, Budd. *Intruders.* Ballantine 1987

Hopkins, Budd. *Witnessed.* Pocket Books 1997

Hopkins, B., Jacobs, D., & Westrum, R. *Unusual Personal Experiences.* Bigelow 1992

Hough, Peter & Randles, Jenny. *Looking for the Aliens.* Blandford 1991

Howe, Linda Moulton. *An Alien Harvest.* LHM Productions 1989

Jacobs, David. Interview in *UFO* Magazine (UK), Nov/Dec 1995

Jacobs, David. *Secret Life.* Simon & Schuster 1992 (UK edition: *Alien Encounters.* Virgin 1994)

Jordan, Debbie [Debbie Tomey] & Mitchell, Kathy. *Abducted.* Dell 1995

Jung, Carl G. *Flying Saucers: A modern myth of things seen in the sky.* (1959) Ark 1987

King, Jeffrey. 'A Tin Ear: A critique of Bullard's Sympathetic

Ear' (unpublished draft 1997).

Kirk, G.S. *Myth*. Cambridge University Press 1971

Klass, Philip J. *UFO Abductions: A dangerous game*. Prometheus 1988

Kottmeyer, Martin. 'The Boundary Deficit Hypothesis', *Magonia #32* (1989)

Kottmeyer, Martin. 'Entirely Unpredisposed', *Magonia #35* (1990)

Kottmeyer, Martin. 'The Eyes That Spoke', *REALL News* Vol 2 #7 (1994)

Kottmeyer, Martin. 'Why Are the Grays Gray?' *MUFON UFO Journal #319* (1994)

Kottmeyer, Martin. 'The Curse of the Space Mummies', *Promises & Disappointments #2* (1994)

La Planche, J. & Pontalis, J.B. *The Language of Psychoanalysis*. Hutchinson 1985

Lawson, Alvin H. 'What Can We Learn From The Hypnosis of Imaginary Abductees?', 1977 MUFON Symposium Proceedings, MUFON *1977*

Lewis, James R. (ed.), *The Gods Have Landed*. State University of New York 1995

Loftus, Elizabeth & Ketcham, Katherine. *The Myth of Repressed Memory*. St Martin's Press 1994

Lorenzen, Coral & Jim. *Flying Saucer Occupants* Signet 1967

Lorenzen, Coral & Jim. *Encounters with UFO Occupants*. Berkley Medallion 1976

Lorenzen, Coral & Jim. *Abducted!* Berkley Medallion 1977

Mack, John E. Foreword to Jacobs, D. *op cit.*

Mack, John E. *Abduction: Human encounters with aliens*. Revised edition: Ballantine 1995

May, Rollo. *The Cry for Myth*. W.W. Norton 1991

McLachlan, Chris. 'Symbolic and Mythical Components of the Abduction Experience', *Bulletin of Anomalous Experience*. Vol 5 #3 (1994)

Méheust, Bertrand. *Science-fiction et soucoupes volantes: une réalité mythico-physique*. Mercure de France 1978

Méheust, Bertrand. *Soucoupes volantes et folklore*. Mercure de France 1985

Mizrach, Steve. 'UFO Abductions and Race Fear', *Bulletin of Anomalous Experience*. Vol 5 #3 (1994)

Newitz, Annalee. 'Alien Abductions and the End of White People', *Bad Subjects #5* (1993). *Bad Subjects* is available on the Internet at: http://english www.hss.cmu.edu/BS/issues.html

Norman, Eric. *Gods, Demons & UFOs*. Lancer 1970

Ofshe, Richard & Watters, Ethan. *Making Monsters: False memories, psychotherapy & sexual hysteria*. Scribner's 1994

Pendergrast, Mark. *Victims of Memory*. Upper Access 1995

Polti, Georges. *The Thirty-Six Dramatic Situations*. The Writer, Boston (n.d.)

Pontolillo, James. 'Demons, Doctors and Aliens', *International Fortean Organization Occasional Paper #2* (1993)

Pritchard, A. et al (eds). *Alien Discussions: Proceedings of the Abductions Study Conference at MIT*. North Cambridge Press 1994

Randles, Jenny. *Aliens: The Real Story*. Robert Hale 1993

Randles, Jenny. *Star Children*. Robert Hale 1994

Rimmer, John. 'Facts, Fraud, and Fairytales', *MUFOB New Series #9* (1977)

Rimmer, John. *The Evidence for Alien Abductions*. Aquarian 1984

Rojcewicz, Peter. 'Fairies, UFOs, and Problems of Knowedge', *Bulletin of Anomalous Experience*. Vol 3 #1 (1992)

Rogerson, Peter. 'Northern Echoes', *Magonia #35* (1990)

Rose, Steven. *The Making of Memory*. Bantam 1992

Royal, Lyssa & Priest, Keith. *Visitors from Within*. Royal Priest Research Press 1992

Sandow, Greg. 'The Abduction Conundrum' (unpublished MS, 1996)

Sandow, Greg. 'The Linda Case' (Parts 1 & 2), *International UFO Reporter* (Spring & Summer 1997)

Sebeok, Thomas A. (ed.) *Myth: A Symposium*. Indiana University Press 1970

Sheaffer, Robert. *The UFO Verdict*. Prometheus 1980

Schnabel, Jim. *Dark White*. Hamish Hamilton 1994

Siegel, Ronald K. *Fire In The Brain*. Dutton 1992

Spencer, John. *Perspectives*. Macdonald 1989

Stacy, Dennis. 'Abductions and Abortions', *Bulletin of Anomalous Experience*. Vol 3 #5 (1992)

Stacy, Dennis. 'Alien Abortions, Avenging Angels', *Magonia #44* (1992)

Stillings, Dennis. *Cyberbiological Studies of the Imaginal Component in the UFO Contact Experience*. (Archaeus Vol 5) Archaeus Project 1989

Story, Ronald (ed) *The UFO Encyclopedia*. New English Library 1980

Strieber, Whitley. *Communion*. Avon 1987

Strieber, Whitley. *Transformation*. Beach Tree 1988

Strieber, Whitley. *The Secret School*. Harper Collins 1997

Thompson, Keith. *Angels & Aliens: UFOs and the mythic imagination*. Addison Wesley 1991

Thompson, Richard L. *Alien Identities*. Govardhan Hill 1993

Vallée, Jacques. *Passport To Magonia*. Henry Regnery 1969

Vallée, Jacques. *Confrontations*. Random House 1990

Walton, Travis. *Fire In The Sky*. Marlowe 1996

Watson, Nigel. *Portraits of Alien Encounters*. Valis 1990

Whitmore, John. 'Religious Dimensions of the UFO Abduction Experience', in James R. Lewis *op cit.*

Wright, Lawrence. *Remembering Satan: Recovered memory and the shattering of a family*. Knopf 1994

Further Reading

Barbour, Ian G. *Myths, Models and Paradigms: a comparative study in science and religion*. Harper & Row 1976

Blackmore, Susan. 'Alien Abduction: The inside story', *New Scientist* (19 Nov 1994)

Campbell, Joseph. *Creative Mythology*. Viking 1968

Cassirer, Manfred. *Dimensions of Enchantment*. Breese 1992

Clarke, David & Roberts, Andy. *Phantoms of the Sky*. Robert Hale 1990

Festinger, L., Riecken, H.W., & Schachter, S. *When Prophecy Fails*. Harper & Row 1956

Hufford, David. *The Terror That Comes in the Night*. University of Pennsylvania 1982

Pervin, Lawrence A. (ed) *Psychological Inquiry Vol 7 #2* (entire issue devoted to articles interpreting the abduction phenomenon, with wide variety of opinion)

Ring, Kenneth. *The Omega Project*. Morrow 1992

Showalter, Elaine. *Hystories: Hysterical epidemics and modern culture*. Columbia University Press 1997

Spencer, John. *Gifts of the Gods?* Virgin 1994

Index

Acknowledgements

Above all others I owe extra special thanks to those whom I interviewed in order to include some of their experiences in this book, and who have greatly enriched it: Clarke Hathaway, David Howard, Kathy, Sue McLaren, Pat Parrinello, and John Velez. Their hospitality and generosity – not least their generosity of spirit – went far beyond the call of duty or friendship, and to them I am deeply grateful, especially for the illustrations they have allowed me to use. To them, with the best and warmest wishes, I dedicate this book.

Special thanks too to Betty Hill, whose unique perspective gives her commentary on today's abduction phenomenon a particular force; and to Stuart Appelle, Dr Susan Blackmore, Janet Bord, Paul Devereux, Hilary Evans, Budd Hopkins, Rebecca Keith, Martin Kottmeyer, Kevin McLure, Karl Pflock, Katherine Photos, Kevin Randle, Bob Rickard, John Rimmer, Greg Sandow and Dennis Stacy, who were more than generous in helping me acquire documents,

information and background material, and in contributing to much stimulating discussion. For hospitality, guided tours, smoothing of ways and good times in general while working on this book in Canada and the USA I'm indebted (in chronological order) to Massad Ayoob, Kathie Photos, Errol Bruce Knapp and Sue Kovios, Greg Sandow, Rebecca Keith, Dennis and Julie Stacy, Julie Presson, Roselynn Towle, Stacy Swenck, and Ronald and Elin Pendleton. And finally, back home, my editor Lesley Riley did a heroic job of keeping me on the strait and narrow to complete the manuscript in good time, and ensuring that what I wrote was what I meant.

**Any reader who suspects he or she has had an
'abduction' or similar experience may find it helpful to visit the Abduction
Information Center website, at: http://www.crossfields.com/~aic/index.html**

Picture Credits

Popperfoto: 160; (Reuters) 4, 158; (AFP/EPA) 166.
Frank Spooner Pictures: (Pugliano) 5; (Rotolo) 11, 57.
Fortean Picture Library: 6, 8, 10, 13, 14, 17, 20, 21, 22, 45, 46, 50, 61, 63, 71, 74, 109, 112, 118, 130, 134, 143, 149, 150, 157, 165; (Clarke Hathaway) 18, 26, 31, 44, 111, 132, 147, 171; (Dennis Stacy) 28, 41, 43, 55, 114;
(Lisa Anders) 47, 51, 124; (John Velez) 62, 67, 70, 128, 129; (Seale Photography) 69; (Rebecca Keith) 73, 100.
Images Colour Library: 90; (Charles Walker Collection) 12, 16, 82, 107.
Mary Evans Picture Library: 24, 78, 98, 140; (Michael Buhler) 53; (Sigmund Freud Copyrights) 84.
Private Collection: 33, 35, 38, 144.
Ronald Grant Archive: 40.
Moviestore Collection: 49, 72, 96.
Philip J. Klass: 56.
Private Collection: (Front cover of *Communion* by Whitley Strieber. Published 1988 in paperback by Arrow Books Limited, an imprint of Random House UK Limited. © Wilson & Neff, Inc. 1987. Illustration on cover © Whitley Strieber.) 59.
Dennis Stacy: 60.
Robert Irving: 65.

Science Photo Library: (Oscar Burriel) 77; (Philippe Plailly) 88; (Francois Gohier) 102; (Keith Kent) 104; (National Library of Medicine) 106; (Petit Format/Nestle) 159.
Dr Susan Blackmore: 83, 97; (David Howard) 79, 81, 127, 168.
Professor Alvin H. Lawson: (Retraced by MUFON artists) 87.
NASA: 92.
Pheasantry/Allied Vision: (Courtesy Kobal Collection) 95.
Project Hessdalen: (Leif Havik) 110.
Nigel Watson: (Norman Harrison) 115.
Erling Strand: 117.
Pat Parrinello: 121.
Image Bank: (Thierry Seray) 123.
E.T. Archive: (Louvre, Paris) 137.
Fotomas Index: 139, 142.
Corbis: (Alison Wright) 145; (UPI/Bettmann) 161.
Private Collection: (cartoon images from *The Collected Works of Buck Rogers in the 25th Century*, edited by Robert C. Dille, published 1969 by Chelsea House Publishers. © Dille Family Trust.) 152-153.
Universal: (Courtesy Kobal Collection) 155.
Sue McLaren: 163.

Every effort has been made to contact the copyright holder in each case. We apologize for any omissions.